Challenging Medicine

Second Edition

Edited by

David Kelleher, Jonathan Gabe and Gareth Williams

Routledge
Taylor & Francis Group

LONDON AND NEW YORK

First edition published 1994
This edition published 2006
by Routledge
2 Park Square, Milton Park, Abingdon, Oxon OX14 4RN

Simultaneously published in the USA and Canada
by Routledge
270 Madison Ave, New York, NY 10016

Routledge is an imprint of the Taylor & Francis Group

© 1994, 2006 David Kelleher, Jonathan Gabe and Gareth Williams,
selection and editorial matter; individual chapters, the contributors.

Typeset in Goudy by
Integra Software Services Pvt. Ltd, Pondicherry, India
Printed and bound in Great Britain by
TJ International Ltd, Padstow, Cornwall

British Library Cataloguing in Publication Data
A catalogue record for this book is available from the British Library

Library of Congress Cataloging in Publication Data
Challenging medicine / edited by David Kelleher, Jonathan Gabe
and Gareth Williams. — 2nd ed.
    p.   cm.
Includes bibliographical references and index.
ISBN 0–415–38954–2 (pbk.) — ISBN 0–415–38953–4 (hardback)
1. Social medicine—Great Britain.   2. Medical care—Great Britain.
3. National health services—Great Britain.
[DNLM: 1. Social Medicine—Great Britain.   2. Delivery of Health
Care—Great Britain.   3. Health Occupations—Great Britain.
4. Social Dominance—Great Britain. WA 31 C437 2006]
I. Kelleher, David, 1935–   II. Gabe, Jonathan.
III. Williams, Gareth, MD.
RA418.3.G7C48 2006
306.4′61—dc22   2005017078

ISBN10: 0–415–38953–4   ISBN13: 9–78–0–415–38953–2 (hbk)
ISBN10: 0–415–38954–2   ISBN13: 9–78–0–415–38954–9 (pbk)

For Charlotte

Contents

Contributors

Ellen Annandale Senior Lecturer, Department of Sociology, University of Leicester.

Michael Bury Professor Emeritus, Department of Health and Social Care, Royal Holloway, University of London.

Robert Dingwall Professor and Director, Institute for the Study of Genetics and Biorisks in Society, University of Nottingham.

Lesley Doyal Professor, School for Policy Studies, University of Bristol.

Mary Ann Elston Reader Emeritus, Department of Health and Social Care, Royal Holloway College, University of London.

Jonathan Gabe Professor, Department of Health and Social Care, Royal Holloway, University of London.

Pru Hobson-West Leverhulme Training Fellow at IGBiS, University of Nottingham.

David J. Hunter Professor, Centre for Public Policy and Health, University of Durham.

David Kelleher Reader Emeritus, Department of Sociology, London Metropolitan University.

Jennie Popay Professor of Sociology and Public Health, Institute for Health Research, University of Lancaster.

Mike Saks Professor and Pro-Vice Chancellor, University of Lincoln.

Gareth Williams Professor, School of Social Sciences, Cardiff University.

Anne Witz Reader, Department of Sociology, University of Leicester.

Preface to second edition

The medical profession has long been thought of as an occupational group that has considerable power, but one that used its power in the best interests of individuals and society. In a world that often appears to be controlled by experts, the medical profession has been among the most powerful of these groups. As the high priests of modern society, doctors have come to be seen as experts not only on the treatment of bodily ills but also on how to live the good life. From time to time their power and status have been challenged, but these challenges have always been easily brushed aside.

Until the late 1960s most sociologists accepted medicine's definition of itself as a profession. Subsequently, the growth of a more critical sociology encouraged an alternative view of medicine as a dominating profession, monopolising the provision of health services or responding to the requirements of the economic system. Indeed, some even suggested that medicine was responsible for creating demand for its services by medicalising everyday life.

This 'professional dominance' model has been extremely influential over the last two decades but is increasingly being questioned. Initially this was couched in terms of what has come to be called 'deprofessionalisation': the proposition that medicine's professional status has been undermined as the 'knowledge gap' between physicians and consumers has diminished and new specialised occupations have arisen around bodies of knowledge and skills that physicians themselves are not competent to employ. Within the general backlash against professional society, lay people have been less willing to accept uncritically the judgements of doctors. More recently, it has been argued that the medical profession is being 'proletarianised'. According to this argument its members are being deskilled, losing their economic independence (becoming wage labourers) and being required to work in bureaucratically organised institutions under the instructions of managers. Another formulation from this perspective talks in terms of corporatisation, on the basis that it is less contentious (doctors do not resemble typical wage labourers) and more illustrative of recent developments than proletarianisation. Both deprofessionalisation and proletarianisation/corporatisation have in turn attracted considerable criticism. For example those associated with professional dominance have claimed that these formulations underplay the significance of the organised character of the medical profession and its increasing internal stratification. Others have argued for a more pluralist approach, rejecting both medical dominance and the alternatives mentioned above, and suggesting that the medical profession should be seen as just one interest group alongside others (such as the state, the health care industry and consumers) competing for power, influence and resources. From this standpoint if one set of interests becomes predominant, a countervailing set of interests will challenge it in time. Yet others have concentrated solely on external challenges to medicine seeing its dominance being threatened by the growth of new social movements, ranging from feminists to anti-vivisectionists, who have questioned the basis of medical knowledge and the techniques used in its production and application.

Given these developments there would seem to be good reason to reassess the position of the medical profession in contemporary Britain and the extent to which it still dominates the health field. How seriously should we take arguments about proletarianisation or deprofessionalisation, which have been developed primarily with the US context in mind? Is the profession's position of power under serious threat from the new social movements? Or is the prime threat to medicine the economically driven rise of managerialism? And how has the medical profession responded to these challenges?

The present book aims to reassess these issues by inviting a number of well-known medical sociologists to reconsider a range of 'challenges' currently being faced by the medical profession from within and outside the health care system. Each contributor has been asked to assess the significance of his or her challenge in relation to the theoretical arguments outlined above and to reflect on recent developments since the first edition was published.

We believe that revisiting these important questions will have an appeal for a number of reasons. First, most of the literature on this issue is to be found in journals or in books whose primary focus is different from the present one. Second, those books that have considered the question of medical dominance in recent times have tended to focus on challenges from within the health care system, especially in the United States, and to have played down or ignored the significance of the range of external challenges to be considered here. Third, the gap in the literature needs to be filled because of the continued widespread interest in the social relations of health care. It is hoped that this book will, as before, appeal not only to medical sociologists but also to a much wider audience including policy analysts, health service workers, medical journalists and interested members of the public.

Understanding medical dominance in the modern world

Jonathan Gabe, David Kelleher and Gareth Williams

The place of medicine

We are so accustomed to thinking of the profession of medicine as a stable institution with considerable power that it is sometimes difficult to imagine that it could ever be otherwise or that it has ever been different. In the eighteenth century, however, patients and the public had little conception of the medical profession as a collective entity. In this unregulated world of medicine the competence and sound judgement of healers, licensed or not, was highly variable (Stacey 1988). What mattered in the formulation of opinions about medicine in the eighteenth century were face-to-face encounters with individual practitioners in what amounted to a free market in healing (Porter and Porter 1989).

Although these interpersonal encounters have remained an important influence, from the middle of the nineteenth century onwards, individual doctors were increasingly incorporated into professions, institutions and bureaucracies which had definite social and cultural relations to civil society and the State. In this process the occupation of healing changed from being frequently seen as a rattlebag of quacks and rogues (Porter and Porter 1989) to a profession with considerable power, authority and status. Two strands developed. The general practitioner (GP), who was part of the same social world as the patient, sometimes playing a key civic role in his or her locality (Tudor Hart 1988). The hospital consultant, meanwhile, was a rare breed to whom the familiar GP occasionally referred patients. He was a more distant figure with access to knowledge which transcended local concerns and was unavailable directly to ordinary people. These medical men and women increasingly became stabilising authorities in a universe prone to occasional disorder. They were the people to whom one turned at times of crisis, after all other sources of help had been exhausted (Berger 1967). Their self-presentation might sometimes be brusque and aloof, but within the class structure and gender order of the time such interpersonal inequalities were seen as part of the way things were, at least as far as most ordinary people were concerned.

In the first half of the twentieth century some important developments occurred in the delivery of health care, the organisation of the medical profession and the scientific foundations of medical practice. The growth of research laboratories and the increasing numbers of hospital patients had put medicine in a strong position to capitalise on the growing concern about the public health (Stacey 1988). First, hospital doctors and later GPs found themselves with more money, higher status and greater political power. The Second World War ushered in significant political changes. Doctors were now part of a public service – the National Health Service (NHS) – at a time when the universally blessed goal of such a service and the professionalism of its workers were largely taken for granted. They were exemplary members of a 'professional society' (Perkin 1989) in which everyone wanted to get professionalised (Wilensky 1964).

After the Second World War doctors' power was further underlined by various social, cultural and technological changes. The validity of medical knowledge had always rested on a degree of trade-off between technicality and indeterminacy (Jamous and Peloille 1970), the former emphasising the solid scientific basis of medicine and the latter stressing the interpretive mysteries of diagnosis and treatment. The decline of organised religion, moreover, has led to doctors being cast more and more in the role of secular priests whose expertise encompassed not only the treatment of bodily ills but also advice on how to live the good life, and judgements on right and wrong behaviour (Zola 1972).

In addition, doctors benefited from being gatekeepers to a whole range of new pharmacological products which were generally perceived as enhancing their ability to save life and minimise personal discomfort. The power and status gained from such pharmacological developments, and the close alliance between doctors and the pharmaceutical industry (Bodenheimer 1984), were further enhanced in the 1950s and 1960s by the introduction of surgical procedures which for the first time facilitated the replacement of diseased organs by transplantation (Stocking 1992).

In recent decades the position of the medical profession appears to have changed. The corporate power of medicine has been increasingly challenged, and doctors, the high priests of modern society, have become increasingly embattled as their position as experts has been challenged from inside and outside the health care arena. In conjunction with direct challenges to their knowledge and expertise and the greater knowledge of patients have come doubts about the nature of their power, stirred by the secularisation of medical mystique and changing perceptions of the dynamics of power in society.

Challenges to medicine

One of the major internal challenges faced by doctors in Britain comes from management. In chronological terms this is not the first challenge, but it is certainly the most salient. Before the Griffiths Report of 1983 (DHSS 1983) the NHS was run by consensus teams with doctors and nurses sharing managerial responsibilities with what were then called administrators (Harrison *et al.* 1990). Griffiths introduced the notion of commercial business management from the private sector and turned administrators into general managers who would have overall responsibility for the delivery of health care. One consequence of this has been that managers, by way of information systems and clinical budgeting, have been expected to establish some control over the activities of doctors and their use of resources (Cox 1991). In practice general managers seemed unable to challenge the medical domain. While they were now able to close hospital beds and make other changes to the service without lengthy consultations, in every other respect they remained unable to curtail doctors' autonomy over their work (Harrison and Pollitt 1994). A further attempt to shift the balance of power more forcefully in the direction of managers was made by the Conservative government in the 1989 White Paper (DH 1989). This White Paper recommended that district general managers should be involved in appointing consultants, allocating merit awards and agreeing detailed job descriptions with consultants on an annual basis (Hunter 1991). At a more general level, the introduction of an 'internal market' into the NHS, with a separation between the purchasers and the providers of health care, set up changes within the system which have had major implications for the autonomy of the medical profession (Flynn 1992).

At the same time a variety of new techniques of managerial evaluation were developed. Quality assurance and performance indicators were developed, made possible by advances in information technology (Flynn 1992). This increased opportunities for the managerial determination of work content, productivity, resource utilisation and quality standards. Following New Labour's election in 1997 'clinical governance' was introduced as a further means to challenge the clinical autonomy of the medical profession (Gabe 2004). Chief executives of hospitals became responsible for clinical as well as financial performance. They were now expected to make sure that their clinicians followed the service guidelines for specific conditions identified by National Service Frameworks and those treatments specified as clinically and cost-effective by the newly created National Institute for Clinical Excellence (NICE). In addition managers were required to provide evidence that doctors in their Trusts were following these guidelines when inspected by the Commission for Health Improvement (Harrison and Ahmad 2000) and its successor (Commission for Healthcare Audit and Inspection).

The response of doctors to this challenge has been mixed. While many medical staff in hospitals have reacted critically to the increased powers of general management and resisted the opportunity to become managers following the Griffiths Report (Harrison 1988), the requirement that doctors be involved in management at every level following the 1989 White Paper has resulted in a change of heart by many who have seen their role as part-time managers as a way of retaining control over the service. Having learnt the language of management, they have been able to use their bilingual skills to interpret and reframe problems. According to Thorne (2002) they have been able to adopt a clinical perspective on managerial issues and a managerial perspective on clinical matters. As a result those members of the medical profession who have become clinical directors have enabled the medical profession to retain a central role in shaping the service and work organisation.

The sources of this managerial challenge are both economic and ideological. The period since 1979 in British politics under both Conservative and New Labour governments has been characterised by a heavy emphasis on 'liberalising' the economy, abolishing the 'dependency culture' and encouraging business values and the disciplines of the market. From this perspective the crisis in the organisation and funding of the NHS in the 1980s was a direct consequence of the restrictive practices of the medical profession and the failure of the old-style administrators to take action on inefficiency and waste. Against this background, developing new policies and targets for health care can be seen as part of a more generalised dilution of the power of those professions and other corporate bodies, which had previously been able to provide a counterweight to government policy.

The introduction of general management poses a challenge not only to the medical profession. As Witz and Annandale argue in this edition, nursing is also challenged by managerial techniques. Nursing, or rather the nursing elite, has embarked on a process of occupational development in recent years, which is threatening to redefine the relationship between nursing and medicine. The history of nursing is full of accounts of struggles to define the role of nurses as something more than handmaidens to doctors (Dingwall *et al.* 1988). In recent times, the introduction of more patient-centred care in hospital is an attempt to make nurses' work less routinised while at the same time being more sensitive to the needs of patients. This 'new nursing' has been informed by a body of theory which has been developed in the newly established academic departments of nursing in Britain, drawing on US nurses' efforts to redefine their role as independent clinical practitioners (Beardshaw 1992). At the same time, nurses working in primary care have had the opportunity to develop new responsibilities, undertaking health promotion, screening and counselling as well as more routine work which has traditionally been undertaken by GPs (Greenfield 1992; Williams *et al.* 1993). Both these developments have been accompanied by a major reform of nursing education, Project 2000, which links nursing more directly with higher education, increases the amount of theoretical knowledge being transmitted to student nurses, and reduces the time which they spend on the wards providing a service. Taken together, such changes may be perceived as an explicit professionalising strategy designed to give skilled nurses a distinct sphere of influence and greater autonomy from doctors, who have traditionally dominated the health care division of labour. Alternatively, they may be perceived, as Salvage (1988) has argued, simply as a 'survival strategy' involving an attempt to construct a new model for occupational authority in the face of an unprecedented combination of threats to their already limited autonomy.

The challenge to medicine can also be seen from groups within the health care arena but outside the boundaries of medical orthodoxy. The growth of interest in and support for activities that are often lumped together as 'complementary' or 'alternative' medicine (Fulder and Monro 1981) is indicative of a challenge to orthodox medicine which is simultaneously ethical and epistemological. These alternatives to orthodoxy can be found not only in the clinics of practitioners, but also on the shelves in the health section of any large bookshop. Some suggest that the growth of alternative medicine is a product of the disillusionment many people feel with the dehumanising effects of 'scientific' medicine: the manifest lack of interest doctors display in treating them as persons with identities, roles and relationships, as well as bodies. For others, the key to alternative medicine's growing attractiveness is quite simply the failure of medicine to match up to the expectation (which it encouraged) that it could deal safely and effectively with a wide range of common symptoms.

The specific criticisms of orthodox medicine exemplified in the popularity of alternatives to it have to be seen against the background of wider social and cultural changes which have altered individuals' expectations about their health. Although these altered expectations are not evenly distributed through the social strata of Western societies, they may nonetheless mark changed cultural and indeed 'theological' concerns about what in human life is taken to be valuable and important. In responding to these changes the medical profession has used a number of strategies (BMA 1986). These range from extreme scepticism about the scientificity of anything lying outside its boundaries to attempted incorporation of some of the techniques of alternative practitioners into its own sphere of work (Fairfoot 1987). Just how serious a challenge alternative medicine poses and whether it is best understood as a reaction to changes in society rather than a series of practices that have arisen in response to shortcomings in medicine are serious questions which are now beginning to be addressed (Saks 1992, 2003; Sharma 1992).

Threats to medical hegemony from outside the health care workforce also need to be considered. These come both from other professionals and from lay people with an interest in medicine and medical care who have organised themselves collectively in order to fight for change. Of those professional occupations now involving themselves increasingly with the practice of medicine perhaps the most powerful are lawyers and journalists.

Lawyers in the UK have benefited financially from the rapid increase in medical negligence claims in recent years, in terms of frequency and severity, following trends in the United States (Dingwall *et al.* 1991; Allsop and Mulcahy 1996; National Audit Office 2001). Moreover, some have actively encouraged such claims by advertising in local newspapers for prospective litigants to seek their firm's advice about their eligibility to participate in current or possible future class actions. Furthermore, although litigation has traditionally been targeted against high-status medical specialities such as surgery or obstetrics, events such as the legal proceedings over the prescribing of benzodiazepine tranquillisers suggest that GPs are also being implicated by lawyers. In such circumstances it is not surprising that there should be growing concern amongst doctors about the possibility of being sued for negligence and about the actions of lawyers in facilitating this process. In response it is claimed that doctors have become more defensive in their medical practice. Hospital doctors are said to order treatments, tests and procedures primarily to protect themselves from criticism or potential litigation (Allsop and Mulcahy 1996). And there is evidence that GPs have refused to treat certain conditions and are engaging in more detailed note-taking and giving more detailed explanations as a result of fears about being sued (Summerton 1995).

While medical negligence claims have been thought to provide the main reason for activity by lawyers in the health care arena in the UK, the involvement of law with medical matters is much more extensive as Dingwall and Hobson-West argue in this edition. They suggest that although the threat of litigation may still hang over doctors, in reality its payment represents a very small part of the NHS budget. They use the MMR scare to illustrate that such events are better understood as changes in society rather than as threats directed only at the medical profession.

Journalists, too, have taken an increasing interest in medicine and medical care in recent years, in part perhaps because of the growth of a consumer culture which treats health as a commodity (Crawford 1984; Williams and Bendelow 1998), and in part because of escalating health care expenditure and thus the increasing political salience of health (Allsop 1995). Available evidence suggests that not only has media coverage of medical and health matters increased, but the proportion of that coverage which makes use of lay as opposed to medical perspectives has also increased (Lund 1992). It is against this background that journalists have not simply accepted medical definitions (Turow and Coe 1985; Karpf 1988), but have developed a more critical view of medical knowledge, medical technology and medical practice (Seale 2002). Although there are still television and radio programmes and newspaper articles which present a narrow, 'technophoric' view of medicine, the creation of a more critical journalistic perspective may be providing a counterweight to medical power, empowering readers, listeners and viewers to challenge medical decision-making and reducing the esteem in which doctors have been held. In the 1990s the medical profession responded to this by including a 'Medicine and the Media' section in the *British Medical Journal*, which reviewed television and radio coverage of medicine in a critical light, often hitting back at what it saw as the sensationalist 'trial by media' characteristic of much reporting. At the same time, it could also be seen more positively as part of a general move by professionals and scientists to use the media for their own ends (Nelkin 1987).

Challenges to medical dominance from outside the health service are not confined to those from other professionals. As we noted earlier, lay people with an interest in medicine and medical care have, since the late 1960s, been increasingly willing to question medical expertise. One illustration of this tendency has been the growth of self-help groups, though their prevalence and rate of growth is difficult to quantify with any confidence. It would be naive to regard self-help as some sort of simple consumer revolt, like the food riots of the eighteenth century. Self-help groups have developed against a backdrop of increasing discontent about the effectiveness of medicine in dealing with chronic morbidity, along with growing political pressure on professionals to be accountable to consumers (as in *The Patient's Charter* (DH 1991)) and on consumers to take greater responsibility for their own health (as in the government White Paper *The Health of the Nation* (DH 1992)). While some of the neo-liberal rhetoric has softened under New Labour, the emphasis on choice appears to be stronger than ever, becoming almost a panacea for all political ills (DH 2004) in Westminster and Whitehall, if not necessarily in Belfast, Cardiff or Edinburgh (Greer 2004).

The pattern of self-help activity has complex origins (Williams 1989). Some self-help groups have been initiated by professionals and have stimulated the growth of statutory services (Robinson and Henry 1977; Trojan 1989). Others have acted as an alternative source of advice and care about which doctors are uneasy (Black 1988; Stewart 1990). Many are large, national organisations with easy access to the media and professional bodies; others are local organisations with limited funds and restricted networks. Whether they are antagonistic or agreeable to orthodox medical services, and whether or not they can be said to constitute a new social movement (Gussow and Tracy 1976; Kelleher 2001), their very existence can be interpreted as a developing challenge to professional power (Klein 1983; Brown *et al.* 2004; Scambler and Kelleher in press).

Alongside the growth in self-help as a means of responding to the unpleasantness of illness comes a lay challenge to the way in which problems of public and environmental health are defined by doctors in these fields. In the face of contemporary hazards to the public health, groups of people in different localities, both in the United States and United Kingdom, are taking action against those individuals or organisations they believe to be responsible for the problems (Brown and Mikkelsen 1990; Martin 1993). For example, families in Grangetown on Teesside have engaged in legal action against ICI for nuisance and negligence in response to what are perceived to be high rates of cancer and respiratory problems in their area which they believe are linked to the toxic emissions produced by local industry (Utting 1991). As will be seen in this book, these lay challenges are sometimes not easily assuaged by simple appeals to either 'experts' or 'evidence'.

What makes this development challenging to medicine is the fact that many groups are doing their own research, or engaging their own 'experts' to provide countervailing perspectives, a phenomenon sometimes referred to as 'popular epidemiology' (Brown 1992). In developing such 'competing rationalities', lay people have found themselves engaged in disagreements with those experts from orthodox epidemiology and public health who insist that the evidence does not support the claims they are making (Williams and Popay 1993). The direction of this challenge leads to the involvement of lay people not just in the process of doing the research or responding to scientific findings produced by others, but in identifying and conceptualising the nature of the risks and how they should be studied. While some may disagree with the idea of the lay expert (Prior 2003), scepticism about science, as well as the increasing availability of online information about diseases and drugs, has changed the dynamics of lay–expert relations.

There are a number of other challenges to medical dominance which can more confidently be described as social movements. These movements are clearly trying by 'collective endeavour to promote or resist change' (Bottomore 1979: 41), and their actions are underpinned by an overt ideology and self-consciousness of purpose (Giddens 1984). One such collectivity, albeit a diverse one, is the women's movement, which has been very vocal in its criticism of the quality and quantity of health services available to women and, in the United States at least, has established alternative services emphasising self-help and minimising professional distinctions (Fee 1983; Ruzek 1986).

In Britain the movement's involvement in health and medicine is said to have changed over time (Doyal 1983). In the late 1960s and early 1970s, attention was concentrated on women as 'consumers' and on the treatment they received at the hands of male doctors. Feminists exposed the sexism inherent in much medical practice and sought to take control of reproductive technology (Stacey 1988). Establishing alternative services, however, was not considered economically or politically viable, mainly because of the existence of the NHS, which provides treatment free at the point of use (Doyal 1983, 1995 (see Chapter 8)).

Subsequently, in the late 1970s and early 1980s, priorities shifted towards attempting to defend the NHS against cutbacks and increasing privatisation. These campaigns involved women not only as users of health services but as producers of health care. New groups of feminist health workers (radical nurses and midwives, and feminist doctors and medical students) joined women's health groups in campaigns to save hospitals, jobs and services (Doyal and Elston 1986). Alongside these changes, some feminists have started to develop an alternative analysis to that underpinned by the biomedical model (Popay *et al.* 1993). Here the aim has been to discover how women's morbidity and mortality can be explained by the capitalist and patriarchal organisation of society, and to develop campaigns to improve their living and working conditions. All this is not to say that earlier priorities have been totally displaced. Recent campaigns around the development and application of new reproductive technologies (Stacey 1988), and attempts to alter NHS Well Women's Clinics to reflect the values of the women's health movement (Craddock and Reid 1993), indicate that the struggles of feminists to challenge medical dominance and the hegemony of the biomedical model continue on a broad terrain.

Another configuration of resistance to orthodox medicine is that represented by the animal rights movement and anti-vivisectionists who have criticised medical scientists for using animals in their experiments and for exploiting such animals for career purposes. The organisations which make up this movement have used various strategies to get scientists and their institutions to stop using animals for research purposes and to recognise these animals' rights by including them within the sphere of social citizenship (Turner 1986). The challenge they represent is not only ethical but epistemological. It threatens the scientific basis of medical knowledge by questioning its reliance on animal models and their relevance to human health. The movement has provoked an increasingly organised, visible response from the medical research community and other interested parties such as the pharmaceutical industry. Educational materials, for example AMRIC's video for schools (see Chapter 9), have been produced for use in schools; learned scientific societies have organised petitions in support of animal experiments and there has been a general attempt to 'go public' in the mass media in order to win the battle for the 'hearts and minds' of the general population.

These developments represent major challenges to medicine. They also raise a number of questions for sociology, perhaps the most fundamental of which is: to what extent are the traditional explanations of medical dominance and more recent propositions regarding 'deprofessionalisation' and 'proletarianisation/corporatism' able to account for the challenges that medicine is currently facing?

Sociological analysis of medicine

Until the late 1960s most sociologists accepted medicine's definition of itself as a profession using its expert knowledge and special skills rationally and benevolently. This progressive and benevolent construction of medicine was supported by its location, from the Second World War onwards within systems of health services and welfare states which were seen as effective, equitable and legitimate environments for the delivery of expertise in the context of modern citizenship (Williams 2004). Thereafter, the development of a more critical sociology stimulated an alternative view of medicine as a dominating profession, monopolising the provision of health services (Freidson 1970) or responding to the requirements of the economic system by narrowly concentrating on sickness and by commodifying medicine (Johnson 1977; Navarro 1978). Indeed, some went beyond this to argue that medicine was itself responsible for creating the need for its services by medicalising the ordinary problems of everyday life (Zola 1972; Illich 1975).

This critique was part of a much larger process during the late 1960s and early 1970s in which the world was, for a short time in certain sectors, turned upside down. In Britain and elsewhere, education, medicine, the law and the police were increasingly found wanting, both in the academy and on the streets. Workers, students and other groups proclaimed the need to be liberated from the shackles of authority in whatever form, and the celebrated tolerance of Western liberal democracies was seen to be a 'repressive tolerance' (Marcuse 1969).

Since those eventful days and the initial critique of professional dominance, the status of medicine and the medical profession has come under renewed attack, as we have seen, from both inside and outside the health care system. Yet sociological explanations of what has been happening have not been very fully developed. One view that has been put forward by Haug and her colleagues (Haug 1973, 1988; Haug and Lavin 1983) is that medicine is being 'deprofessionalised', as part of a more general trend of rationalisation and codification of expert knowledge and a rejection of professional paternalism. Writing about recent developments in the United States and the consequences for doctoring, Haug has argued that the relationship between doctors and patients has changed as the 'knowledge gap' between them has reduced. On this argument the popularisation of medical knowledge by the media, increased literacy and the computerisation of medical diagnoses and treatment are combining to undermine patients' unquestioning trust and increase their willingness to shop around for medical services as consumers in a health care market. In addition, doctors' autonomy is said to have been curtailed as new specialised occupations have arisen around bodies of knowledge which doctors themselves are not competent to use.

With the general backlash against professional society, lay people have been less willing to accept uncritically the opinions of doctors, less happy to grant unquestioning trust and more likely to object to their autonomy, power and rate of remuneration (Watkins 1987). In spite of the continuing 'magic' of medical technology there have been specific challenges to medicine's ethics, politics and epistemology:

> At the very time when physicians can diagnose the inner reaches of the brain with magnets, disintegrate kidney stones using sound waves instead of scalpels, and command an increasingly impressive techno-logy, the profession is feeling besieged.
>
> (Stoeckle, quoted in Light and Levine 1988: 10)

Other writers have argued that the medical profession is being 'proletarian-ised', in line with the requirements of advanced capitalism (Oppenheimer 1973; McKinlay and Arches 1985; McKinlay and Stoeckle 1988). Not only do people no longer believe in doctors' special status, but the very material basis of their work is changing. On this view, the profession's members are being deskilled, losing their economic independence (becoming wage labourers) and being required to work in bureaucratically organised institutions under the instructions of managers. Or, to put it another way, they are becoming technically, economically and organisationally alienated (Larson 1977) in a system restricted by increasing state control of the financing of health care and by the growth of corporate provision of health care for profit (Elston 1991). A more recent formulation by McKinlay and Marceau (2002) substitutes 'corporatization' for 'proletarianization', in recognition of the growing significance of corporate provision and because of a hostility to the equation of doctors with wage slaves which was detracting from the explanatory power of the underlying thesis. In the United States, where this argument was first developed, many doctors work in hospitals or health maintenance organisations (HMOs), paid not on a fee-for-service principle, but in terms of a pre-payment plan with a third-party payer such as Blue Cross/Blue Shield. The financial interests of these organisations stand above the interests of individual clinicians (however charismatic their authority may be), and the introduction of diagnostic related groups (DRGs) and HMOs requires doctors to tailor treatment to the organisations' contractual responsibilities. Not surprisingly there has been a backlash to such restrictions, by doctors and middle-class patients (Mechanic 2004), but 'managed care' in some form or other is likely to continue with a significant number of doctors continuing to work for large corporations.

There are different slants on these arguments. First, it can be contended that as medical knowledge becomes codified and routinised and subject to audit, less imagination and less space are required for the autonomous physician to use his or her intellectual powers (Armstrong 1990). Second, the harsh fact is that medicine has simply become too expensive and is being squeezed. In this regard, in Britain at least, the health service and the medical profession are exposed to the same trends towards privatisation that have affected many other areas of public sector activity (Marsh 1991).

Given the developments outlined in the previous section there would seem to be good reason to reassess the usefulness of existing theories in explaining the position of the medical profession in contemporary Britain and other industrialised countries. How seriously should we take arguments about proletarianisation/corporatisation or deprofessionalisation, which have been developed primarily with the American context in mind? Is deprofessionalisation a general process, or are we seeing the decline of some professions, such as medicine, and the rise of others, such as accountancy? (Perkin 1989; Crompton 1990). Is the profession's position of power under serious threat from the new social movements, alternative medicine or the media, as a reconstituted deprofessionalisation thesis might suggest? Or is the prime threat to medicine the economically and ideologically driven rise of managerialism, an explanation which fits better with the proletarianisation thesis? At the same time we need to consider how medicine has responded to such managerialism. Has it been incorporated or has it resulted in restratification (Freidson 1994) with an elite group of medical managers increasingly dominating rank-and-file professionals? More recently some commentators, such as Light (2000), have taken a more pluralistic view, starting from the assumption that society consists of numerous 'countervailing powers' with interests of one kind or another in health care. Medicine is one of these, and not necessarily the dominant one (Elston 2004; Light 2000); but allowing medicine to remain free from too heavy a weight of political or organisational shackles may work to the advantage of not only doctors, but patients and the State as well.

Alternatively, should the various developments we have identified be reconceptualised as part of a deregulated and essentially post-modern world? From this standpoint the challenges to the expert system of modern medicine could reflect the breakdown of legitimised authority, permitting any number of challenges to be made. Thus, the proliferation of innumerable groups and movements could be understood as part of the freedom of expression possible in a post-modern world in which the exploration of the self and the body in new ways are encouraged as part of a 're-enchantment of the world' (Bauman 1991).

Our objectives in editing this collection are twofold: first, to represent the state of play with regard to the sociological analysis of medicine in society; and second, to illuminate the situation that doctors and other health care workers find themselves in. The book does this by exploring the changes taking place in the relationships between the State, the public and institutions that constitute civil society, the health care system and the medical profession. In this way, medicine is seen as part of society rather than simply an institution experiencing internal strains. At the same time, contributors have been asked to write their chapters in such a way that their contents are accessible to a wider public who might be searching for ways of understanding and coming to terms with a changing health care system, which seems to be in a state of fiscal crisis (O'Connor 1973), as well as an ideological one (Williams 1991).

In the light of these concerns, we have invited a number of social scientists to reconsider the challenges we believe medicine now faces in Britain, and to assess whether they parallel developments in other advanced capitalist societies such as the United States. Their contributions should be seen as attempts to develop specifically sociological analyses of complex and rapidly changing situations. For that reason, although the chapters each deal with one substantive issue, they all relate these issues to broader theoretical and political concerns. It is hoped that the book will contribute to an informed overview of what is happening to medicine and health care in Britain and other advanced capitalist societies at a time that may well prove to have been a watershed in the history of the medical profession.

The first chapter, by David Hunter, examines the strength of the managerial challenge to medical dominance. He describes the rise of managerialism in the NHS from 1974 onwards, and notes that it is of recent origin in health care systems generally. The main purpose of the chapter is to chart the management thrust of the British NHS reforms since 1991 and to assess their implications for medical practice. Hunter argues that for all the plausibility of sociological arguments about proletarianisation, it would be unwise to overestimate the extent to which doctors' influence has been seriously eroded by developments in management. Doctors are perfectly capable of transforming themselves into managers and exerting their power in such a way that no fundamental challenge is mounted to their view of the health service.

Chapter 2, by Anne Witz and Ellen Annandale, examines the changes taking place in nursing. Reminding us of the long and chequered history of nurses' attempts to establish a distinct sphere of competence within the health care division of labour, they advocate a cautious stance to the challenge which nursing poses. They suggest that recent changes in the organisation of the NHS may offer some nurses the possibility of higher professional status, but this will be at the expense of the majority, who will be deskilled. They argue that the main difficulty faced by nurses in challenging doctors is that while the former may claim caring as the centre of their profession, caring is traditionally seen as women's work and accorded low status. The problem *for* nursing, therefore, has been and continues to be the problem of gender.

In Chapter 3 Robert Dingwall and Pru Hobson-West consider the effect that working within a culture, which defines relationships in legal terms, has on doctors. They begin with a review of the formal legal environment within which the medical profession operates and, in particular, its experience of tort litigation. They argue that this litigation is a problem for the profession rather than for the NHS, and that it is part of a wider shift in the status of the professions rather than being unique to medicine. From this perspective the medical profession's response is best understood as a status protest and as a symbolic expression of its discontent with other social and cultural changes. Dingwall and Hobson-West note the part played by law in such case studies as the MMR vaccine but go on to argue that the real challenge to the medical profession is not from law but from governmentality, which favours law as its operative strategy of social control.

Chapter 4, by Michael Bury and Jonathan Gabe, considers the way in which the medical profession and medical work are portrayed on television. It starts by outlining the argument that medicine has come to dominate media coverage of health and illness. On this view, any challenges to medicine's knowledge base and power as a profession have largely been absorbed and therefore neutralised. The authors then proceed to test empirically the assumptions behind this argument by considering three examples of television's portrayal of medicine, employing different programme formats: the exposé (*The Cook Report*), the documentary (*Operation Hospital*) and the drama serial (*Casualty*). They also examine briefly recent developments in television and the media, which have eroded some of the boundaries between these formats and consider the greater attention now being paid to the Internet. Their analysis suggests that the proposition that the 'box is doctored' is difficult to sustain in its original form when exposed to empirical tests. While it is still possible to find television coverage which displays clear ideological support for the medical profession and medical practice, it is also clear that the media are acting as carriers and amplifiers of a more challenging position.

In Chapter 5 Mike Saks explores the challenge that the increasingly popular alternatives pose to orthodox medicine in a consumer-based society. He examines the occupational strategies employed by the medical profession in defending its position against external competitors and the ideological arguments that are deployed to underpin these strategies. Saks argues that the authority of the British medical profession has been thrown into question by the growing public demand for alternative therapies, and suggests how this may provide openings for some alternatives to be incorporated into the health service. The main conclusion of this chapter is that while alternative therapies pose important challenges to medicine, they have not yet significantly reduced its dominance.

In Chapter 6 David Kelleher examines the challenge of self-help groups to modern medicine. He starts by describing some of the activities of self-help groups, using the distinction between 'inner focused' and 'outer focused' groups. This demonstrates that groups often engage in both kinds of activity to varying degrees, and that while much of what goes on can be interpreted as complementary to medicine, there is nevertheless a subversive readiness to question the status of medical knowledge and assert the value of lay knowledge. Kelleher then goes on to explore the ways in which the relationship between self-help groups and modern medicine has been influenced by changes in contemporary culture. Against this background it is suggested that self-help groups can also be seen as part of a new social movement, resisting the dominance of medicine's instrumental-cognitive rationality and, by valuing experiential knowledge, retaining the possibility of seeing things differently.

In a much-extended Chapter 7 Gareth Williams and Jennie Popay examine the challenge posed by lay perspectives in the field of public and environmental health. They note how, in recent years, there has been an increase in lay challenges not just to those institutions seen to be responsible for causing environmental health problems, but also to those experts whose role is to explain and suggest solutions to these problems. Beginning with an examination of lay knowledge about health issues, they go on to consider the phenomenon of 'popular epidemiology' using the events surrounding the contamination of the public water supply at Camelford, North Cornwall in 1988 as a case study. They argue that such community responses to environmental health problems pose a challenge to the dominance of conventional biomedical perspectives that is both epistemological and political – a difference between 'narrative based' and 'evidence based' knowledge.

In Chapter 8 Lesley Doyal considers the feminist challenge to medicine. She starts by describing briefly the range of feminist critiques of medicine. This leads to a consideration of the evidence of gender inequalities in the control of the formal health care system and the consequences for women's subjective experience of care. Doyal then considers the male bias in the production of medical knowledge and its relationship to medical treatment, before turning to whether there have been any changes in practice as a result of feminist analyses and the campaigns they have generated. Overall she suggests that while women have collectively mounted an important challenge to the medical profession, they have not been powerful enough to bring about any major change in medical practice. The newly established Commission for Equality and Human Rights is seen as a step in the right direction.

In Chapter 9 Mary Ann Elston considers the extent and the nature of the challenge to medicine from the anti-vivisectionist movement and the dangers in extrapolating results of tests on animals to humans. She begins by outlining the links between the rise and fall of the movement and the medical profession's rise in status from the 1870s to the 1960s. Against this backcloth she considers the marked revival of anti-vivisectionist activity over the last twenty-five years. She notes that initially the emphasis was primarily on the moral status of animals and their alleged widespread use in laboratories for non-medical purposes. During the 1980s, however, the focus switched to making the kinds of claims about the morality and value of animal experiments for human health that had been voiced in the late nineteenth century, providing a renewed challenge to medical science. Medicine's response, she suggests, has been much more vigorous than in the past, and has involved mounting a campaign to win the 'hearts and minds' of the public in the face of the perceived success of the animal rights movement in integrating some of its concerns into public consciousness and political life in Britain.

In conclusion, while none of the authors in this collection predict the impending emasculation of the power of medicine as a result of the challenges surveyed, they all point to changes taking place in society that are likely to bring about a reconfiguration of professional power. These changes, which some might describe as a shift from modernity to post-modernity, are having an impact on the wider environment in which the medical profession and the health service operate. While these developments offer little support to the deprofessionalisation and proletarianisation/corporatisation theses, they do, at the very least, suggest the need for a re-examination and reworking of our traditional ideas about professional dominance.

Acknowledgements

We should like to thank Mary Ann Elston and Mike Saks for their comments on an earlier draft of this introduction.

References

Allsop, J. (1995) *Health Policy and the NHS Towards 2000*, Longman: London.

Allsop, J. and Mulcahy, L. (1996) *Regulating Medical Work*, Open University Press: Buckingham.

Armstrong, D. (1990) 'Medicine as a profession: Times of change', *British Medical Journal*, 301: 691–3.

Bauman, Z. (1991) *Intimations of Postmodernity*, London: Routledge.

Beardshaw, V. (1992) 'Prospects for nursing', in Beck, E., Lonsdale, S., Newman, S. and Patterson, D. (eds), *In the Best of Health?*, London: Chapman & Hall.

Berger, J. (1967) *A Fortunate Man*, London: Allen Lane.

Black, M. (1988) 'Self-help groups and professionals – what is the relationship?', *British Medical Journal*, 296: 1, 485–6.

Bodenheimer, T.S. (1984) 'The transnational pharmaceutical industry and the health of the world's people', in McKinlay, J. (ed.), *Issues in the Political Economy of Health Care*, London: Tavistock.

Bottomore, T.B. (1979) *Political Sociology*, London: Hutchinson.

British Medical Association (Board of Science and Education) (1986) *Alternative Therapy*, London: BMA.

Brown, P. (1992) 'Popular epidemiology and toxic waste contamination: Lay and professional ways of knowing', *Journal of Health and Social Behaviour*, 33: 267–81.

Brown, P. and Mikkelsen, E.J. (1990) *No Safe Place: Toxic Waste, Leukemia and Community Action*, Berkeley: University of California Press.

Brown, P., Zavestoski, S., McCormick, S., Mayer, B., Morello-Frosch, R. and Altman, R. (2004) 'Embodied health movements: New approaches to social movements in health', *Sociology of Health and Illness*, 26: 50–80.

Cox, D. (1991) 'Health service management – a sociological view: Griffiths and the non-negotiated order of the hospital', in Gabe, J., Calnan, M. and Bury, M. (eds), *The Sociology of the Health Service*, London: Routledge.

Craddock, C. and Reid, M. (1993) 'Structure and struggle: Implementing a social model of a well woman clinic in Glasgow', *Social Science and Medicine*, 36: 67–76.

Crawford, R. (1984) 'A cultural account of "health": Control, release and the social body', in McKinlay, J.B. (ed.), *Issues in the Political Economy of Health Care*, New York: Tavistock Publications.

Crompton, R. (1990) 'Professions in the current context', *Work, Employment and Society*, Additional Special Issue: 147–66.

Department of Health (DH) (1989) *Working for Patients*, London: HMSO.

—— (1991) *The Patient's Charter*, London: HMSO.

—— (1992) *The Health of the Nation. A Strategy for Health in England*, London: HMSO.

—— (2004) *Choosing Health: Making Healthier Choices Easier*, London: TSO.

Department of Health and Social Security (DHSS) (1983) *NHS Management Enquiry (Griffiths Report)*, London: HMSO.

Dingwall, R., Rafferty, A.M. and Webster, C. (1988) *An Introduction to the Social History of Nursing*, London: Routledge.

Dingwall, R., Fenn, P. and Quam, L. (1991) *Medical Negligence. A Review of the Literature*, Oxford: Centre for Socio-legal Studies, Wolfson College.

Doyal, L. (1983) 'Women, health and the sexual division of labour: A case study of the women's health movement in Britain', *International Journal of Health Services*, 13: 373–87.

—— (1995) *What Makes Women Sick? Gender and the Political Economy of Health*, Basingstoke: Macmillan.

Doyal, L. and Elston, M.A. (1986) 'Women, health and medicine', in Beechey, V. and Whitelegg, E. (eds), *Women in Britain Today*, Milton Keynes: Open University Press.

Elston, M.A. (1991) 'The politics of professional power: Medicine in a changing health service', in Gabe, J., Calnan, M. and Bury, M. (eds), *The Sociology of the Health Service*, London: Routledge.

—— (2004) 'Decline of medical autonomy', in Gabe, J., Bury, M. and Elston, M. (eds) *Key Concepts in Medical Sociology*, London: Sage Publications.

Fairfoot, P. (1987) 'Alternative therapies: The BMA knows best?', *Journal of Social Policy*, 16: 383–90.

Fee, E. (ed.) (1983) 'Women and health care: A comparison of theories', *Women and Health: The Politics of Sex in Medicine*, Farmingdale, New York: Baywood.

Flynn, R. (1992) *Structures of Control in Health Management*, London: Routledge.

Freidson, E. (1970) *The Profession of Medicine*, New York: Dodd Mead.

—— (1994) *Professionalism Reborn: Theory, Prophecy and Policy*, Cambridge: Polity Press.

Fulder, S. and Monro, R. (1981) *The Status of Complementary Medicine in the UK*, London: The Threshold Foundation.

Gabe, J. (2004) 'Managerialism', in Gabe, J., Bury, M. and Elston, M. (eds) *Key Concepts in Medical Sociology*, London: Sage Publications.

Giddens, A. (1984) *The Constitution of Society: Outline of the Theory of Structuration*, Cambridge: Polity Press.

—— (1990) *The Consequences of Modernity*, Cambridge: Polity Press.

Greenfield, S. (1992) 'Nurse practitioners and the changing face of general practice', in Loveridge, R. and Starkey, K. (eds), *Continuity and Crisis in the NHS*, Buckingham: Open University Press.

Greer, S. (ed) *Territorial Politics and Health Policy*, Manchester: Manchester University Press.

Gussow, Z. and Tracy, G. (1976) 'The role of self-help clubs in adaptation to chronic illness and disability', *Social Science and Medicine*, 10: 407–14.

Harrison, S. (1988) 'The workforce and the new managerialism', in Maxwell, R. (ed.), *Reshaping the NHS*, London: Policy Journals.

Harrison, S. and Ahmad, W. (2000) 'Medical autonomy and the UK state', *Sociology*, 34: 129–46.

Harrison, S., Hunter, D. and Pollitt, C. (1990) *The Dynamics of British Health Policy*, London: Unwin Hyman.

Harrison, S. and Pollitt, C. (1994) *Controlling Health Professionals: The Future of Work and Organisation in the NHS*, Buckingham: Open University Press.

Haug, M. (1973) 'Deprofessionalization: An alternative hypothesis for the future', *Sociological Review Monograph*, 20: 195–211.

—— (1988) 'A re-examination of the hypothesis of deprofessionalization', *Milbank Quarterly*, 66 (Suppl. 2): 48–56.

Haug, M. and Lavin, B. (1983) *Consumerism in Medicine: Challenging Physician Authority*, Beverly Hills: Sage.

Hunter, D. (1991) 'Managing medicine: A response to the "crisis"', *Social Science and Medicine*, 32: 441–9.

Illich, I. (1975) *Medical Nemesis*, London: Calder & Boyars.

Jamous, H. and Peloille, B. (1970) 'Changes in the French University-Hospital System', in Jackson, J.A. (ed.), *Professions and Professionalization*, Cambridge: Cambridge University Press.

Johnson, T. (1977) 'The professions in the class structure', in Scase, R. (ed.), *Industrial Society: Class, Cleavage and Control*, London: Allen & Unwin.

Karpf, A. (1988) *Doctoring the Media*, London: Routledge.

Kelleher, D. (2001) 'Problematic identities and health', in May, M., Page, R. and Brunsdon, E. (eds) *Understanding Social Problems*, Oxford: Blackwell Publishers.

Klein, R. (1983) *The Politics of the National Health Service*, London: Longman.

Larson, M.S. (1977) *The Rise of Professionalism*, Berkeley: University of California Press.

Light, D. (2000) 'The medical profession and organizational change': From professional dominance to countervailing power', in Bird, C.E., Conrad, P. and Fremont, A.M. (eds) *Handbook of Medical Sociology*, 5th edition, Upper Saddle River, NJ: Prentice Hall.

Light, D. and Levine, S. (1988) 'The changing character of the medical profession: A theoretical overview', *Milbank Quarterly*, 66 (Suppl. 2): 10–32.

Lund, A.B. (1992) 'Health care users as news producers', unpublished paper presented at a scientific workshop on The User Perspective in Health Services Research, Denmark, September.

McKinlay, J. and Arches, J. (1985) 'Towards the proletarianization of physicians', *International Journal of Health Services*, 15: 161–95.

McKinlay, J. and Marceau, L. (2002) 'The end of the golden age of doctoring', *International Journal of Health Services*, 32: 379–416.

McKinlay, J. and Stoeckle, J. (1988) 'Corporatization and the social transformation of doctoring', *International Journal of Health Services*, 18: 191–205.

Marcuse, H. (1969) *An Essay on Liberation*, London: Allen Lane.

Marsh, D. (1991) 'Privatization under Mrs Thatcher: A review of the literature', *Public Administration*, 69: 459–80.

Martin, J. (1993) *The Public Perception of Risk from Industrial Hazards: Case Studies of Halton, Cheshire and Halebank, Merseyside*, unpublished MSc dissertation, University of Salford.

Mechanic, D. (2004) 'The rise and fall of managed care', *Journal of Health and Social Behaviour*, 45 (extra issue) 76–86.

National Audit Office (2001) *Handling Clinical Negligence Claims in England*, London: TSO.

Navarro, V. (1978) *Class Struggle, the State and Medicine*, London: Martin Robertson.

Nelkin, D. (1987) *Selling Science: How the Press Covers Science and Technology*, New York: Freeman.

O'Connor, J. (1973) *The Fiscal Crisis of the State*, New York: St Martin's Press.

Oppenheimer, M. (1973) 'The proletarianization of the professional', *Sociological Review Monograph*, 20: 213–37.

Perkin, H. (1989) *The Rise of Professional Society: England since 1880*, London: Routledge.

Popay, J., Bartley, M. and Owen, C. (1993) 'Gender inequalities in health: Social position, affective disorders and minor physical morbidity', *Social Science and Medicine*, 36: 21–32.

Porter, D. and Porter, R. (1989) *Patient's Progress: Doctors and Doctoring in Eighteenth-Century England*, Cambridge: Polity Press.

Prior, L. (2003) 'Belief, knowledge and expertise: The emergence of the lay expert in medical sociology', *Sociology of Health and Illness*, 25 (Silver Anniversary Issue): 41–57.

Robinson, D. and Henry, S. (1977) *Self-Help and Health: Mutual Aid for Modern Problems*, London: Martin Robertson.

Ruzek, S. (1986) 'Feminist visions of health: An international perspective', in Mitchell, J. and Oakley, A. (eds), *What is Feminism?*, Oxford: Basil Blackwell.

Saks, M. (ed.) (1992) *Alternative Medicine in Britain*, Oxford: Clarendon.

—— (2003) *Orthodox and Alternative Medicine*, London: Sage Publications.

Salvage, J. (1988) 'Professionalization – or struggle for survival? A consideration of current proposals for the reform of nursing in the United Kingdom', *Journal of Advanced Nursing*, 13: 515–19.

Scambler G. and Kelleher D. (in press) 'New social and health movements: Issues of representation and change', *Critical Public Health*.

Seale, C. (2002) *Media and Health*, London: Sage Publications.

Sharma, U. (1992) *Complementary Medicine Today: Practitioners and Patients*, London: Routledge.

Stacey, M. (1988) *The Sociology of Health and Healing*, London: Unwin Hyman.

Stewart, M.J. (1990) 'Professional interface with mutual aid self-help groups: A review', *Social Science and Medicine*, 31: 1, 143–58.

Stocking, B. (1992) 'The introduction and costs of new technologies', in Beck, E., Lonsdale, S., Newman, S. and Patterson, D. (eds), *In the Best of Health?*, London: Chapman & Hall.

Summerton, N. (1995) 'Positive and negative factors in defensive medicine: A questionnaire study of general practitioners', *British Medical Journal*, 310: 27–9.

Thorne, M. (2002) 'Colonizing the newworld of NHS management: The shifting power of professionals', *Health Service Management Research*, 15: 14–26.

Trojan, A. (1989) 'Benefits of self-help groups: A survey of 232 members from 65 disease related groups', *Social Science and Medicine*, 29: 225–32.

Tudor Hart, J. (1988) *A New Kind of Doctor*, London: Merlin Press.

Turner, B.S. (1986) *Citizenship and Capitalism*, London: Allen & Unwin.

Turow, J. and Coe, L. (1985) 'Curing television's ills: The portrayal of health care', *Journal of Communication*, 35: 36–51.

Utting, D. (1991) 'Battle over the breath of life', *Guardian*, 3 July: 25.

Watkins, S. (1987) *Medicine and Labour: The Politics of a Profession*, London: Lawrence & Wishart.

Wilensky, H.L. (1964) 'The professionalization of everybody', *American Journal of Sociology*, 70: 137–58.

Williams, G.H. (1989) 'Hope for the humblest? The role of self-help in chronic illness: The case of ankylosing spondylitis', *Sociology of Health and Illness*, 11: 135–59.

—— (1991) 'Disablement and the ideological crisis in health care', *Social Science and Medicine*, 32: 517–24.

—— (2004) 'Citizenship and health', in Gabe, J., Bury, M. and Elston, M. (eds) *Key Concepts in Medical Sociology*, London: Sage Publications.

Williams, G.H. and Popay, J. (eds) (1993) 'Researching the people's health: Dilemmas and opportunities for social scientists', *Social Research and Public Health* (Salford Papers in Sociology, No. 13), Department of Sociology, University of Salford.

Williams, S.J. and Bendelow, G. (1998) *The Lived Body: Sociological Themes, Embodied Issues*, London: Routledge.

Williams, S., Calnan, M., Cant, S. and Coyle, J. (1993) 'All change in the NHS? Implications of the NHS reforms for primary care prevention', *Sociology of Health and Illness*, 15: 43–67.

Zola, I.K. (1972) 'Medicine as an institution of social control', *The Sociological Review*, 20: 487–503.

1 From tribalism to corporatism

The continuing managerial challenge to medical dominance

David J. Hunter

> In the case of prophesizing, or projecting trends into the future, due caution requires being aware of the danger of mistaking short-term, ephemeral trends for long-term trends and cyclical change for linear, progressive change.
>
> (Freidson 1993)

Introduction

A constant theme running through successive reorganisations of the NHS since the mid-1970s has been the search for improved management. The search has been accompanied by growing centralisation, with occasional lapses into decentralisation and the application of market principles to the delivery of care (Hogget 1991; Hunter 1994). As Hoggett observes more generally in the restructuring of the public sector in Britain, elements of decentralised, hands-off, market-based approaches to delivering public services have been 'dwarfed by visible elements of centralization...and the extended use of hands-on systems of performance management creating a form of "evaluative state"' (Hoggett 1996).

Since Labour took office in 1997, these developments have both intensified and been modified. Most recently, attention has focused on combining a strong performance management culture with competitive impulses resulting from the application of market-style practices and the engagement of the private sector in the direct provision of services alongside state-run ones. However, following political devolution to Wales and Scotland (it is presently suspended in Northern Ireland), there is growing divergence in health policy within Britain (Greer 2001). What follows describes developments in England, and although there is some overlap with those occurring in Wales and Scotland the relationship between management and medicine in general terms is less fraught and adversarial in those places.

Thirty years ago, in his classic analysis of the organisation of health care systems, Robert Alford characterised reformers as falling into one of two camps: 'market reformers', who hold state involvement in health care and bureaucratic complexity responsible for the ills apparent in health care systems; and 'bureaucratic reformers', who claim that the defects are all the fault of those who subscribe to markets and competition which obstruct the orderly planned provision of effective health care and have no place in medicine (Alford 1975). The successive waves of reform that have swept over the National Health Service (NHS) represent varying mixes of these two competing notions. The Conservative government, which held office for some 18 years from 1979 to 1997, introduced the internal market changes which put policy-makers firmly in the camp of Alford's 'market reformers'. Towards the end of their term of office, the Conservatives retreated from their market-based ideology and reintroduced a range of more orthodox bureaucratic reforms which tightened the centre's managerial grip on the NHS. When Labour took over in 1997, its approach to the NHS during the early years could firmly be located in the category of bureaucratic reforms. But by 2001 or so, the government began to move in the direction of devolution and localism accompanied by the introduction (or, to be more precise, re-introduction) of market mechanisms and competition thereby putting it in Alford's first camp as well.

If there has been a consistent thread running through the numerous changes imposed on the NHS, it has been a never-ending fascination with economic rationalism and a belief that market-style incentives are necessary in some form to temper the excesses and producer-focused nature of public sector practices (Evans 1997). There is little to divide the two main political parties on this point. Nor is the issue confined to the UK. The prevailing wisdom that has taken root in many countries in recent years is that as long as the state controls the funding of health care then it matters rather less who provides it. Indeed, the UK government has pushed such pragmatism further asserting that what matters is what works, not whether it is publicly or privately managed and delivered. The introduction of pluralism and a mixed economy of care are believed to inject healthy competition to drive up standards and make services more responsive to users. Public–private partnerships are in high fashion as exemplars of the end of ideology, demonstrating a pragmatic commitment to efficient and effective delivery of care.

But, as Alford argues, reform strategies based on either market or bureaucratic models are unlikely to succeed because they neglect the way in which groups within health care systems develop vital interests which sustain the present system and vitiate attempts at reform. The two types of reform are not mere ideological constructs. They are also analyses of the structure of health care which rest upon different empirical assumptions about the nature and power of the health profession, the nature of medical technology, the role of the hospital, and the role of the patient...as passively receiving or actively demanding a greater quality and quantity of health care.

(Alford 1975)

It is a failure on the part of policy-makers to appreciate this feature of both market and bureaucratic reform models that accounts for the disappointment that quickly sets in when reforms do not match expectations.

Alford's 'structural interest' perspective remains useful in understanding the organisational life of health care systems regardless of whether they are predisposed to market or bureaucratic ideal types, or a mix of the two. According to this view, powerful interests benefit from the health care system precisely as it is. This applies regardless of whether it is a US-style market system or a UK national health service. In either model, the 'dominant' interests (clinicians – the 'professional monopolists') manage to do rather nicely and exercise considerable power to preserve their privileges. For their part, the challenging interests (managers – the 'corporate rationalisers') are party to a constant expansion of their functions, powers and resources justified by the need to control the professional monopolists. Meanwhile, the goal of easily accessible, low cost and equitable health care remains elusive and the source of repeated reform efforts on the part of frustrated policy-makers restless for results.

An intrinsic feature of successive reforms has been the role of management and managers as the means by which the changes, whether market-based or of a more bureaucratic type, are implemented in pursuit of the desired goal. A principal feature of the evolution of management in the NHS has been the struggle between doctors and managers for control of the health policy agenda. Each of the major reorganisations that have convulsed the NHS since 1974 has sought to shift the frontier between medicine and management decisively in favour of management. The various reorganisations all have in common the attempt to modify the individualism, and often sectionalist tribalism, which characterises medicine (Freidson 1993), and to subject it to the corporate disciplines of management (Griffiths 1983; Hunter 2002). On one reading, it can be argued that the reforms that have been taking place almost continuously since the early 1990s have virtually completed the bureaucratisation, or proletarianisation, of medicine and its penetration by management (McKinlay 1988). Doctors are being compelled to account for their working practices which have hitherto remained hidden from public scrutiny and to subject themselves to regular assessment and validation to ensure that their skills keep them 'fit for purpose' in an age of ever-greater complexity and rapid technological change. At the same time, exercising professional judgement in respect of who should receive clinical treatment is being superseded by a managerial target culture which places a premium on meeting nationally set targets over waiting times and access to care. In practice, except where there is non-compliance or 'gaming' to meet targets, these targets take precedence over clinically defined priorities in respect of individual cases.

Many observers believe that such practices, irrespective of their merits and alleged success, are having a corrosive effect on the medical profession, in particular undermining professional values and an ability to act in accordance with these values. For example, Simon Jenkins believes that the Thatcher reforms of the NHS in the early 1990s 'left an uneasy feeling that a professional relationship of trust between patient and doctor and hospital and community had been broken' (Jenkins 1995). He contrasts these managerial reforms with Aneurin Bevan's original model for the NHS: 'His health service was concerned simply with offering doctors and nurses an administrative apparatus "for them freely to use in accordance with their training for the benefit of the people of the country"' (Jenkins 1995). But therein lies the rub for recent governments, often goaded by sections of the media and a more critically aware public, who have remained unconvinced that the professional ethos is as altruistic and self-less as it is portrayed to be. For them, it is an appealing, but ultimately flawed, myth. They suspect, not without some justification, that the NHS has been run more for the convenience of those providing services than for those receiving them with the result that restrictive practices abound.

The Kennedy report on the Bristol Royal Infirmary, following the fatalities in the paediatric cardiac surgical service, pointed to the 'insular "club" culture, in which it was difficult for anyone to...press for change or to raise questions and concerns' (Bristol Royal Infirmary Inquiry 2001: 302). Furthermore, such a culture was not unique to Bristol but evident across the NHS. Another more recent high-profile inquiry into the deaths of hundreds of patients under the care of general practitioner (GP) Harold Shipman was also extremely critical of the way complaints against doctors were handled and of the weaknesses in rooting out poorly performing doctors (The Shipman Inquiry 2004). The entire system of professional self-regulation has come under the spotlight and pressure brought to bear on the medical establishment to remedy its own practices or risk having its freedom to self-regulate replaced by external scrutiny.

Whether, to use Alford's terms, the professional monopolists have begun to see their power base significantly curbed in recent years in the face of the challenge from the corporate rationalisers is a matter for empirical inquiry and the subject of some debate among researchers (Hafferty and

McKinlay 1993; Harrison and Pollitt 1994; Harrison 1999). The questions being addressed include: How far is medical dominance under serious or lasting threat? Will the changes irreversibly modify the prevailing power structures in health care systems? Or is the relentless managerial onslaught causing doctors to pause and regroup around a set of countervailing practices and tactics which may be aimed at blunting the impact of the new managerialism or, more radically, wresting back control by colonising the management function and becoming the new managers in future?

It is the purpose of this chapter to explore these questions by charting the managerial thrust of the NHS reforms as these have been pursued since the 1980s when the management grip really began to be felt. The analysis draws upon recent studies of managers and management in the NHS and their impact on the medical profession. The chapter is organised into three sections. First, there is a brief review of the progression of NHS reform through the 1980s, 1990s and early years of the twenty-first century with particular emphasis on developments since 1997. Second, the impact of the management revolution on the medical profession is considered. In the final section, an attempt is made to look beyond the immediate preoccupations of doctors and managers and consider a scenario that would enable doctors to reoccupy, albeit in a new guise, territory they increasingly feel is being wrested from them. The central theme of this section is that although management and managers are clearly in the ascendancy, and have been for many years, it remains possible for the overall balance of power still to operate in favour of doctors and the medical paradigm to which they subscribe (Mechanic 1991; Harrison 1999).

The rise of managerialism

Management is a fairly recent phenomenon in health care systems and follows from a perception by policy-makers of all political hues over the years that health services, like other public services, have tended to suffer from being over-administered and under-managed thereby failing to hold professionals to account (Hunter 1980, 1998; Harrison *et al.* 1992). Excluding the first major NHS reorganisation in 1974 which is not considered here, there have been three significant waves of change that are briefly described below. These have tended to roll into each other with the result that the NHS has been in the grip of a permanent revolution for most of its life.

From consensus to general management, 1982–1988

Bevan's model of the NHS in 1948 was the profession-dominated one which survived largely intact until the first half of the 1980s, when the

model was questioned by a businessman, Roy Griffiths, the then head of
the supermarket chain, Sainsbury's. He was brought in by the government
of the day to advise on the future management of the NHS. Griffiths
sought to strengthen management and to shift the emphasis, and ostensibly the balance of power, from producers to consumers, in line with
commercial practice. He was tapping into a trend that was becoming
established globally not only in health care but throughout the public
sector. The tenets of what became known as 'new public management'
(NPM) entered the public sector reform lexicon (Hood 1991; McLaughlin
et al. 2002). It was notable for the following distinctive features or
doctrines:

- explicit standards and measures of performance
- greater emphasis on outputs and results
- disaggregation of public bureaucracies into agencies operating on a
  user-pay basis
- greater competition through use of quasi-markets and contracting
- stress on private sector styles of management practice
- stress on performance incentives for managers
- stress on discipline in resource use and cost improvements
- emphasis on the public as customer.

Of particular importance was NPM's emphasis on standard setting,
performance management and target-setting in the sphere of professional
influence. But Griffiths went further in his critique of NHS management.
He diagnosed the management problem as having four components:
(1) management influence was low in relation to clinicians and medicine;
(2) the managerial emphasis was on reacting to problems instead of antici-
pating them; (3) maintaining the status quo was seen as the extent of the
management task; and (4) the NHS was producer, rather than consumer,
oriented (Harrison et al. 1992).

Unlike previous reorganisations, the Griffiths proposals were more
concerned with changing cultures and the prevailing balance of power
than with rejigging structures. Intended explicitly to modify the chemistry
and balance of power between the key stakeholders in the NHS, the
prescription offered by Griffiths, and accepted wholesale by the government, centred on the introduction of general managers at all levels of the
Service with a consequent diminution of the power of veto by doctors
which had been a feature of the previous consensus management arrangements. Day and Klein (1983: 1813) described the changed approach to
management as a 'move from a system that is based on the mobilisation of
consent to one based on the management of conflict – from one that has

conceded the right of groups to veto change to one that gives the managers the right to override objections'.

But if the Griffiths management revolution ushered in during the early 1980s was intended to shift the balance of power in favour of managers, little evidence for it could be detected during the latter half of the decade. A conclusion from a study of the impact of general management was that it had not significantly challenged the prevailing medical hegemony (Harrison *et al.* 1992). Doctors' training and career patterns remained largely unchanged with the consequence that their basic beliefs and attitudes remained more or less unaffected. While the authority of doctors may have been bruised, their power and status both within the NHS and in society at large remained largely intact.

The internal market, 1989–1997

The next wave of significant change, in the late 1980s, acknowledged that the management changes following the Griffiths inquiry while laying the foundations did not go far enough. It was the purpose of the *Working for Patients* changes introduced in 1991 to address this unfinished business at the medicine-management interface (Department of Health *et al.* 1989). Holding doctors more explicitly accountable for their actions and providing incentives to modify their behaviour so that they responded to patient wishes and preferences were key themes of the changes. The government wished to move from a producer-led to a user-driven NHS and sought to do so by adopting quasi-market thinking and concepts.

First, it introduced the purchaser–provider separation and, second, it set great store on consumerism. Conflating the purchaser and provider functions in a single organisation was regarded as resulting in a potential conflict of interest between the preferences of providers on the one hand and those of users on the other. By making the commissioning health authorities the 'champions of the people', the government hoped to break the mould and create new incentives for providers to become more responsive to the needs and wishes of local people and less susceptible to provider capture. The system of contracts between purchasers and providers entailed the introduction of a quasi-, or what became known as an internal, market wholly operated by public funds and intended to spur providers to offer improved and more user-friendly services. The focus on consumers led to attempts to ensure that resources followed patients in the belief that the patient should be in the driving seat. Such thinking underlay the GP fundholding scheme that was both welcomed and detested in almost equal measure by the medical profession and others (Le Grand *et al.* 1998).

The NHS reforms introduced during the early 1990s provided managers with a range of instruments and levers to challenge the medical dominance that was widely perceived as constituting a major barrier to change. Managers were granted powers to participate in the selection of consultants and other senior posts. They were also empowered to discuss contracts and job plans with doctors to establish with them their responsibilities and duties. Furthermore, the merit awards to which doctors are entitled to supplement their salaries had to demonstrate management competence and not only clinical excellence. Clinical and medical audit became obligatory for all hospital doctors at this time. Although primarily conceived as educational tools, they reinforced the general trend evident in the reform agenda that no longer are doctors wholly free agents. The micro-management of their work at the level of instrumental procedures holding them to account, such as those just noted and others like evidence-based medicine, served to strengthen the managerial grip on their work and prepare the ground for what was to follow with a change of government in 1997.

At this point in the history of NHS reform, commentators disagreed over the degree to which the 'corporate rationalisers' (i.e. managers) had conquered, or were in the process of conquering, the 'professional monopolists' (i.e. doctors). For example, Flynn believed that the battery of management techniques introduced following the introduction of general management was further strengthened in the 1991 reforms, the upshot being a reduction in clinical autonomy. This analysis was in line with his overall thesis that the tendency over the period had been towards 'an erosion of professional dominance in the face of increased . . . managerial power' (Flynn 1992: 50). In contrast, Dent (1993) argued that while it was true that doctors were no longer the sole arbiters of health care delivery, they had not foregone their dominant position. He employed the notion of 'responsible autonomy' to describe the changed relationship between doctors and managers. While doctors' autonomy may be limited at the level of the individual practitioner, it does not follow that the collective autonomy of the profession is limited. Dent's position is akin to that of Freidson (1990), Evans (1990) and Mechanic (1991) who all argue that little has changed fundamentally to erode medical dominance and the ability of doctors to determine health care priorities while remaining wedded to a medical model of delivery.

If this was the somewhat ambivalent assessment of the medicine–management interface in the early 1990s, the issue some dozen years later is whether it requires major reassessment in the light of the further rounds of reform commencing in 1997 with the arrival of a Labour government committed to the NHS as the embodiment of all it stood for in terms of fairness and social justice.

New Labour and NHS modernisation, 1997–

The incoming Labour government, which embarked upon a programme of continuous reform in public services, adopted the term 'modernisation' as a euphemism for bringing powerful professional groups like doctors to heel. It proved to be the most managerial and technocratic of any British government, fluent in the language of management and, from the prime minister down, seemingly endlessly fascinated by the latest management fads and fashions imported from the US (Marmor 2004). After 17 years in opposition, ministers were impatient to put their imprint on public services and to demonstrate their commitment to them. However, the strong managerial style involving tough targets centrally set and monitored did not endear the government to professional groups who had hoped that a Labour government would restore their pre-eminence in shaping and implementing policy.

At first, Labour's reform agenda took the form of appearing to dismantle its predecessor's controversial internal market changes and restoring a public service ethic to the NHS (Department of Health 1997). As the health minister at the time put it, 'we are replacing the internal market with a system we are calling "integrated" care' (Dobson 1999: 41). But, a few years on, Labour ended up retaining, or reintroducing, more of the internal market changes than it abolished (Department of Health 2004). As if to demonstrate the point, the prime minister appointed as his health adviser one of the staunchest advocates of the internal market, Professor Julian Le Grand (Le Grand 1999). The government introduced some new market-style changes designed to put doctors on their mettle as well as to give the public more voice and choice. The changes focused on making the NHS a primary care-led organisation with the introduction of primary care organisations which it was hoped GPs would lead or contribute to managing.

There was also a strong emphasis on performance and quality improvement to be achieved through a plethora of targets and performance indicators set and managed from the centre (Department of Health 1998). They were to be achieved through a transformation in how medicine was practised and poor performance was dealt with. The principal vehicle to achieve this was 'clinical governance' which Scally and Donaldson (1998: 61) define as 'a system through which NHS organizations are accountable for continuously improving the quality of their services and safeguarding high standards of care by creating an environment in which excellence in clinical care will flourish'. Clinical governance was the centrepiece of the government's 1997 white paper and demanded 'the re-examination of traditional roles and boundaries – between health professions, between doctor and patient, and between managers and clinicians' (Halligan and Donaldson 2001: 1413).

Key elements in the NHS quality strategy comprised a focus on standards, assuring quality of individual practice, scrutiny and patient empowerment with underpinning strategies in respect of R&D and evidence-based medicine, and investment in information systems and technology. Standards were developed by a new organisation, the National Institute for Clinical Excellence (NICE), and by the publication of national service frameworks (NSFs) governing particular disease categories and care groups. There are NSFs covering cancer, coronary heart disease, mental health, diabetes, elderly people and children's health. They are evidence-based and costed, and embrace prevention as well as primary and secondary care.

The NICE is charged with assessing the evidence base for particular interventions and with providing cost-effective guidance to the NHS in England and Wales (two bodies in Scotland perform a similar function). NICE provides guidance both in terms of individual health technologies (such as medicines, medical devices, diagnostic techniques and procedures) and the clinical management of specific conditions. It provides three main types of guidance:

1   technology appraisals of new and existing health technologies
2   clinical guidelines and protocols for the management of specific diseases and conditions
3   safety and efficacy decisions about new interventions.

Local health organisations are expected to act on NICE guidance when determining local priorities and making resource allocation decisions. Taken together, NSFs and NICE recommendations are expected to form a sound basis for the setting of clinical standards. From April 2005, NICE became known as the National Institute for Health and Clinical Excellence and is responsible for producing similar guidance in respect of public health interventions.

A second new organisation – the Commission for Health Improvement (CHI) – was established at the same time to scrutinise the delivery of the NSFs and the operation of clinical governance. Finally, partly as a consequence of a series of failures in standards of care which threatened to undermine public confidence in the NHS in general and in doctors in particular, the government put considerable pressure on the medical profession through the General Medical Council to put its house in order by introducing annual appraisal and revalidation for all doctors. The move towards greater transparency and accountability begun under the Conservative government was continued with even greater determination and vigour under Labour.

All these changes were presented as positive, developmental and educational but they had an edge to them unprecedented in the management of health care. When combined with targets over waiting lists and access to care which the government ruthlessly set about achieving, it seemed that the medical profession's traditional autonomy had all but vanished and the frontier had all but shifted to managers. Indeed, it was seen to be the price that had to be paid for the injection of new funds announced shortly after Derek Wanless's report, advisor to the Chancellor of the Exchequer, appointed to investigate the future funding of the NHS up to 2022 (Wanless 2002). Wanless concluded that the NHS was under-funded, but that a tax-funded system remained viable at least over the next 20 years. He also endorsed the government's belief that if the public was to support additional investment then it would expect to see a return on it. This meant changes in the way health care was practised and delivered. Effective management was central to the reform programme. At the same time, Wanless was mildly critical of the degree of central control and tendency to micro-manage the NHS from the Department of Health and, increasingly, from No. 10 itself. He supported giving more local discretion to those delivering care to nationally set standards, and reported discussions with NHS staff who had expressed the view that there should be greater local responsibility for delivery, 'ensuring an appropriate balance between central direction and local autonomy' (Wanless 2002: para. 6.34, 105). But the government, aided by its army of advisers seized of the need for reform and impatient for results, seemed to regard clinicians as part of the problem rather than the solution.

Little wonder, then, that despite the commitment to additional funding and to overcoming many of the NHS's weaknesses in terms of providing high quality care for those in need, there was growing unrest and unease among doctors and others at what they perceived to be excessive and inappropriate central control and direction. Many believed clinical priorities were being skewed by the requirement to meet government targets and that care was suffering as a result. In the words of a professor of geriatric medicine, the alleged disempowerment of the medical profession was seen by many as a 'political triumph and therapeutic disaster'.

There were concerns that doctors were becoming frustrated with the relentless pressures upon them and the flood of demands emanating from the Department of Health, not to mention the permanent revolution underway in the organisation and delivery of health care. Many felt they were becoming 'technical monkeys' and no longer considered themselves professionals trained to use judgement and develop craft skills. They felt oppressed by the demands of a mechanistic, reductionist style of management and the creation of a low trust, unforgiving blame culture. It was all a far cry from the ideals of clinical governance set out by its principal architect, the Chief Medical Officer, Liam Donaldson. Indeed, the preoccupation with top-down performance management seriously undermined the development potential of clinical governance (Gray and Harrison 2004). The term 'unhappy doctors' entered the vocabulary to describe the deep malaise evident not only in the British NHS but in other health care systems going through similar changes (Edwards et al. 2002).

The government responded to the charge of adopting an overbearing, command-and-control style by devolving power and responsibility, and by introducing (or perhaps re-introducing would be more accurate) market-style competitive mechanisms not only to increase capacity in order to clear waiting lists for elective treatment, but also to act as a spur to encourage doctors and others to raise their game. It also introduced the notion of 'earned autonomy' so that NHS organisations who achieved the targets and performed well received a lighter touch in terms of central control and inspection. From 2002, therefore, a top-down centralised system of management began to give way to a more hands-off, devolved style of management with fewer targets and a new inspectorate – the Healthcare Commission – established to replace CHI which was accountable not to ministers but to Parliament.

Whether the emphasis on devolution and localism and the restriction of inspection to a few key targets will restore confidence in government on the part of an increasingly suspicious and unhappy clinical workforce seems unlikely. For all the talk of letting go and localism, the government has made reform of the NHS a key plank of its electoral platform. As long as the NHS remains a focus of major public attention and concern and is funded through taxation, it seems unlikely that either this or any government can truly let go. But, the degree to which it can do so will become a true test of its commitment to a new and different NHS in which ministers meddle less and allow managers to get on with the job.

The impact of managerialism on the medical profession

Three broad strategies are available to doctors, managers and politicians seeking to improve health services (Ham and Hunter 1988). These are set out in Table 1. First, it is possible to encourage self-help among doctors to raise professional standards through medical audit, the use of standards and guidelines, the accreditation of hospitals and other services, and the revalidation of doctors to ensure their competence. A second strategy is to seek to involve doctors in management by delegating budgetary responsibility to them, and appointing doctors as managers. A third strategy is more assertive and interventionist and seeks to strengthen external management

Table 1 Strategies for managing clinical activity

• *Raising professional standards*	Medical audit Standards and guidelines Accreditation Revalidation
• *Involving doctors in management*	Budgets for doctors Doctor-managers
• *External management controls of doctors*	Managing medical work Changing doctors' contracts Extending provider competition

Source: Adapted from Ham and Hunter (1988: 7).

control of doctors by changing their contracts and encouraging managers to supervise medical work more directly.

Elements of all these strategies may be found operating within the NHS at different times in its history although, until recently, attention has concentrated on the first two. The desire has been for compliance rather than confrontation and to create a culture in which doctors regard themselves as having a legitimate management role rather than one thrust upon them. But in recent years, and especially at the present time, the third strategy has come to the fore as governments have sought to quicken the pace and scale of change. New contracts for doctors, while generously funded, do begin to set out what doctors will, and by the same token will not, do. The extension of provider competition through the introduction of independent treatment centres within a publicly funded health care system will inevitably bring doctors under tighter management control.

The issue is whether the shift from tribalism to corporatism can be achieved with the doctors or without them. And even if it occurs with them, there remain difficult issues about the exact nature of the engagement. Will doctors comply in order, as many see it, to collude in the erosion of their freedom? Will they do so in order to secure a new equilibrium with managers? Or will they cooperate in order to ensure that any erosion of their power base is resisted or halted? (Hunter 1992). If it is the third option, then doctors becoming managers is a perfectly rational stratagem for ensuring that no fundamental challenge is successfully mounted to their prevailing view of the world. If colonising the strange, and somewhat alien, world of management becomes the means for securing such an outcome then so be it. But perhaps it is not quite so simple.

As preceding sections have demonstrated, a consequence of the various management reforms on the medical profession has been closer bureaucratic control of its activities. Hence the observation that a cause of unhappiness among doctors is the intrusion of management into their working lives in ways neither foreseen nor regarded as helpful or in line with professional beliefs and values. Nevertheless, the perception of a profession whose autonomy is under threat from politicians and managers is real and can only add to the unhappiness doctors feel even if it cannot all be laid at the door of politicians and managers. The changes occurring among patients and in society at large are also responsible for the shift in the way doctors are regarded. There has been a decline in deference for all professions and a perceived loss of trust coinciding with a more hostile media. In fact, despite the overall loss of trust in experts, and the high-profile failures in clinical practice resulting from the Bristol and Shipman cases among others, repeated surveys show doctors are still held in high regard by the public. At the same time, patients are also increasingly active consumers and they demand, and have been encouraged to expect by reforming governments, enhanced services including extended hours and rapid access. In addition, there are also unrealistic expectations about the power of medicine to solve the ills of modern life, a development which doctors have often encouraged (Edwards *et al.* 2002).

With some exceptions, relations between doctors and managers remain at an all time low. The issue does need to be addressed because, if left unresolved, it threatens the future of the NHS (Edwards and Marshall 2003). Part of the problem in creating the conditions for a constructive dialogue between the two camps lies in the very different approaches to issues such as accountability, use of guidelines, and resources which arise from their respective training, beliefs and experiences. Also, in the case of managers, their increasing politicisation in recent years has made them appear in the eyes of doctors as the agents or mouthpieces of the centre with no opportunity to exercise independent thought or judgement.

While it seems unlikely that the move towards greater managerial control over doctors is going to go away or be reversed, the impact of such developments on clinical practice and behaviour remains little understood and should not be overstated. Health care organisations like the NHS are complex and contain strong professional bureaucracies that remain strong despite recent developments. The micro-management of medical work is weaker than is sometimes thought and seems likely to remain so unless, or until, doctors manage themselves and their work. Some evidence for this is borne out by a study of clinical governance in Wales which suggested that it was more about rhetoric than substance as far as doctors were concerned (Degeling *et al.* 2002).

Also, despite the claims for NICE that it is impacting upon clinical practice and driving up quality through the implementation of its guidance in respect of interventions that are deemed to be cost-effective, a study of the implementation of NICE guidance and its impact on quality of care and variations in practice concluded that it has been variable and mixed (Sheldon *et al.* 2004). Guidance seems more likely to be adopted when there is strong support, a stable and convincing evidence base and no increased or unfunded costs, and where the professionals involved are not isolated thereby demonstrating the importance of clinical context. The researchers suggest that change is 'heavily dependent on the actions of groups of professionals and individual clinicians' (Sheldon *et al.* 2004).

At issue may also be the extent to which doctors actually want to be managers, with opinions varying on this point. For example, Lee-Potter (1997), a former chairman of the British Medical Association (BMA) Council, maintains that 'relatively few' doctors want to be managers. It is an assessment that receives strong support from numerous surveys, among them a survey of young doctors' views of their core values conducted by the BMA (Allen 1997). The survey found considerable hostility towards management, whose apparently conflicting culture and different ethos and value base, doctors believed, prevented them from practising medicine to the benefit of their patients. The respondents were particularly concerned about the demands to maintain throughput and numbers, and to account for their time. The young doctors also saw management as becoming increasingly intrusive and aggressive in questioning the commitment of doctors through their working practices. Many felt 'hassle' from management to speed up their consultations and to see more patients. Overall, the doctors questioned presented a bleak picture of misunderstanding and territorial separation which illustrated the width of the gulf between them and managers. Managers were perceived as individuals who 'don't know what we do and they don't want to know either' (Allen 1997: 8). But the differences go deeper with other factors at work. Lee-Potter touches on these when he asserts:

> doctors are unavoidably elitist. They have been used to being amongst the brightest in their schools, they have had to work longer and harder while at university.... The lot of a junior doctor is a hard one, and it does not get much easier during the rest of a medical career, whether in hospital or general practice. From this point of view, the path to chief executive of a trust hospital, on a salary equal to or higher than that of a consultant with at least a 'B' merit award...looks much easier. If the truth were told it probably is.
>
> (Lee-Potter 1997: 249)

Whatever the salience of Lee-Potter's analysis, the relationship between the medical profession and managers is characterised by different sets of aims and objectives, as well as different values. Empirical evidence has been produced by Degeling and colleagues comparing professional subcultures in English and Australian hospitals (Degeling *et al.* 1998). The subcultures comprised five occupational groups: medical clinicians, medical managers, nurse clinicians, nurse managers and lay managers. The study elicited views on various themes such as strategies for dealing with hospital resource issues, the causes of clinical practice variation, who should be involved in setting clinical standards, how clinical units should be managed, and the accountability and autonomy of clinicians. The views obtained were placed alongside the four elements comprising the reform agenda in each country that followed a similar trajectory (Degeling *et al.* 2001). These require health care professionals and managers to:

1   recognise interconnections between the clinical and financial dimensions of care;
2   participate in processes which will increase the stematisation and integration of clinical work and bring it within the ambit of work process control;
3   accept the multidisciplinary and team-based nature of clinical service provision and the need to establish structures and practices capable of supporting this;
4   adopt a perspective which balances clinical autonomy with transparent accountability.

The findings point to significant profession-based differences on each of the four elements of the reform agenda. For instance, clinical purists proceed from the view that efforts to link clinical and resource issues, and make transparent the resource implications of clinical practice, will be detrimental to care. For them, patient need as determined by clinical judgement should be the only determinant of how resources are allocated, and that clinicians should not be held directly responsible for the resource implications of their practices. In contrast, financial realists argue that clinical decisions are also resource decisions and that the two are inherently interconnected. Among the different professional groups, lay managers are strongly financial realists while nurse clinicians tend to be clinical purists. Nurse managers are only marginally financial realists while medical managers (e.g. clinical directors), in keeping with their location at the boundary of clinical and managerial identities, although recognising that all clinical decisions are resource decisions, reject work process control and the systematisation of clinical work.

These findings, and the dissonances they reveal, indicate the barriers that face those seeking to introduce changes in the delivery of health care. For those changes to happen there needs to be a common sense of purpose and a set of core values shared by the key stakeholders. For the most part, these prior conditions do not exist thereby contributing to the state of unhappiness among doctors and others noted earlier. The point to stress is that all attempts to impose managerial controls on clinical work are doomed to failure unless a different approach to managing change is adopted. This is the subject of the final section.

The medicine–management interface: A third way?

As has been shown, the deteriorating relationship between doctors and managers over recent years, coupled with evidence of a growing unhappiness on the part of doctors, are not indicators of a healthy or well-managed organisation. While the final outcome may not be a total collapse of professional autonomy, the bad feeling resulting from the fractured relationship could be sufficient to render the NHS a sick organisation that is rendered incapable of performing optimally. Short-term gains in respect of meeting waiting times and other targets may come at too high a price and prove unsustainable in the long-term. Compounding the dilemma for doctors is a realisation that if they do not take action themselves to participate in management then they are likely to find external management controls over clinical activity strengthened and imposed on them. Indeed, an element of the unhappiness doctors feel is an awareness that this erosion of their responsibility is already occurring.

Yet, at the same time, there are glimmers of a backlash against a reform agenda that allegedly undermines the notion of professionalism in public services like health care (Caulkin 2005). For instance, the chief executive of BP, Lord Browne, is critical of the reckless co-mingling of public and private domains while ignoring their differences. He believes that using market forces inappropriately to deliver public services could damage the professional ethos in health care and elsewhere.

The starting point for breaking out of the downward spiral is an acknowledgement that health care managers need the active participation of doctors to implement changes at the level that clinical work is done (Degeling *et al.* 2003). If 'the systematisation of clinical work' is truly to re-engineer the way health care is managed and delivered, then this can only occur if an accommodation is reached between the differing cultures evident among doctors and managers (Degeling *et al.* 2003). Important, too, are other clinicians, notably nurses, who may often share a more collectivist ethos with managers in place of a medically focused individualistic ethos.

Only then can 'responsible autonomy' flourish. Under such an arrange-ment, in return for more explicit accountability, professionals will be able to exercise professional judgement, determine resource use and ply their craft in an atmosphere of mutual trust. This, after all, is the essence of the philosophy underpinning clinical governance. As Degeling *et al.* (2004) assert, because clinicians are at the core of clinical work, they must be at the heart of clinical governance. 'Recognition of this fact by clinicians, managers, and policy makers is central to re-establishing "responsible autonomy" as a foundation principle in the performance and organization of clinical work' (Degeling *et al.* 2004: 679).

In the light of such evidence, the impact of managerialism on medicine remains equivocal. At a macro-level, there is only limited evidence of a shift in the collective power base of doctors. At a micro-individual level the picture is more mixed. That clinical practice has been changed by the encroachment of management is probably not in doubt at one level, although how much of this may prove to be superficial and short-lived if achieved in the teeth of opposition and weak or non-compliance remains unclear. As exemplars of 'street level bureaucrats', doctors continue to wield considerable influence and exercise discretion over the dispensation of services and the allocation of resources enjoying relative autonomy from organisational authority, despite the raft of government initiatives designed to alter their practices and blunt their power (Lipsky 1980). Doctors may have lost a few minor skirmishes and even some battles but it is still by no means self-evident they have lost the war.

As Mechanic (1991) among others has argued, regardless of the reforms enacted by governments and their differential impact on professional groups either within medicine or between medicine and other occupa-tions, the changes all fall within a continuing medical paradigm thereby perpetuating its intellectual dominance and assuring the power of doctors. Paradoxically, at precisely the time when medical power is being challenged, there is a growing medicalisation of personal and social problems, and strong media interest in biomedical advances as witnessed, for example, by the interest in genetics. The notion of 'a pill for every ill', and vice versa, has arguably never been more prevalent as people search for the quick fix in an age of instant gratification and consumer choice. The application of Lukes's three faces of power is instructive to this analysis, especially his third face which allows for consideration of the many ways in which potential issues are kept out of politics and off the agenda (Lukes 1974). The play of power in this sense can occur in the absence of actual, observable conflict.

The standard objection to Lukes's position is that, since by defini-tion the third dimension of power involves B's values and preferences being shaped by A, there remains no observable conflict of values and therefore no observable exercise of power. It becomes difficult in such circumstances to demonstrate the third dimension empirically. Lukes defends his position by arguing that it is valid for an observer to make a judgement about the 'real' ('objective') interests of actors: to reach, for instance, a conclusion that B has been manipulated into adopting preferences which are actually against B's interests. A classic indicator of the presence of third-face medical power is the phrase 'Doctor knows best' (Harrison *et al.* 1992).

But Lukes's conceptualisation of power is helpful in illuminating and explaining the seeming paradox noted above of a medical profession allegedly under attack and having its power and freedoms curbed on the one hand while, on the other, societal views about doctors, and their status, and about the nature of medicine and health care generally, reinforce the prevailing orthodoxy and serve to blunt attempts to challenge it. Even recent efforts to shift the health policy paradigm in favour of 'upstream' interventions designed to improve the public's health appear to take second place to the relentless drive to invest in downstream curative treatment services and meet ever more challenging targets (Hunter 2003; Wanless 2004). Managers often collude with doctors in the mobilisation of bias. The medical profession, despite the failures at Bristol and the antics of Shipman together with other examples of medical negligence, continues to enjoy high social status and respect. The public would still prefer to put their faith in doctors in preference to managers and politicians (Harrison 1999).

Conclusion

Looking at future options for addressing the tribalism versus corporatism dichotomy, there appear to be three. First, doctors might seek to preserve their current status and freedoms by simply resisting attempts by managers to curtail them and by opting to work around the constraints, game-playing and generally continuing with the ploys that accompany their 'street level' status. Second, doctors could choose to join the ranks of managers in order to thwart, deflect or neutralise the changes being directed at them in the tradition of poacher turned gamekeeper (Hunter 1992). Indeed, if doctors do not participate in management they run the risk of having controls and other intrusions imposed on them. Paradoxically, this may require them having to adopt the trappings of corporatism while at the same time seeking to resist the corporate embrace. Finally, doctors might decide to become managers not only to embrace elements of the reform agenda but to lead, drive and reshape them. This option lies behind the notion of 'responsible autonomy' and entails doctors relinquishing outmoded features of their professional status but in return acquiring new power and influence over the reform agenda. It may even result in a different form of management culture taking root in health care with a shift from a mechanistic target-based approach to one that acknowledges the particular challenges posed by managing complex organisations (Chapman 2004). The losers under this option become the lay or non-medical managers.

The future seems poised between the second and third options. But, as was noted above, whatever the outcome of the tussle between doctors and managers, on another level medicine will be the ultimate victor since the very terms of the reform agenda, and the parameters governing health care systems and their operation, have already been determined by a medical mindset. Neither politicians nor managers have succeeded in challenging this manifestation of medical dominance. Indeed, they show few signs of wishing to do so since the collusion between doctors and the public remains unchallenged. The overall balance of power, therefore, seems likely to remain in doctors' favour even if this means exercising it within a managerial modality.

References

Alford, R. (1975) *Health Care Politics*, Chicago: University of Chicago Press.

Allen, I. (1997) *Committed but Critical: An Examination of Young Doctors' Views of Their Core Values*, London: British Medical Association.

Bristol Royal Infirmary Inquiry (2001) *Learning from Bristol: The Report of the Public Inquiry into Children's Heart Surgery at the Bristol Royal Infirmary 1984–1995*, Cm. 5207 (Chairman: Ian Kennedy), London: The Stationery Office.

Caulkin, S. (2005) 'Management: Time for a commercial break', *The Observer*, 6 March.

Chapman, J. (2004) *System Failure: Why Governments Must Learn to Think Differently*, Second edition, London: Demos.

Day, P. and Klein, R.E. (1983) 'The mobilization of consent versus the management of conflict: Decoding the Griffiths Report', *British Medical Journal*, 287: 1813–15.

Degeling, P., Kennedy, J. and Hill, M. (1998) 'Do professional subcultures set limits to hospital reform?', *Clinician in Management*, 7: 89–98.

Degeling, P., Hunter, D.J. and Dowdeswell, B. (2001) 'Changing health care systems', *Journal of Integrated Care Pathways*, 5 (2): 64–69.

Degeling, P., Macbeth, F., Kennedy, J., Maxwell, S., Coyle, B. and Telfer, B. (2002) *Professional Subcultures and Clinical Governance Implementation in Wales: A Report for the National Assembly for Wales*, Durham: Centre for Clinical

Management Development, University of Durham, and College of Medicine, University of Wales.

Degeling, P., Maxwell, S., Kennedy, J. and Coyle, B. (2003) 'Medicine, management, and modernization: A "danse macabre"?', *British Medical Journal*, 326: 649–52.

Degeling, P.J., Maxwell, S., Iedema, R. and Hunter, D.J. (2004) 'Making clinical governance work', *British Medical Journal*, 329: 679–81.

Dent, M. (1993) 'Professionalism, educated labour and the State: Hospital medicine and the new managerialism', *The Sociological Review*, May: 244–73.

Department of Health (1997) *The New NHS: Modern, Dependable*. Cm. 3807, London: HMSO.

—— (2004) *The NHS Improvement Plan*, London: Department of Health.

Department of Health, Welsh Office, Scottish Home and Health Department, and Northern Ireland (1989) *Working for Patients*. Cm. 555, London: HMSO.

Dobson, F. (1999) 'Modernising Britain's National Health Service', *Health Affairs* 18 (3): 40–1.

Edwards, N. and Marshall, M. (2003) 'Doctors and managers', *British Medical Journal*, 326: 116–17.

Edwards, N., Kornacki, M.J. and Silversin, J. (2002) 'Unhappy doctors: What are the causes and what can be done?', *British Medical Journal*, 324: 835–8.

Evans, R.G. (1990) 'The day in the night-time: Medical practice variations and health policy', in Mooney, G. and Andersen, T.S. (eds), *The Challenge of Medical Practice Variations*, Basingstoke: Macmillan.

—— (1997) 'Health care reform: Who's selling the market and why?', *Journal of Public Health Medicine*, 19 (1): 45–9.

Flynn, R. (1992) *Structures of Control in Health Management*, London: Routledge.

Freidson, E. (1990) 'The centrality of professionalism to health care', *Jurimetrics Journal of Law, Science and Technology*, 30: 431–45.

—— (1993) 'How dominant are the professions?', in Hafferty, F.W. and McKinlay, J.B. (eds) *The Changing Medical Profession: An International Perspective*, New York: Oxford University Press.

Gray, A. and Harrison, S. (eds) (2004) *Governing Medicine: Theory and Practice*, Buckingham: Open University Press.

Greer, S. (2001) *Divergence and Devolution*, London: The Nuffield Trust.

Griffiths, R. (1983) 'NHS Management Inquiry', *Report*, London: DHSS.

Hafferty, F.W. and McKinlay, J.B. (eds) (1993) *The Changing Medical Profession: An International Perspective*, New York: Oxford University Press.

Halligan, A. and Donaldson, L. (2001) 'Implementing clinical governance: Turning vision into reality', *British Medical Journal*, 322: 1413–17.

Ham, C. and Hunter, D.J. (1998) *Managing Clinical Activity in the NHS*, Briefing Paper 8, London: King's Fund Institute.

Harrison, S. (1999) 'Clinical autonomy and health policy: Past and futures', in Exworthy, M. and Halford, S. (eds), *Professionals and the New Managerialism in the Public Sector*, Buckingham: Open University Press.

Harrison, S. and Pollitt, C. (1994) *Controlling Health Professionals: The Future of Work and Organisation in the NHS*, Buckingham: Open University Press.

Harrison, S., Hunter, D.J., Marnoch, G. and Pollitt, C. (1992) *Just Managing: Power and Culture in the National Health Service*, Basingstoke: Macmillan.

HM Government/Department of Health (1998) *A First Class Service: Quality in the New NHS*, London: The Stationery Office.

Hoggett, P. (1991) 'A new management in the public sector', *Policy and Politics* 19 (4): 243–56.

—— (1996) 'New modes of control in the public service', *Public Administration*, 74 (1): 9–32

Hood, C. (1991) 'A new public management for all seasons?', *Public Administration*, 69 (1): 3–19.

Hunter, D.J. (1980) *Coping with Uncertainty: Policy and Politics in the National Health Service*, Chichester: Research Studies Press/Wiley & Sons.

—— (1992) 'Doctors as managers: Poachers turned gamekeepers?', *Social Science and Medicine*, 35 (4): 557–66.

—— (1994) 'From Tribalism to Corporatism: The managerial challenge to medical dominance', in Gabe, J., Kelleher, D. and Williams, G. (eds), *Challenging Medicine*, London: Routledge.

—— (1998) 'Medicine', in Laffin, M. (ed.), *Beyond Bureaucracy? The Professions in the Contemporary Public Sector*, Aldershot: Ashgate.

—— (2002) 'A tale of two tribes: The tension between managerial and professional values', in New, B. and Neuberger, J. (eds), *Hidden Assets: Values and Decision-Making in the NHS*, London: King's Fund.

—— (2003) *Public Health Policy*, Cambridge: Polity.

Jenkins, S. (1995) *Accountable to None: The Tory nationalization of Britain*, London: Hamish Hamilton.

Le Grand, J. (1999) 'Competition, cooperation, or control? Tales from the British National Health Service', *Health Affairs*, 18 (3): 27–39.

Le Grand, J., Mays, N. and Mulligan (eds) (1998) *Learning from the NHS Internal Market*, London: King's Fund.

Lee-Potter, J. (1997) *A Damn Bad Business: The NHS deformed*, London: Gollancz.

Lipsky, M. (1980) *Street-Level Bureaucracy*, New York: Sage.

Lukes, S. (1974) *Power: A Radical View*, London: Macmillan.

McKinlay, J.B. (1988) 'Introduction', *Milbank Quarterly*, 66 (Suppl. 2): 1–9.

McLaughlin, K., Osborne, S.P. and Ferlie, E. (eds) (2002) *New Public Management: Current Trends and Future Prospects*, London: Routledge.

Marmor, T. (2004) *Fads in Medical Care Policy and Politics: The Rhetoric and Reality of Managerialism*, London: The Nuffield Trust.

Mechanic, D. (1991) 'Sources of countervailing power in medicine', *Journal of Health Politics, Policy and Law*, 16 (3): 485–506.

Scally, G. and Donaldson, L. (1998) 'Clinical governance and the drive for quality improvement in the new NHS in England', *British Medical Journal*, 317: 61–5.

Sheldon, T., Cullum, N., Dawson, D., Lankshear, A., Lowson, K., Watt, I., West, P., Wright, D. and Wright, J. (2004) 'What's the evidence that NICE guidance has been implemented? Results from a national evaluation using time series analysis, audit of patients' notes, and interviews', *British Medical Journal*, 329: 999.

The Shipman Inquiry (2004) *Safeguarding Patients: Lessons from the Past – Proposals for the Future, fifth report*, Cm. 6394 (Chair: Dame Janet Smith), London: The Stationery Office.

Wanless, D. (2002) *Securing Our Future Health: Taking a Long-Term View*, Final Report, London: HM Treasury.

—— (2004) *Securing Good Health for the Whole Population*, Final report, London: HMSO.

2   The challenge of nursing

Anne Witz and Ellen Annandale

This chapter takes stock of some of the changes that have been taking place in British nursing over the past two decades and asks whether these changes, together with the changing role of medicine over the same period, suggest the need to reassess the relation between nursing and medicine. Overall, we are wary of any claim that these changes necessarily pose a challenge to medicine. Certainly major changes have been taking place in nursing. And certainly these changes pose challenges *for* nursing, notably the need to be proactive rather than reactive in the context of the ongoing restructuring of the National Health Service (NHS). But we need to be wary of assuming that these changes can – and, as some may assume, should – constitute a challenge *to* medicine. The work of nurses is changing in major ways: many are developing specific clinical skills which parallel those of doctors; gaining mandates to exercise independent clinical judgement in some areas of practice; undertaking independent prescribing; and assuming managerial positions which give them authority in relation to doctors' everyday work.

It is by no means self-evident that these, and other developments, should be considered 'challenges to medicine'. There is no *prima facie* reason to expect that gains in professional autonomy within nursing will reduce or encroach upon the professional powers of medicine in any simple or straightforward way. We will argue instead that developments in nursing have been harnessed to the new public management agenda currently driving reform in the NHS. This agenda is concerned as much, if not more, with economic efficiency as it is with the professional autonomy of medicine or nursing. Indeed, the achievement of economy efficiency is predicated on unsettling the health care division of labour to meet local workforce demands. As the health care division of labour is increasingly fragmented, contestation is likely to be between *individuals* as much, if not more, than between doctors or nurses *as groups*. This suggests that, while it remains important to consider the corporate bodies of medicine and nursing since they are integral to an understanding of health politics, now more than ever we need to also appreciate the multiple divisions within each occupational group and to be alert to the influence of local contexts upon any challenges that nursing might pose to medicine (and vice versa).

Nurse professionalisation: Past and present

Historical continuities as well as discontinuities are evident in nurses' long-standing 'professional project', which has taken the form of an occupational strategy of dual closure (Witz 1990, 1992). This is a double-edged occupational strategy which has its roots in the nineteenth century and has sought not only to challenge medical definitions and control over what nurses know and do (this is its *usurpationary* dimension), but also to create mechanisms of occupational closure that will clearly distinguish who and who might not practice as a nurse (this is its *exclusionary* dimension). In addition, the defining feature of a profession is generally considered to be its distinctive body of knowledge, based on credentials gained through advanced training (Annandale and Field 2003). So credentialism will be a central plank of any professional project. Demarcationary strategies which shape the content of and boundaries between different occupations engaged in the delivery of health care have historically also been central to the professional projects of health care occupations (Witz 1990, 1992; Sandall 1999). To what extent, then, are strategies of closure and demarcation, once so central in shaping the occupational jurisdictions of health care occupations, still relevant to an analysis of the health care division of labour today, and particularly to the relation between nurses and doctors?

One of the main features of the 'new nursing' in Britain has been the reorganisation of nurse education set in train by *Project 2000* (UKCC 1987). The radical reform of nurse education associated with *Project 2000* can be seen as a pulling through of a long-standing credentialist tactic – that is, one that seeks to establish a link between education and practice, ensuring a uniform programme of education and examination for all nurses. This concern with credentialism lay at the heart of Mrs Bedford-Fenwick's vision of nurse autonomy in the late nineteenth century.

Mrs Bedford-Fenwick's struggle for nurse registration was kick-started by her disagreement with the Hospital Association's reluctance to countenance more than 12 months training for nurses. This led her to set up the British Nurses' Association in 1887 to campaign for a system of registration for nurses who had undergone not less than three years training. Here we see how credentialist tactics went hand in hand with legalistic ones, as Mrs Bedford-Fenwick believed that a system of state-sponsored registration was the only way in which 'a general standard of education and a definite system of professional control can be obtained' (*British Journal of Nursing* 1904: 47). Her main objective in campaigning for a state-sponsored system of registration and a Central Nursing Council run by nurses that would prescribe the nurse training curriculum and oversee examinations was to challenge the discretionary powers then enjoyed by hospitals over the length, standard and content of nurse training, as well as over the conditions of nursing labour (Dingwall *et al.* 1988; Witz 1990, 1992; Rafferty 1996).

The *Project 2000* initiative represented a realisation, 100 years on, of many of Mrs Bedford-Fenwick's key demands. Essentially, the *Project 2000* reforms centred on the education of nurses, enabling greater control by nurses over what is taught, how it is taught and where it is taught. The introduction of a single educational route to registration and a three-year education programme followed by specialist branch programmes is very much in line with Mrs Bedford-Fenwick's vision of a single register and a common nursing curriculum followed by specialisation in, for example, midwifery or mental health. One major difference is that midwifery has not been fully absorbed within nursing, as Mrs Bedford had hoped it would be. Like nursing, midwifery has now become an academic (diploma or degree level) undergraduate subject, retaining its own direct-entry programmes as well as separate and distinct competencies.[1]

Furthermore, *Project 2000* introduced nursing control over where and how nurses are trained, prioritising educational over service needs and effectively disentangled nurse education and training from the institutional location of the hospital, relocating this in institutions of higher education and transforming the student nurse from a probationer on a salary into a super-numerary learner with a bursary. This dissociation of nurse education and training from the service needs of hospitals is yet more evidence of historical continuity in nurses' professional project as it too was one of the foremost aims of Mrs Bedford-Fenwick and, indeed, the voluntary hospitals proved the most powerful and vocal opponents to her campaign for nurse registration.

Indeed, we might consider whether, in fact, nurses' professional projects past and present have represented more of a challenge to hospital's service priorities than they have to medicine. There has been a much greater emphasis in recent years on the delineation of the *content* of the nursing role. Whereas legalistic and credentialist tactics are concerned mainly with *occupational control*, any attempt to delineate the content of nursing work necessarily raises the issue of the relation between the nurse and other professionals in the health division of labour and touches more on the issue of jurisdictional powers (Abbott 1988) as well as foregrounding the issue of *demarcation* of inter-occupational relations between different groups involved in the delivery of health care (Witz 1992). *Project 2000* defined the nurse of the future as a ' "knowledgeable doer" able to marshal information to make an assessment of need, devise a plan of care and implement, monitor and evaluate it' (UKCC 1987: 2), as well as exercise individual judgement in applying principles to practice (UKCC 1992). In short, there was a firm expectation that the nurse would be actively involved in and trusted with patient care, not merely supervising its delivery on terms dictated by medicine.

Continuities in nurses' professional project have been noted, but what about discontinuities? *Project 2000* and subsequent nursing reforms have paid far more attention to the nurse's practice, defined not simply in terms of tasks, but of scope, where the emphasis is on professional competencies and individual judgement (hence *accountability*) in applying principles to practice. Still regarded as a watershed in the development of nursing in the UK, the UKCC's (1992) document *The Scope of Professional Practice* did not seek to define the limits to practice in terms of particular tasks to be or not to be performed by nurses, but declared the limits of practice to be 'determined by the knowledge and skills required for safe and competent performance, and that the nurse is accountable for whatever he or she decides or does' (RCN 2002: 26). It is fair to say that the *Scope of Practice* generated not only enthusiasm, but also anxieties. There remains wide-spread confusion over accountability for the new roles which has undoubtedly led some nurses to retreat from undertaking them (Annandale *et al.* 1999; Dowling *et al.* 2000).

When crossing the boundary from traditional nursing work into the medical domain, nurses are held not to the general standards of care expected of a nurse, but to what would be expected of the person, traditionally a doctor, undertaking the task concerned (i.e. the rule of negligence). These anxieties have been all too apparent to those responsible for encouraging new roles in order to deal with service delivery problems. So much so that the Department of Health recently held a series of 'myth busting events' to identify the perceived obstacles to practice innovation in emergency care, an area targeted for major workforce reconfiguration in the UK. This has included laying emphasis on the legal context of practice and emphasising the kinds of tasks that nurses with the appropriate competencies can undertake, such as nurse-led assessment, nurse-initiated thrombolysis, nurse-initiated and nurse-interpreted X-rays, and nurse-initiated interventions based on blood results (RCN/DoH 2003).

But this may do little to allay the anxieties of nurses who work in a complex division of labour, often in low-trust environments (Annandale and Field 2003). This makes clear that defining the scope of practice is not simply a matter internal to nursing; it is also influenced by the *environment* within which nursing takes place and that this is significantly influenced by changing expectations on the part of government, employers and the public, as well as by changes in the practice of other health professions (RCN 2002). It is in this context that nursing's professional bodies have long sought to define the 'new nursing'.

The 'new nursing'

Discourses of the 'new nursing' emerged out of the nursing process philosophy that developed in the USA in the 1950s and began to take hold in Britain in the late 1970s. Basically, the nursing process has underpinned moves to replace a routinised, task-oriented approach to nursing care with a problem-solving, patient-centred approach which defines nursing through a defined domain of 'expertise' which has as its core skill the exercise of judgement to 'match the knowledge base' to an individual client's needs (RCN 2002: 5). It also draws upon knowledge and techniques derived from the humanities and the physical, social, medical and biological sciences (WHO 1991). This emphasis on the core skills of clinical decision-making and clinical judgement certainly takes nursing close – at least in theory – to the ideal-typical core traits of professionalism associated with medicine.

Nursing process philosophy fundamentally redefined the core tasks and responsibilities of the nurse. The traditional demarcations between 'cure' and 'care' were seen as increasingly untenable and blurred by the mid-1980s, the new nursing was seen as posing a threat to medical dominance and the extent to which doctors would be willing to exchange their traditional 'handmaidens' for true clinical partners, or even substitutes, became a key concern (Beardshaw and Robinson 1990). Nonetheless, it was argued that, as nurses became better at advocacy and explaining their actions, doctors would be much more receptive to innovative nursing care and less anxious about nurses interfering in treatment regimes (Kershaw 1992). The 'nursing nineties' was heralded as the decade when nurses would become 'professionals of care' rather than 'handmaidens of cure' (Pashley and Henry 1990: 46). There is no doubt that the nursing process philosophy was used by nurse leaders on both sides of the Atlantic as a means of enhancing their professional status and autonomy. In Britain, the Royal College of Nursing (RCN) was becoming increasingly concerned that post-war nursing roles were becoming *extended* rather than *expanded*. The *extended* role typically describes the extension of nurses' sphere of competence to encompass medically derived, largely routine technical tasks that are delegated by doctors to nurses (Orlando 1987). The new nursing process philosophy, on the other hand, opened up a completely different definition of nurses' role as an *expanded* (or *enhanced*) one encapsulated in the notion of a people-centred rather than a task-centred approach to patients, who are treated as partners in, rather than the passive recipients of, care. So nursing process philosophy has been concerned with redefining the core tasks and responsibilities of the nurse and disrupting received understandings of the relationship between nurses and their patients and between nurses and doctors.

The 'new nursing' advocated a distinctive 'carative' route forward rather than a derivative 'curative' one. The former has often been developed through an explicit critique of the dominant model of medical practice as masculinist. Mimicking a biomedical model of practice, extended roles for nurses are seen by Davies (1995, 2000) and others as inappropriately adopting a masculinist approach to practice, premised on personal autonomy and self-management, impartiality and emotional distance. This may turn upon the historical use of gender to justify nurses' jurisdiction over caring work (Witz 1990, 1992; Gamarnikov 1991). Davies, for example, argues that, rather than seeking inclusion in such a masculine model, nursing should seek to transcend it by adopting an enhanced model of nursing that positively values feminine traits and a patient-centred philosophy of care (see also Salvage 1992). In similar, though less explicitly feminist terms, Hart remarks that the nursing role has developed so that it

> fits within that structure of doing bits that the patriarch – and others – doesn't want to do, rather than defining the role through the work of caring, by helping patients adapt, cope or change through the way in which they work with them and placing all of this on nursing terms.
>
> (Hart 2004: 103)

Yet it also has to be recognised that the discourse of caring is embedded within a discourse of sexual/gender difference (see Chua and Clegg 1990; Witz 1992). How can a discourse of professionalism, with its recourse to qualities such as autonomy, accountability, decision-making and so on be re-centred around a concept of caring – as the new nursing has attempted to do – and yet escape the disruptive and disempowering equivalence between gender and caring? As Reverby (1987) identifies, a crucial dilemma in contemporary nursing is that it is a form of labour shaped by the obligation to care, but exists in a society that refuses to value caring.

In sum, there has been considerable and long-standing discussion on both sides of the Atlantic, and indeed worldwide, about whether expanded and extended roles are mutually exclusive and incompatible. There appears to be an emerging consensus among nurses that change is not acceptable and should not be supported if it means 'picking up the work or tasks that others leave behind or choose to delegate' (RCN 2003b: 7), and that technical task-oriented work is in the interests of neither nurse nor patient. At the same time, it is increasingly emphasised that the 'carative' approach is not necessarily inimical to nurses taking on diagnostic and treatment care, and practices such as independent prescribing,[2] particularly at advanced or higher levels of practice such as in the work of advanced nurse practitioners, clinical nurse specialists and nurse consultants (RCN 2002, 2003a, 2003b).

The compatibility/incompatibility of extended and expanded roles has been particularly debated in primary care, where the pace of change in the organisation of care has been swifter, so much so that it has been argued that 'role delegation and substitution between and within professional groups is changing the face of inter-professional relations' (Hart 2004). Delivering government's *The NHS Plan* (Department of Health 2000b) is contingent on a shift to a primary care or community-led health service which has changes in nursing roles and patient roles at its core. Dent and Burtney (1997) argue that the impetus for redrawing boundaries between medicine and nursing roles has seen new demands placed by health authorities on general practitioners (GPs) and that this has meant, once again, that the expansion of practice nurses has been propelled by state sponsorship rather than nurses' professionalising discourse.

It is significant that the major development to date in primary care has been the increase in practice nurses – there has been a phenomenal growth in the number of practice nurses, in England alone rising from 9600 in 1993 to 13,000 in 2003 (DoH 2004) – rather than nurse practitioners, which appears to provide evidence of nurses extending, rather than expanding, their role. Writing in the early 1990s, for example, Williams *et al.* (1993: 58) asked the significant question of 'whether the practice nurse will perform an instrumental role acting as a complement, probably a subordinate, to the general practitioner or if they will act as a substitute to the doctor becoming more fully involved in health education and counselling as a nurse practitioner?' There is at least a suggestion that the new framework for nursing in primary care has the potential to take us beyond both these scenarios via nurse-led primary medical services, such as minor injuries clinics, rapid response teams, Walk In Centres and lead roles in supporting patients with chronic illnesses. In these terms, the Department of Health emphasises three core functions for primary care nurses, which have the potential for both extension and expansion. These are: (1) at *first contact*, acute assessment, diagnosis, care, treatment and referral; (2) *continuing care*, including rehabilitation and chronic disease management; and (3) the *delivery of health protection and promotion* programmes that improve health and reduce health inequalities (DoH 2002c: 8). Significantly, it is in primary care that we have witnessed the most vocal opposition from doctors to nurses' 'encroachment' on their domain. Back in the mid-1980s, The Cumberledge Report (DHSS 1986) on neighbourhood nursing recommended the appointment of nurse practitioners, yet doctor's response to this report revealed strong resistance to the idea of nurses acting autonomously in the field of primary care. In the early 1990s, General Medical Guidelines on nurse prescribing and other forms of task delegation to nurses remained ambiguous and the General Medical Council (GMC) was bombarded with letters requesting advice and clarification from GPs. More recently, we have witnessed a 'chorus of doctors' disapproval' to nurse practitioner roles and the introduction of NHS Direct (a nurse-led 24-hour telephone helpline) (Hart 2004). In summary, this suggests on the one hand that recent developments – notably those in primary care – offer the potential for (some) nurses to combine extended and expanded roles and thereby draw to a close the long-standing debate within the profession about 'which route' nurses should take. Yet, on the other hand it makes clear the context-specific character of new roles and hence the context-specific nature of interprofessional relations and any 'challenge' to medicine by nursing. As Peckham and Exworthy explain, the boundaries of GPs' work are being fundamentally redrawn through new relationships with hospital consultants, primary care nurses and others. 'However, it would be premature to interpret all these "boundary" changes as being inimical to medical autonomy' (2004: 107).

The challenge to medicine?

As important as these debates within nursing are – and here it should be stressed that they are taking place between nurses 'on the ground' as well as at the level of professional bodies such as the RCN – we would argue that they would have had little or no chance of impacting the power and autonomy of medicine without external challenges to medicine through health care reform from the 1980s onwards.

The past 15 years have seen seismic change in the NHS in the UK (although, since getting its own parliament, Scotland now has autonomous control over budgets and policy). This has been a crucial period in changing the ways in which health care is organised and delivered, not simply in terms of re-demarcation between different occupational groups, but also in terms of the broader political, economic and organisational changes in the health service. Significant pronouncements on the decline of the medical profession go back within medical sociology to at least the mid-1980s and make reference (particularly in the USA) to the corporatisation and bureaucratisation of the profession (e.g. in managed care environments) as the state, insurance companies and health care companies attempt to cut costs and raise revenues by holding doctors accountable for practice decisions (e.g. Freidson 1986; McKinlay and Marceau 2002). Most commentators see new nursing roles as a central plank in this process. McKinlay and Marceau, for example, remark that physicians 'had the playing field to themselves for most of the 20th century, but the last several decades witnessed the arrival of a group of ever more powerful and legitimate new players who are threatening the physician's traditional game' (2002: 391). The point of course is that non-physician providers often cost significantly less and there is growing (although not uncontested) evidence that, under optimum conditions, they can provide quality of care equivalent to that of doctors. In the USA, in particular, the concern is that this can challenge physician autonomy where it arguably hurts most: in their financial pockets during a time of economic physician over-supply. But these conditions hardly pertain in the UK which has fewer doctors per head of the population than many other Western countries and currently does not have enough doctors to deliver a comprehensive, high-quality service (Wanless 2002). Nevertheless there is every reason to argue recent policy changes are a state-sponsored attempt to challenge medicine and resolve workforce shortages (following key changes such as the statutory reduction in junior doctors' hours) through changes to nursing practice.

One might have expected the 'New Labour' government's modernisation agenda to have intensified the alleged shift from Fordist or hierarchicalised and bureaucratised modes of work organisation towards a post-Fordist mode of governance which enhances functional flexibility in the NHS (Walby *et al.* 1994). Certainly, health policy documents and workforce planning are currently driven by a post-Fordist rhetoric of functional flexibility that espouses the more flexible deployment of staff 'as teams of people rather than as different professional tribes' (DoH 2000a: 9). Emphasis is placed on team working across professional boundaries, on flexible working, on 'maximising the contribution of all staff to patient care, doing away with barriers which say only doctors or nurses can provide particular types of care', and on developing new, more flexible careers structures for staff too. The anti-professionalism rhetoric is couched in terms of 'liberating' skills, and the prime benefactor is the patient who 'will get more flexible, faster and effective care' (DoH 2000a: 5, 11). This is by no means a new discourse, though, and attempts have been made to dismantle traditional demarcations between nurses and doctors, and between nurses and health/care assistants for well over a decade now (Annandale *et al.* 1999). Indeed, there is political expediency in portraying health service staff as a conservative force for it deflects undivided attention away from 'the thorny question of resource allocation' (Allen and Hughes 2002: 101), while providing a solution to it framed in terms of staff recalcitrance to move forward in innovative ways. In a recent Fabian Society paper the Prime Minister Tony Blair offered front-line staff a 'new partnership' based on, from the government's side, 'more investment, more recruitment, better pay and conditions', in expectation in return of 'high standards of professional engagement [and]...a new flexibility in the professions that break down old working practices, old demarcations' (Blair 2002: 23).

However, it is one thing to point to policy changes that intend the breaking of professional boundaries to challenge medical prerogatives and thereby cut costs and help resolve workforce shortfalls, but quite another to say that *nurses* are in practice challenging medicine at the present time. As remarked upon at the start of the chapter, perhaps the most telling outcome of these changes has been the generation of a more fragmented and contested health care division of labour. Taken alongside the increasing specialised and divided characters of both nursing and medicine, it is premature to suggest that the former is successfully 'challenging' the latter. The waters become very muddied when we try to build up a coherent picture of the various ways in which 'new nursing' practice might impinge on medicine and this is even before we attempt to assess medicine's response and whether any challenge should be viewed in a positive or negative light. Although there is a strong central policy steer, developments have been local and piecemeal. Not surprisingly therefore, considerable energy has been expended trying to formulate a coherent framework for new roles. The new pay system (DoH 2002a, 2003a) which applies one set of terms and conditions for all NHS staff groups may go some way towards this, as might the introduction of a stronger leadership role in the form of the new modern matrons who are charged, among other things, with empowering nurses to take on a wider range of clinical tasks (DoH 2003b). The Department of Health's Chief Nursing Officer has provided a list of ten key roles for nursing (DoH 2000b) which includes: ordering diagnostic investigations, admitting and discharging certain patients for specified conditions under agreed protocols, running clinics such as ophthalmology or rheumatology, and performing minor surgery and outpatient procedures. Nonetheless, we are faced at the present time with a bewildering array of 'new roles'. One mapping exercise by Read *et al.* (2001) identified 838 new nursing roles across 40 acute trusts alone. Moreover, they found that individuals in these roles were often isolated and lacked support, and that managerial accountability and role boundaries were often unclear and misunderstood by stakeholders. Specific examples are legion. For example, the Department of Health has produced (DoH 2002b: 1) a booklet to provide practical examples of nurses and midwives who are, as they put it, 'working smarter to provide services that patients want and which help to meet NHS objectives'. The booklet describes a number of 'new role' case studies as they have developed in specific settings, and also provides general guidelines for 'getting started' in developing these roles.

The anxieties that lack of role clarity generates are likely to be exacerbated by the new managerialism which sets new organisational conditions within which nurses carry out their work and exercise their newfound professional autonomy. In any assessment of the impact of the new public management on nursing it is important to note variances in management strategy at the hospital level as managers devise different kinds of strategic responses to, for example, the statutory reduction in junior doctors' hours. It has been suggested that management is not encroaching significantly on nursing autonomy and is continuing to utilise fully trained nurses, but on different employment contracts and surrounded by increasing numbers of bank and agency nurses (Ackroyd and Bolton 1999; Bolton 2004). The tendency has been for managers to extend the nursing role than to encroach significantly on the existing autonomy of doctors by expanding their expertise (Bolton 2004). It has also been argued that there has been a reduction in the proportion of qualified nurses to less qualified health/care assistants (Grimshaw 1999; Daykin and Clarke 2000). In this context, it is not simply a matter of 'less skilled' staff taking on tasks shed by nurses, but also assuming responsibilities for those shed by doctors. For example, a new clinical aid who might be focused on venepuncture or a receptionist in primary care settings undertaking blood glucose testing. These developments are taken by Daykin and Clarke (2000) in their study of skill mix projects to indicate that post-Fordist practices of de-skilling are leading to the diminishing of nurse authority and the increase in managerial control over the nursing labour process.

Post-Fordist flexibility and the associated complexity, indeed confusion, over the nature and scope of 'new roles' and their interface with medicine all add up to a picture of local variability. This leads us to stress the point raised earlier, that any notion of 'challenge' at the level of practice (rather than the discourse of professional bodies) is likely to be context-specific. Most important for individual doctors and nurses then are the 'challenges' that mark everyday work be this on the hospital ward, the outpatient clinic or primary care setting. Moreover, it is argued that this contestation is fostered by the boundary-breaking managerial agenda which envisages individuals holding *each other* to account for actions under conditions of low trust and relatively high anxiety (Annandale 1996).

Making the point that contestation is context-specific continues a long-standing tradition of conceptualising medical and nursing work as 'negotiated' action (see Annandale *et al.* 2004). This work makes clear that doctors are far less omniscient and nurses far less subservient than Stein's original (1967) analysis of the 'doctor–nurse game' – where nursing input to doctors' decisions was not acknowledged. If not completely dead, the doctor–nurse game has become more complex (see Porter 1995). For example, Svensson (1996) argued (on the basis of a study of five Swedish hospitals) that changes in the structural context of health work have facilitated inter-occupational negotiation between nurses and doctors and that this has augmented the influence of nurses *vis-à-vis* doctors. He identifies three key drivers of change: the increasing prevalence of chronic illness; the shift from task- to team-based nursing; and the introduction of 'sitting rounds' which provide the opportunity for discussion between nurses and doctors prior to 'walking rounds'. Allen (1997, 2001) builds on Svensson's analysis, but focuses on features of nurses' and doctors' work that inhibit inter-occupational negotiation. She argues that, in fact, there has been *little* negotiation between nurses and doctors in a climate of change but a lot of non-negotiated boundary-blurring by nurses. Allen argues that this type of boundary-blurring by nurses, which has taken the form of nurses extending their scope of practice to mop up the shortfall in junior doctors' hours and encompasses administration of intravenous antibiotics, venepuncture, ECGs, male catheterisation and intravenous cannulation, is a taken-for-granted feature of normal nursing practices, facilitated by the organisational turbulence of the work environment. Other research (e.g. Annandale *et al.* 1999) also indicates that nurses' willingness to undertake extended roles is not only context-dependent (e.g. related to work-load), but also related to their inter-personal relationships – notably feelings of trust or lack of trust – between colleagues.

Conclusion

The Department of Health sees the workforce fit for the twenty-first century as one that abandons its preoccupation with professional demarcation and embraces team working based on patients' needs (DOH 2004). The paradoxical situation where nurses' rhetoric of professionalisation seems to be fairly resilient in the face of the more general attack on professional monopolies and demarcation may well have more to do with the cost-cutting potential of a nursing service with its core of highly skilled, registered nurses surrounded by a peripheral workforce of cheaper care assistants than with the re-demarcation of medical and nursing roles and any significant challenge to medical dominance by nurses. Certainly, the shift away from a task-centred division of labour towards a patient-centred form of care that has driven NHS management through the 1990s and into the twenty-first century maps neatly onto nurses' professionalising rhetoric of nurse–patient partnerships in care, as does the shift away from a definition of nursing in terms of 'certificates for tasks' and towards 'principles for practice'.

Significantly, in the light of the above discussion of nurses' professional project as a strategy of dual closure, pursuit of the expanded (or enhanced) nursing role entails both exclusionary and usurpatory dimensions. It might be seen as exclusionary in the sense that the new, expanded nursing role also entails a vision of a new division of labour in caring, where diagnostic autonomy in relation to care in illness and in health becomes the privilege of the few surrounded by lesser skilled health care assistants (HCAs). Research is currently underway to assess the impact of the new public management on the composition of the nursing workforce, particularly whether the core of skilled or elite nurses is diminishing whilst the periphery of lesser skilled care assistants is growing (see, for example, Ackroyd and Bolton 1999; Grimshaw 1999; Daykin and Clarke 2000; Thornley 2001; Bolton 2004). The expanded nursing role might also be seen as usurpatory because it entails a renegotiation of diagnostic and decision-making responsibilities *vis-à-vis* the patient, with certain areas of decision-making becoming the domain of nurses, with others retained by doctors. Furthermore, the new nursing set in train by *Project 2000* is not simply about redefining the scope of nursing practice, but also raises the issue of *demarcation* between different groups in the health division of labour – not simply doctors and nurses, but also nurses surrounded by a constellation of lesser and differently skilled HCAs.

Notes

1 We focus in this chapter on nursing rather than midwifery. However, as Sandall (1999) shows, it is possible to explore midwifery's relationship to medicine through Witz's 'dual closure' model. Historically, midwives have been subject to demarcationary closure from medical men. This has revolved around an ongoing struggle over definitions of 'normal' and 'abnormal' birth and the boundaries between them. Recent policy changes which stress continuity of care and partnership between midwife and client provide the opportunity for midwives to carve out a discrete sphere of knowledge and practice. However, as Sandall explains, this potential challenge to medicine by a professionalising elite may exclude the rank and file midwife, that is, it has exclusionary as well as usurpatory dimensions.

2 All first level registered nurses may legally train to independently prescribe from the *Nurse Prescribers' Extended Formulary*. Extended formulary nurse prescribing is a central plank in the development of the role of nurses (see DoH 2005).

References

Abbott, A. (1988) *The System of Professions*. Chicago: Chicago University Press.

Ackroyd, S. and Bolton, S. (1999) 'It Is Not Taylorism: Mechanisms of Work Intensification in the Provision of Gynaecological Services in a NHS Hospital', *Work, Employment & Society*, 13(2): 369–87.

Allen, D. (1997) 'The Nursing-Medical Boundary: A Negotiated Order', *Sociology of Health and Illness*, 19(4): 498–520.

—— (2001) *The Changing Shape of Nursing Practice*. London: Routledge.

Allen, D. and Hughes, D. (2002) *Nursing and the Division of Labour in Healthcare*. Basingstoke: Palgrave Macmillan.

Annandale, E. (1996) 'Working on the Front Line: Risk Culture and Nursing in the New NHS', *The Sociological Review*, 44(3): 416–51.

Annandale, E. and Field, D. (2003) 'The Division of Labour in Nursing', in S. Taylor and D. Field (eds), *Sociology of Health and Health Care* (3rd edition). Oxford: Blackwell.

Annandale, E., Clark, J. and Allen, E. (1999) 'Interprofessional Working: An Ethnographic Case Study of Emergency Health Care', *Journal of Interprofessional Care*, 13(2): 139–50.

Annandale, E., Elston, M. and Prior, L. (eds) (2004) 'Medical Work, Medical Knowledge and Health Care. Themes and Perspectives', *Medical Work, Medical Knowledge and Health Care*. Oxford: Blackwell.

Beardshaw, V. and Robinson, R. (1990) *New for Old? Prospects for Nursing in the 1990s*, London: King's Fund Institute.

Blair, T. (2002) *The Courage of Our Convictions*. Fabian Ideas 603. London: The Fabian Society.

Bolton, S. (2004) 'A Simple Matter of Control? Hospital Nurses and New Management', *Journal of Management Studies*, 14(2): 317–33.

Chua, T. and Clegg, S. (1990) 'Professional Closure: The Case of British Nursing', *Theory and Society*, 19(2): 132–72.

Davies, C. (1995) *Gender and the Professional Predicament in Nursing*. Buckingham: Open University Press.

—— (2000) 'Care and the Transformation of Professionalism', in Davies, C., Findlay, L. and Bullman, A. (eds), *Changing Practice in Health and Social Care*. London: Sage, pp. 343–540.

Daykin, N. and Clarke, B. (2000) ' "They'll Still Get the Bodily Care". Discourses of Care and Relationships between Nurses and Health Care Assistants in the NHS', *Sociology of Health and Illness*, 22(3): 349–64.

Dent, M. and Burtney, E. (1997) 'Changes in Practice Nursing: Professionalism, Segmentation and Sponsorship', *Journal of Clinical Nursing*, 6: 355.

Department of Health (2000a) *A Health Service of All the Talents. Developing the NHS Workforce*. London: DoH.

—— (2000b) *The NHS Plan*. London: DoH.

—— (2002a) *Agenda for Change*. London: Stationary Office.

—— (2002b) *Developing Key Roles for Nurses and Midwives*. London: DoH.

—— (2002c) *Liberating the Talents. Helping Primary Care Trusts and Nurses to Deliver the NHS Plan*. London: DoH.

—— (2003a) *The New NHS Pay System. An Overview*. London: DoH.

—— (2003b) *Modern Matrons – Improving the Patient Experience*. London: DoH.

—— (2004) *The NHS Workforce in England 2003*. London: HMSO.

—— (2005) *Medicine Matters. A Guide to Current Mechanisms for the Prescribing, Supply and Administration of Medicines*. London: DoH.

Department of Health and Social Security (DHSS) (1986) *Neighbourhood Nursing: A Focus for Care, a Report of the Community Nursing Review in England* (chairperson, Julia Cumberlege), London: HMSO.

Dingwall, R., Rafferty, A.M. and Webster, C. (1988) *An Introduction to the Social History of Nursing*. London: Routledge.

Dowling, S., Martin, R., Skidmore, P., Doyal, L., Cameron, A. and Lloyd, S. (2000) 'Nurses Taking on Junior Doctors' Work: A Confusion of Accountability', in Davies, C., Finlay, L. and Bullman, A. (eds), *Changing Practice in Health and Social Care*. London: Open University/Sage.

Freidson, E. (1986) *Professional Powers*. Chicago: University of Chicago Press.

Gamarnikov, E. (1991) 'Nurse or Woman: Gender and Professionalism in Reformed Nursing 1860–1923', in Holden, P. and Littlewood, J. (eds), *Anthropology and Nursing*. London: Routledge.

Grimshaw, D. (1999) 'Changes in Skills-Mix and Pay Determination among the Nursing Workforce in the UK', *Work, Employment & Society*, 13(2): 295–328.

Hart, C. (2004) *Nurses and Politics*. Basingstoke: Palgrave.

Kershaw, B. (1992) 'Models of Nursing', in Jolley, M. and Bryhezynska, G. (eds), *Nursing Care: The Challenge to Change*. London: Edward Arnold.

McKinlay, J. and Marceau, L. (2002) 'The End of the Golden Age of Doctoring', *International Journal of Health Services*, 32(2): 379–416.

Orlando, I.J. (1987) 'Nursing in the 21st century; Alternate paths', *Journal of Advanced Nursing*, 12: 403–12.

Pashley, G. and Henry, C. (1990) 'Carving out the Nursing Nineties', *Nursing Times*, 86: 45–6.

Peckham, S. and Exworthy, M. (2004) *Primary Care in the UK*. Basingstoke: Palgrave.

Porter, S. (1995) *Nursing's Relationship with Medicine*. Aldershot: Avebury.

Rafferty, A.M. (1996) *The Politics of Nursing Knowledge*. London: Routledge.

Read, S., Jones, M.L., Collins, K., McDonnell, A., Jones, R., Doyal, L., Masterton, A., Dowling, S., Vaughan, B., Furlong, S. and Scholes, J. (2001) *Exploring New Roles in Practice* (ENRip). SSHAR, University of Sheffield.

Reverby, S. (1987) *Ordered to Care: The Dilemma of American Nursing 1850–1945*. Cambridge: Cambridge University Press.

Royal College of Nursing (2002) *Defining Nursing*. London: RCN.

—— (2003a) *The Future Nurse*. London: RCN.

—— (2003b) *The Future Nurse*. Interim report. London: RCN.

Royal College of Nursing/Department of Health (2003) *Freedom to Practise: Dispelling the Myths*. London: DoH/RCN.

Salvage, J. (1992) 'The New Nursing: Empowering Patients or Empowering Nurses?', in Robinson, J., Gray, A. and Elkan, R. (eds), *Policy Issues in Nursing*. Milton Keynes: Open University Press.

Sandall, J. (1999) 'Choice, Continuity and Control: Changing Midwifery towards a Sociological Perspective', in Van Teijlingen, E., Lowis, G., McCaffery, P. and Porter, M. (eds), *Midwifery and the Medicalization of Childbirth*. Science Publishers, Inc: Huntington, New York.

Svensson, R. (1996) 'The Interplay between Doctors and Nurses – a Negotiated Order Perspective', *Sociology of Health and Illness*, 18(3): 379–98.

Thornley, C. (2001) Divisions in Health-Care Labour', in Komaromy, C. (ed.), *Dilemmas in UK Health Care* (3rd edition). Buckingham: Open University Press.

UKCC (1987) *Project 2000: The Final Proposals*. London: UKCC.

—— (1992) *The Scope of Professional Practice*. London: UKCC.

Walby, S., Greenwell, J. and Soothil, K. (1994) *Medicine and Nursing. Profession in a Changing Health Service*. London: Sage.

Wanless (2002) *Securing Our Future Health: Taking a Long-Term View*. Final Report. London: HM Treasury.

Williams, S.J., Calnan, M., Cant, S.L. and Coyle, J. (1993) 'All Change in the NHS? Implications of the NHS Reforms for Primary Care Prevention', *Sociology of Health and Illness*, 15: 43–67.

Witz, A. (1990) 'Patriarchy and Professions: The Gendered Politics of Occupational Closure', *Sociology*, 24: 675–90.

—— (1992) *Professions and Patriarchy*. London: Routledge.

World Health Organisation (1991) *Nursing in Action Project: Mission and Functions of the Nurse*. Copenhagen: WHO.

3 Litigation and the threat to medicine

Robert Dingwall and Pru Hobson-West

In 1984, *Sociology of Health and Illness* published an article by Philip Strong on 'The academic encirclement of medicine'. This continued his attack on sociologists' uncritical adoption of the thesis of medical imperialism (Strong 1979a). On the contrary, he argued, medicine occupied such a large space in contemporary society that it had become a major target for jurisdictional entrepreneurs in other fields. Law was a newcomer to this enterprise. The 1980 Reith Lectures by Ian Kennedy (1981), a prominent academic lawyer, had staked a public claim to legal jurisdiction over large areas of health care. Kennedy has repeatedly returned to these themes, most recently as Chair of the inquiry into perioperative deaths in paediatric cardiac surgery at the Bristol Royal Infirmary during the early 1980s (Bristol Royal Infirmary Inquiry 2001). Dingwall and Strangleman (2005) note how the final report repeats his earlier criticisms of medicine for persistent paternalism, hierarchy, excessive clinical freedom, underman-agement and lack of accountability, and urges that it should become more open, accountable, quality-oriented and patient-centred, using National Health Service (NHS) employment discipline to achieve these goals. Much the same might be said of the report by Dame Janet Smith, a senior judge, on the implications for the regulation of health care professionals arising from her inquiry into the murderous practice of Dr Harold Shipman, who is believed to have killed more than 500 elderly patients between 1974 and 1998 (Shipman Inquiry Fifth Report 2004). As Eliot Freidson (1982: 97) remarked, however, in a contemporary review of Kennedy's Reith Lectures:

> Merely attacking the pathologies of medical authoritarianism...does not help because it does not give us a sensitive and informed under-standing of how and why they are so persistent even in the face of their massive cost...The broad public too has colluded with medicine, capital and the state in preserving the system...Are [there dangers in] merely

substituting... 'professional' laymen for professional 'experts'... becoming at least as coercive and elitist as what [is] replaced?

Dame Janet Smith conceded, in her covering letter on her Fifth Report to the Secretary of State for Health and the Home Secretary, that

> [The GMC] cannot be held responsible for the fact that Shipman was free to practise although he was regularly killing his patients. The fact that no concerns were ever raised about his treatment of any of the patients that he killed must be attributed partly to Shipman's cunning and plausibility but also in part to the culture within the medical profession and within our society as a whole. The profession was held in such deference that people were unwilling to question the actions of a doctor.

This did not, however, prevent her from recommending wholesale reforms of the General Medical Council (GMC) designed to transfer effective regulatory power from the GMC to the NHS and the courts, much as Kennedy had done and despite the fact that the ink was barely dry on the implementation of the NHS Reform and Health Care Professions Act 2002 and the GMC's Fitness to Practice Rules 2004, both of which responded to Kennedy's Bristol Royal Infirmary report.

Strong (1984: 354) saw Kennedy's original challenge as 'little more than legal imperialism in populist clothing' and many medical sociologists would apply the same analysis to subsequent developments, uncritically adopting the medical profession's own perception. In his conclusion, though, Strong hints at another direction when he links the challenges to medicine to changes in the forms of governmentality, the interlocking systems of values and institutions constitutive of the ordering of a society (Foucault 1979; Burchell *et al.* 1991). The threats from legal imperialism are trivial compared with the process of reconstructing the bases of authority in Anglo-American society, which he could only glimpse in 1984 and which has now run much further.

It is undeniable that British doctors feel threatened by law. They analyse it as a constraint on clinical autonomy, something that forces them to act in ways that they would not choose to. But it can be argued that this mistakes both the real character of law and the real threat that it represents to the role of medicine in social life. Law is also a creative force, constitutive of the social and economic orders in which medical practice occurs. This chapter, then, will deal with the obvious challenges from law, in the form of litigation and regulation, mainly by way of an introduction to the shifting cultural environment created by the substitution of legalisation for medicalisation as the paramount mode of governmentality.

The legal environment of medical practice

Law suffuses modern medical practice. Doctors engage in a host of legal transactions every working day. They make contracts of employment, they lease premises and equipment, and they try to avoid committing torts. Doctors interpret and enforce laws, deciding who can get an abortion or who can get compensation from the social security system for certain industrial diseases. They collect evidence for criminal prosecutions and authorise the detention of people with mental disorders in secure places. They are regulated by laws requiring the notification of births, deaths and specified diseases, governing the availability of organs for transplantation and restricting the right to carry out certain treatments or prescribe certain substances. Modern medicine is a profoundly socio-legal activity. But to list these entanglements is also to underline the inadequacy of a view of law, whether by doctors or medical sociologists, as a purely constraining force: doctors are also users of law. Every general practice relies upon the law of partnership to create the organisational forms that make this mode of professional relationship possible. The NHS was created by statute and is governed by a mixture of administrative legal means. All health professions are legal inventions.[1]

Nevertheless, in most medical discourse, the presence of law tends to be identified with its use to challenge individual practitioners. This perception conflates three lines of legal development. The first is the legal form of the profession itself, the body of statutes and delegated legislation that constitute the profession as a distinctive socio-legal entity, defining its membership, establishing the terms of its licence and specifying the means by which compliance will be monitored and enforced through a governance structure. The second applies only to doctors working in the public sector or under contract with the public sector. This is the body of administrative law that provides for the redress of patient grievances through complaints to the bodies managing the service or holding the contracts.[2] The third is the general body of common law, particularly the tort of negligence. Of these, the first has been left relatively uncontested by the profession itself since the revolts against the governance structure of the GMC in 1970–72 and the subsequent reforms (Stacey 1992: 29–44), although there are indications of growing unrest about the impact of the NHS Reform and Health Care Professions Act 2002. This has given the government much greater power to control professional regulatory bodies and, in particular, introduced a super-regulator in the Council for Healthcare Regulatory Excellence (CHRE) (formerly the Council for the Regulation of Healthcare Profes-sionals). The CHRE's interventions in the procedures and decisions of the individual bodies seem likely to become a significant source of friction.

The CHRE can introduce double jeopardy – trying a practitioner twice for the same allegations – by referring the conclusions of professional tribunals to the courts for further review ('section 29 referrals'). It has also proved hostile to the professions' emphasis on the reintegration and rehabilitation of offenders, tending to press for a more punitive approach. Despite the CHRE's origins in the promptings of legal critics like Kennedy, both of these practices conflict with contemporary legal understandings of human rights and effective penology.[3] Everyday professional anxieties, however, tend to be most closely bound up with concerns about the third type of legal intervention – tort litigation.

Medical negligence litigation in the UK

The tort action is the oldest means of legal redress available to dissatisfied patients. It rests on the theory that members of a society owe each other a duty of care, to avoid harming each other, whether the injury is to the person or to their legitimate interests. If someone fails in this duty, they should pay sufficient compensation to their victim to restore them to their previous condition. The risk of such a payment is a deterrent, an incentive for potential wrongdoers to take their duty of care seriously and to try to behave in a way that limits the possibility of harm. It is important to emphasise that there is nothing special about the position of doctors in tort law. The principles involved are exactly the same for all citizens.

The most relevant type of tort here is *negligence*, where someone has failed to use reasonable care in the performance of a duty or obligation and has caused a material injury to another person. In the specific instance of medicine, this means that an injury has been caused to a patient by a doctor's failure to act in accordance with the profession's customary standards. Both the causal connection and the departure from practices 'accepted as proper by a responsible body of medical men skilled in that particular art' (*Bolam v. Friern Hospital Management Committee* [1957] 2 All ER 118) must be proven for an action to succeed.

The profession has clearly felt under threat from tort litigation since the early 1980s. Although exposure to the risk of litigation varies considerably by specialty (Dingwall and Fenn 1992), most of the Royal Colleges and the British Medical Association (BMA) had conferences and working parties reviewing the situation during the 1980s. These institutional concerns were paralleled by grass-roots correspondence to medical journals and coverage in the trade press. The partnership between the NHS and the medical defence organisations in managing negligence claims, established in 1954, fell apart under the pressure and responsibility for claims against NHS-employed doctors was nationalised in 1990. Since 1995, this has taken the form of a pooling arrangement known as the Clinical Negligence Scheme for Trusts (CNST). This is administered by the NHS Litigation Authority (NHSLA) and meets claims arising from incidents since April 1995. (An Existing Liabilities Scheme covers outstanding liabilities for events prior to 1995.) Initially, trusts could select an excess figure, below which they would meet all the costs of a claim but since April 2002 the NHSLA has taken over the entire responsibility for claims against the NHS. This change was justified on the grounds that the decentralisation of responsibilities for low-value claims was unduly burdensome for hospital management and led to difficulties in producing consolidated estimates for the NHS accounts. It was also argued that the transfer would place the NHSLA in a better position to report national trends in the frequency and cost of medical litigation, and to identify risky activities and procedures.

Nationalisation initially deflected some of the pressure for more fundamental changes, reflected in two Private Members Bills, in 1990 and 1991, and the 1992 Labour Party election manifesto. However, continuing concern about the capacity of a tort-based approach to either provide fair compensation or create effective deterrence has revived interest in reform (Bristol Royal Infirmary Report 2001; National Audit Office 2001; House of Commons Public Accounts Committee 2002). The Secretary of State for Health established an Advisory Group in 2001 to examine the situation, and published a consultative paper in June 2003 (DoH 2003). This proposed a partial 'no-fault' scheme, where compensation would be based solely on demonstrating an adverse outcome caused by NHS treatment without having to prove that any particular individual or organisation had been negligent in a legal sense. A 'Redress Scheme' would offer a fast procedure for resolving 'small claims' (under £30,000) and a full no-fault scheme would be available for compensating birth-related neurological injuries (which currently account for most of the high-cost and high-complexity litigation). Victims would retain the right to sue through the courts but (except for neurologically impaired babies) would be expected first to apply to the NHS Redress Scheme. Those accepting packages of care (where possible to be provided by the NHS) and compensation under the scheme would waive their right to litigate on the same case.

In fact the claims of a litigation crisis have always been somewhat exaggerated (Towse and Danzon 1999; Fenn *et al.* 2000). The Public Accounts Committee's 2000–01 estimate of an outstanding liability of £4.4 billion, for example, assumed that every single claim notified to the NHS would be paid immediately in full, in contrast to the insurance industry's practice of discounting claims by the probability of a pay-out and by their future value. Since medical negligence claims have a relatively low probability of success and tend to be quite slow in closure, because of the difficulties in establishing fault and causation, this approach is particularly misleading.

Paul Fenn and various colleagues have produced the best estimates of trends in the frequency of negligence claims and in their severity, the cost of settlement (Ham *et al.* 1988; Fenn and Dingwall 1990; Fenn *et al.* 1994; Fenn *et al.* 2000; Fenn *et al.* 2004). These suggest that claims frequency grew slowly during the 1970s, accelerated during the first part of the 1980s and then continued to rise at about 7 per cent per year during the 1990s, adjusting for increasing hospital activity. Costs increased from £50 million in 1990 to £294 million in 2000–01 on the same basis. However, NHS funding has also increased rapidly over the same period so that, on our estimate, this remains around 0.2 per cent of the total budget. By contrast, Fenn *et al.*'s (2004) modelling of the effects of a shift to full no-fault compensation suggests a potential for costs to increase to £2.4 billion per year, and that even the more limited scheme proposed in 2003 by the Department of Health would see costs increase by around 10 per cent. While there are important arguments about the efficiency, effectiveness and equity of the tort system as a means of either compensation or deterrence, negligence claims are relatively rare events, whose total cost should be no more than a minor irritant to the NHS. The frequency is around 0.8 per 1000 consultant episodes, adding a cost of about £5 per episode. At hospital level, claims are, at worst, an occasional financial embarrassment if the trust is in a part of the country with higher frequency or severity rates, or is hit by the once in a 7–10-year chance of a pay-out in excess of £0.25 million.

The medical profession, however, may experience the threat differently. Clearly, the near-collapse of the medical defence organisations in the late 1980s was a traumatic event. With hindsight, however, this looks far more explicable in terms of their undercapitalisation and lack of insurance expertise, which left them unprepared for the sudden change in their environment. The English medical profession may also feel the pressures of litigation more acutely because of its relatively small size in relation to the population served. Although more recent data are not available, the intensity of litigation in 1990–91, at 10.5 new claims per 100 hospital doctors, was quite close to US rates.[4] However, it is not just a problem for the medical profession. One of the most striking, and neglected, findings in this area has been that almost all British professions have had a similar experience in the same period (Ham *et al.* 1988). If there is a challenge here, it is a challenge to all professions and the explanation seems likely to be found in some wider process of social or cultural change. Nevertheless, litigation against doctors has been successfully presented as a problem *sui generis*, a phenomenon peculiar to medical practice and requiring special remedies.

MMR vaccination – a case study

Litigation over the safety of MMR (measles, mumps and rubella) vaccination offers an opportunity to look at some of these issues in more depth – although this action was actually based on the Consumer Protection Act 1987, arguing that MMR was a 'defective product' (LSC 2003), rather than claiming negligence by either the manufacturers or the Department of Health.

Vaccination has a long socio-legal history in the UK, beginning with nineteenth-century attempts to compel participation under threats of fine or imprisonment (McGuire 1998). Vaccines are generally considered 'a cornerstone of preventive medicine' (Streefland 2001) and 'one of the greatest public health success stories' (Poland and Jacobson 2001). Through herd immunity, the benefit of mass vaccination to the community may be seen as greater than the sum of individual benefits (Hobson-West 2003: 277). It has, however, long been acknowledged that some individuals may also be harmed in the pursuit of this collective good. In the UK this recognition is institutionalised in the Vaccine Damage Payment Act 1979. This provides for a one-off payment (originally £10,000 but currently up to £100,000) for those who are assessed as suffering 80 per cent disability (recently amended to '60 per cent')[5] as a result of a prescribed vaccine. The scheme is funded out of general taxation and administered on behalf of the Department of Work and Pensions by the Vaccine Damage Payment Unit.

The MMR vaccine controversy is usually dated to the 1998 *Lancet* paper by Dr Andrew Wakefield, a gasteroenterologist based at the Royal Free hospital in London (Wakefield *et al.* 1998). This was based on clinical examination of 12 children who were displaying both autism-like symptoms and severe bowel problems. It hypothesised that the two problems might be linked and that the autistic symptoms displayed could be defined as 'late-onset autism', following initially normal development. It also reported that some parents of these children believed that the condition's onset was associated with the MMR vaccine. This claim was given added publicity at a press conference held to mark publication. Wakefield's claims, and the media coverage that they attracted, are often blamed for the sharp decline in national MMR uptake from 92 per cent in 1996 to 82 per cent by 2002 (Health Protection Agency 2004). The institutionalised solution to the problem of individual vaccine risk under the Vaccine Damage Payment scheme was seen as insufficient by parents who believed that their child had suffered damage as a result of MMR vaccination. One reason is that the likelihood of a successful claim through this scheme is very low. Very few awards have been made since 1988 (when MMR was introduced) and only 6 per cent of MMR claims have been successful, a lower rate than for other vaccines (Pywell 2002: 80–83). Given this, a group of around 1000 parents pursued the matter through the courts in a multi-party action against the three manufacturers of the vaccine. Legal Services Commission (LSC) funding for those cases relating to autism and bowel disease was finally withdrawn on 29th September 2003, after a reported £15 million (Dyer 2003) had been spent on the case.

This episode is relevant to our discussion for three main reasons. The first relates to the status politics of medicine: despite Wakefield's situation on the margins of the epistemic community around vaccination issues, the profession's elite could not successfully trump his arguments (Hobson-West 2004). Statements of support for MMR vaccination by leading members of the Royal Colleges and the Chief Medical Officer failed to dampen media interest in the claims of Wakefield and the affected parents and tended to be portrayed as evidence of an establishment 'cover-up' motivated either by fear of successful litigation or by an identification with the commercial interests of the vaccine manufacturers. The profession saw its leadership being publicly humiliated, while enterprising individual doctors, providing single vaccines obtained through an international grey market for significant fees, were hailed as humanitarian benefactors. For many journalists, MMR vaccination seemed to be yet another accountability scandal, fitted into the frame set by the Bristol Royal Infirmary inquiry. Secondly, we can identify the parents' choice of a legal strategy rather than a political campaign to influence the workings of the Vaccine Damage Payment Act. This Act is essentially a *social security* provision, where individual costs are shared by the community that benefits from them. This contrasts with litigation that focuses on an individual's *right to redress*.

Finally, the eventual collapse of the litigation is instructive in terms of the limits of legalisation. The LSC eventually withdrew legal aid from the families, a decision upheld on appeal and at judicial review, citing the Legal Aid Act 1988, which obliges the LSC to cease funding 'where a case no longer meets the legal merit test. Cases must have reasonable prospects of success' (LSC 2004). This 'chance of success' rested on the ability to demonstrate *causation*. The litigation would need to establish that the MMR vaccine, or some component, caused or 'materially contributed to' the symptoms experienced. Withdrawal of funding was widely interpreted as an indication that causation had not been established, although, as Pywell (2002: 79) notes: 'The current state of research is such that the evidence for most postulated links between vaccines and injuries is insufficient to accept or reject a causal hypothesis, so it is inevitable that claims in respect of such injuries will fail.' The LSC also conceded that it had over-reached by funding a pilot 'viral detection' study by Andrew Wakefield *et al.* (2004). This had crossed the line between an investigation based on accepted principles in preparation for trial and *new scientific research*. In retrospect, the LSC (2003) admitted, 'it was not effective or appropriate...to fund research. The courts are not the place to prove new medical truths.'

What is the challenge to medicine?

Both negligence and MMR litigation emerge as more complex stories than the simple view of legal imperialism suggests. We need to think about what their representation as a challenge to medicine signifies and, in particular, how this representation may form part of a strategy of collective action. Both may be better understood as moral panics, where 'a condition, episode, person or group of persons emerges to become defined as a threat to...values and interests' (Cohen 1973: 9; see also Critcher 2004). The promoters, the moral entrepreneurs in Becker's (1963: 147–63) termi-nology, adopt a real set of behaviours as a basis for a symbolic crusade in defence of certain status interests which are under threat. These crusades commonly involve partnerships and alliances with mass media in order to generate public pressures on political actors. Their promoters are pursuing 'attempts toward cultural hegemony, to control and define the proper and expected way of life....Social, economic and cultural groups struggle over the ceremonial and ritual dimensions of state action because these estab-lish one or other modes of experiencing life as more valid and more rewarding than another' (Gusfield 1986: 209). Gusfield developed the idea of status politics as a way of understanding the response of social groups to a loss or denial of esteem to which they felt entitled:

> The self-esteem of the group member is belied by the failure of others to grant him the respect, approval, admiration and deference he feels that he justly deserves. This may occur when a segment of the society is losing status and finds that prestige-givers withhold expected deference.
> (Gusfield 1986: 18)

The vaccination litigation – a large-scale, high-profile, high-cost mass action – fits into a pattern of developments that British doctors often portray as emblematic of the Americanisation of their relationship with their patients. This dystopian depiction of the USA, of an American medical profession beset by litigation, has little more validity than the standard account of the British experience, and demonstrates a very limited under-standing of the complex interactions between law, health care and insurance against personal misfortune in a country with meagre public provision for ensuring equal access to any of these institutions (Dingwall *et al.* 1991). However, as W.I. Thomas pointed out, it is what people take to be real that has real consequences. In this case, the focal assertion is that 'we (the UK medical profession) have looked at the US and seen a possible future for ourselves that we reject'. This assertion is noteworthy on two grounds.

The first ground is that it represents a marked shift from earlier, positive images of the USA as the beacon of technically advanced medicine, clinical autonomy and handsome remuneration for doctors. While there is still admiration for the technical achievements of American clinical research, even if tempered by some questions about the quality of life produced by its interventions, American doctors are now seen as beset by pressures for additional tests, documentation and practice review which have compromised their ability to act in the best interests of their patients. There is a collapse of trust between doctor and patient, a move from medical paternalism and individualised care to a regime where consumers are treated as formally identical units with certain entitlements and where the provision of the entitlement needs to be documented in order to defend the treatment against *post hoc* review. While there is some envy of the money incomes of doctors in the USA, this is also balanced by recognition that there may be little to be gained from high earnings if a large chunk of these has to be spent on liability insurance.[6]

The second ground is that it is so much at odds with the admiration for American models of culture and social organisation which have had such an influence on the development of UK social and economic policies under both Conservative and Labour administrations since the early 1980s. Rightly or wrongly, the USA has been held up as the model of a dynamic society and economy whose features should be copied by others in the hope of emulating its achievements. Given this, the privatisation of social insurance by the use of the tort system, instead of reliance on social security, ought to be a cause for celebration. The profession has, instead, been urging the adoption of schemes for the public funding of liability, copied from social democratic innovations in countries like Sweden and New Zealand. The parental dissatisfaction with the Vaccine Damage Compensation scheme, which is, in some respects, a prototype for this approach, has important lessons for the reformers, in the sense that compensation in the absence of redress for the underlying grievance may be unacceptable in an environment where individual rights are privileged over collective interests.

The medical profession's litigation crisis is as much a protest against wider changes in the social and cultural environment, their repeated humiliation as self-centred and self-serving, as it is a specific reaction to a specific threat. This is a challenge that runs far deeper than a few court appearances and the diversion of a small fraction of the NHS budget. What is the problem to which the 'litigation crisis' is the answer?

Medicine, law and social control

Many traditional approaches to the study of medicine and law present them as conflicting institutions. Law may be invoked to counter the power of medicine, as in Kennedy's work cited above: medicine may be invoked to mitigate the harshness of law as in the arguments of writers like Barbara Wootton (1959) that delinquency might be better managed by treatment than punishment. Classically, however, sociologists have been more impressed by their complementarity. This is an insight that is particularly associated with the work of Talcott Parsons (1952: 249–325), although his treatment of the issue is clearly indebted, if unacknowledged, to Herbert Spencer.

Although Spencer is easily the most important sociologist ever produced in England, his work has been largely ignored since his death in 1903. His approach was based upon a huge corpus of historical and ethnographic data, from which he tried to induce and test a theory of social organisation and social change. He concluded that all societies needed to develop institutionalised solutions to three problems: regulation, operation and distribution. *Regulation* refers to the political integration of the whole society; *operation* to the co-ordination and control of the various units of material and cultural production; and *distribution* to the transmission of the outputs to all members. In the smallest and simplest societies, there is a low level of differentiation between these systems, but the increasing scale of social organisation leads to a division of labour that generates problems of co-ordination.

This is a familiar narrative in nineteenth-century sociology. However, two elements are unique to Spencer. One is his insistence on the relative autonomy of the various sub-systems that emerge. All confront the same problems of regulation, operation and distribution in microcosm but their local solutions do not necessarily produce societally appropriate results. Advanced societies derive much of their dynamism from the loose coupling between their units, which accentuates the problems of co-ordination. The space is important for innovation and flexibility: the cost is the risk of disintegration. An important example is the relationship between professions and the state.

The other unique element is Spencer's account of the evolution of medicine and law. In traditional societies, the maintenance of order and the co-ordination of activities is a rather diffuse activity. The political and the religious may be hard to distinguish. With the growth of scale, however, they become more discrete as religious ideas are elaborated into symbolic legitimations for the political order. Religion takes on two aspects as it becomes the basis of the operative system: the 'medicine man' who drives away evil ghosts, the defender of the cultural order against external threats, and the 'priest' who invokes supernatural powers in support of the political order. But the religious and the political are always potentially in conflict. The role of religion as a supplier of legitimation gives it an independent source of power, which may be abused for sectional gain or be set against the State. As the State evolves, it creates alternative bases of legitimation and breaks the monopoly of religion. The definition of a secular realm of law is a particularly important part of this process.

The 'medicine man', the specialist in the prevention of cultural disorder, is the ancestor of most modern professions. Professions are producers and orchestrators of culture or, more precisely, those elements of culture that may be of importance to the legitimation and co-ordination of the public order (Dingwall 1999; Evetts and Dingwall 2002). Their work is both material and symbolic: the evil ghosts stand both for the forces of nature, which constantly threaten to destabilise the system of transactions between human beings and their environment that furnishes the material context for any particular society, and for the anarchy which rests in the arbitrary relationship between signifier and signified. Art, music and literature are socially sanctioned arrangements of signs that bear no necessary relationship to the stream of sense-impressions that reach the human eye or ear. In their maintenance of this order, professions manage the relations between people, creating and defining a language for the sharing of experience.

The loose coupling of modern societies, however, means that the definition of culture itself has areas of uncertainty. Different cultural producers generate different possibilities for the co-ordination of the public order. At any given moment, cultural consumers can pick and choose amongst these. Shifts in consumer preferences are likely to lead to shifts in production. Some preferences are, of course, likely to be backed by authority or material resources derived from other sub-systems, so they may have a disproportionate effect. Nevertheless, it is part of the evolutionary dynamic of these societies that such variations exist and represent a potential for change and adaptation.

This is, of course, a sketchy summary of a complex theoretical scheme. Nevertheless, it should help to establish how medicine and law co-exist as choices of operative systems of cultural management which can be used by the regulatory system as practical means of legitimation and integration.[7] What are the implications of choosing one rather than the other?

Parsons's (1952: 309–21) elaborations are helpful here. He identifies two strategies for the maintenance of social order. One is *insulation*, preventing alternative versions becoming the basis for self-supporting groups. The other is *isolation*, denying the possibility of any alternative having a claim to legitimacy. Law, he suggests, is primarily concerned with isolation. Criminals are excluded from society, with little prospect of reintegration, and become the basis of projections of institutionalised values. Here, Parsons closely follows Durkheim and his discussion of the functionality of crime as a means of symbolising the boundaries of the society. Parsons's original contribution comes in his discussion of insulation and the role of medicine. The sick enjoy a conditional legitimacy for their challenge to the social order and a route to reintegration through their compliance with treatment. While there are some significant differences, both cases respond to the problem of illegitimate gains. The criminal may violate the bodily integrity of victims as means to some personal gain or gratification or sequestrate the product of their labour. The sick person fails, for reasons beyond his or her control, to manage his or her body in accord with social expectations and is excluded from productive activity. Both cases are positive statements about cultural values: respect for the human body; avoidance of dependency; the spheres of nature and culture. The difference lies in the capacity ascribed to the people concerned. Criminals are volitional actors; the sick are overwhelmed by the 'evil ghosts'.

In reality, the cases may not be so pure. There is more to law than crime and more to medicine than sickness. There are complex bodies of jurisprudence around questions of intentionality in law and claims to the sick role are notoriously provisional. Nevertheless, if we want to characterise them as competing modes of social intervention, we can see that they cast their shadows in rather different ways.

Medical imperialism: Legal colonialism

The choice between medicine and law as a preferred strategy for operative co-ordination is, then, a choice between two different accounts of human nature, of the relationship between human beings and their material environment and of the relationships between human beings. Some of the difference is captured by the different metaphors used by sociologists of medicine and of law to describe their extensions: medical *imperialism* and legal *colonialism*. Imperialism implies the incorporation of a territory and its people into the metropolitan culture and economy; colonialism the outposting of citizens to subjugate a territory and impose an economic relationship without affecting its everyday life more than necessary to achieve these objectives. It is important to note that these are both metaphors about economy and culture: the values and ideas which frame particular kinds of material relationship and which are, in turn, shaped by that material transaction.

After 1948, medicine in the UK became an increasingly collectivist enterprise. While there are, clearly, still freebooting segments of the profession, its leadership, whether in the BMA, the Royal Colleges, the

GMC or the Department of Health, has recognised that their constituents' interests are best served by a 'medicine of the social'. From another perspective, however, one could see this as a reflection of the political sponsorship of the social in the bipartisan collectivist politics of the same period (Armstrong 1983: 40). Social medicine has emerged in a transaction between the profession and its environment.

The argument, then, is that social medicine is an aspect of the governmentality that produced the welfare state. As such, it articulated some of the core values of that regime. These, however, marked less of a discontinuity with the past than might otherwise have been anticipated. As Strong (1979b: 183–225) has noted, the medical transactions of state medicine were essentially a nationalisation of bourgeois practice. In this respect, they were the local embodiment of the compromise between professional interests and the labour–bureaucrat coalition that shaped the NHS in 1948 (Webster 1990). The result was to perpetuate many inefficiencies and inequities and to create many opportunities for professional and corporate gain. The existing organisational cultures were also left in place (Dingwall 1979). While this removed the stigma of charity from large areas of service to the poor, it did not establish the service as an entitlement. It became a non-market transaction in which a benevolent and paternalist profession was funded by the State to care for those without other resources. The persistence of these elements did much to make the service acceptable to traditional conservatives who could accept the idea of a collective obligation towards the less fortunate, particularly those disadvantaged by some random natural event. It was a restatement of the values of *Gemeinschaft*, of the interdependency of human beings in local communities and of the responsibilities of the more favoured to protect those afflicted through the vulnerability of the human organism to contingent environmental occurrences. Social medicine sought to embrace these groups, to articulate values of community and to draw everyone into membership, without fundamentally changing the existing structures of social relations.

Medicalisation, then, may be better understood less as a professional project than as one aspect of the governmentality of social democracy where 'the imperfections of the market are...tempered by measures of social reform based on the values of an enlightened bourgeoisie' (Dingwall 1979: 17). Social democracy in practice did not elaborate a theory of citizenship to which the values of medicine and other welfare services would be subordinated. The limitations of this approach were spelled out by a number of critics in the late 1960s and 1970s, of whom the best known is probably Ivan Illich (1975, 1977). Illich targeted the power of the medical profession within the social structure and the cultural effects of encouraging dependency rather than self-reliance. Medicine was merely one site for his general critique of modern society from the perspective of a libertarian anarchist.

> That society which can reduce professional intervention to the minimum will provide the best conditions for health. The greater the potential for autonomous adaptation to self, to others and to the environment, the less management of adaptation will be needed or tolerated.... Healthy people need no bureaucratic interference to mate, give birth, share the human condition and die.... Man's (sic) consciously lived fragility, individuality and relatedness make the experience of pain, sickness and death an integral part of his life. The ability to cope with this trio autonomously is fundamental to his health. As he becomes dependent on the management of his intimacy, he renounces his autonomy and his health *must* decline.
>
> (Illich 1975: 169, original emphasis)

Illich's words were the harbingers of a major reappraisal of the values that had created societies in which medicalisation could progress. These calls for deprofessionalisation ushered in a very different model of human nature and social organisation, where the diffuse bonds of community gave way to the more calculating alliances of autonomous individuals. Although Illich often held out a vision of community, it was a stunted growth beside his celebration of personal autonomy. Human relations were founded on the rights of those entering into them and became specific agreements around narrow purposes. Although Illich would not necessarily have endorsed the consequence, they prepared the ground for the introduction of a mode of governmentality more congenial to the colonial aspirations of law.

Law casts human beings as self-sufficient individuals, intentional actors and guardians of their own interests. The sanctions attendant on a wrong decision, in commerce, domestic relations or interpersonal conduct, are the incentives to behave well.

> The individualism embodied in modern law stresses above all that individuals are the makers of their own destiny.... Thus, in its purest form, it takes no account of social or cultural factors that may remove the possibility of choice from individual actors, or severely limit the choices open to them, or determine the way these choices are interpreted.
>
> (Cotterell 1992: 119)

Law is associated with one pole of the classic sociological dichotomies within which modernity is defined: *Gemeinschaft/Gesellschaft*; community/association; status/contract. A modern society is a society formed by law and its impersonal model of relations between people, where traditional societies rested on diffuse ties of mutual obligation and sentiment. The authors of these dichotomies thought they were witnessing a dramatic social change as traditional society gave way to the *laissez-faire* market economy of nineteenth-century Europe. But it is arguable that the contrast was overstated, or perhaps short-lived, that the rise of the welfare state in response to the failures of the market as a basis for social organisation created an environment in which the values of community could be preserved. Only at the point when economic troubles, and international competition from producers that had yet to test their stability against the limits of the market, called the welfare state into question did the values of individualism begin to flourish again. The revolutionary agenda of neo-classical economics had been left incomplete, or betrayed, depending upon which version an author preferred. Law might be summoned as a tool to complete the programme.

As with medicine, it is important to recognise the diversity of law. Law has also discovered the social, and Armstrong's (1983) history of changes in medical thought could be paralleled for legal thinking and socio-legal studies. The level of analysis here is symbolic and focuses on the way in which a traditional rhetoric of law has been selected to challenge the post-war language of medicine. As Hughes and Dingwall (1990) pointed out, the rhetoric of NHS reorganisation since the 1980s has been heavily legalised although the 'contracts', 'trusts' and 'foundations' bear little relationship to any contemporary legal form of the same name. They are better understood as rather specific signals to organisation members about the cultural changes they are expected to accept. These are the official values to be adopted by the 'hands-on, value-driven' manager or clinician. In their legal connotation, they emphasise the break with the past traditions of the service. They constitute signs of a change to a culture modelled on classical capitalist enterprise. This is the language within which these terms acquire their meaning.

As stressed earlier, this is not a narrow shift from a cultural form, imperialism, to an economic form, colonialism. It is, rather, a shift from a mode of governmentality which reaches out to embrace the population in a moral community, a holistic vision of a welfare society, as opposed to one which segments individuals into bundles of discrete interests pursued through specific and limited agreements.[8] Embedded within social medicine's imperialism is a holistic vision of the patient whose life can be made better by the interventions of others. Law's colonialism does not explicitly seek to reach into the hearts and minds of individuals so much as to render them accountable for their breaches of agreements with others or to offer a framework for them to pursue those who have broken commitments. Law does not claim to prescribe the agreements that are to be made. In practice, of course, the programme does aspire to change people's values. Under the real historical conditions of colonialism, it may be possible to trade with indigenous peoples without touching their culture, although even this may be questionable if we think of the effects of introducing a cash economy to a society based on exchange or barter. In the conditions of developed societies with extensive systems of state welfare, colonialism is a challenge to the norms of the population.

In the present context, then, the rhetoric of law is being used to effect a shift in the world of health care towards a narrower conception of the responsibility of the system:

> the modern commercial contract is marked by limited commitment. Terms and conditions are specified closely, and the cost of nonperformance is calculated. Furthermore, with some exceptions, the obligation is not necessarily to *fulfill* the agreement, but only to make good losses that may be incurred in case of an unjustified breach.
>
> (Selznick 1992: 479, original emphasis)

Medicine is no longer to be afforded the imperial space to deal with the 'complete physical, mental and social well-being' of the population. It is, rather, to be directed towards the servicing of human bodies under a series of specific agreements between purchaser, provider and consumer, an automobile mechanic's model of medicine, in Silverman's phrase (personal communication to first author). The intervention of law becomes a way to limit the apparently infinite demand for a health care that represents a collective panacea.

The challenge from law

To return to our earlier question: what is the problem to which the litigation crisis is the answer? This argument suggests that it could be viewed as a status protest against colonisation, the subordination of social medicine to individual law. The analysis could be further sustained if we were to consider the remedies proposed. A no-fault response to claims of injury, whether from negligence or vaccination, is a classic collectivist remedy, a paternalist provision for those in need rather than an acknowledgement of their individual rights to redress. The Vaccine Damage Payment Scheme provides a particularly graphic example of this: compensation symbolises the recognition that individuals should be cared for as a result of injuries incurred in pursuit of the collective good. While such collectivist schemes deal with the economic needs of patients, they do so on a basis of social goodwill rather than entitlement. The victim of an injury would, of course, still have to satisfy the eligibility criteria: the existence of the scheme, however, would represent the beneficence of medicine and state welfare. The tort system, on the other hand, is the social insurance of a market society. But it would be a mistake to concentrate too narrowly on the specifics of the site. Although there has not been space to argue the case here, the restructuring of medicine forms part of a restructuring of all professions, including the legal profession itself.[9] The inarticulacy of the protest is symptomatic of the entanglement of the professions with the social democratic order whose legitimacy has faded. This lack of form, however, should not conceal the substance. The fundamental challenge to medicine is not from law but from the governmentality that favours law as its operative strategy. But we should be reluctant to round up the usual suspects too quickly. The real rise in individual claims against all professions might suggest that the shift in governmentality has followed rather than led a shift to a less deferential and more interest-oriented culture in which the individualist model of law is an obvious resource.

Acknowledgements

This paper draws heavily on research conducted by Dingwall in collaboration with Paul Fenn with the assistance of Lois Quam and Dymphna Hermans. The influence of conversations with Philip Strong should also be recognised. Hobson-West's work on vaccination resistance in the UK is supported by funding from the Leverhulme Trust. The original version of this chapter was scanned for the present revision by Edward Dingwall.

Notes

1 An important element of the sociology of law is the emphasis that it takes from Weber about the importance of law as a tool for thinking new social and economic forms into existence. Much of the legal profession's work is in the role of what Cain (1983) calls *conceptive ideologists*, people who devise the cultural conditions within which actors formulate their projects.

2 It is, in fact, arguable that some aspects of administrative law may also be relevant to private institutions operating in a public fashion. However, this refinement will not be explored here.

3 The European Convention on Human Rights Protocol 7 Article 4 specifies that 'No one shall be liable to be tried or punished again in criminal proceedings under the jurisdiction of the same State for an offence for which he has already been finally acquitted or convicted in accordance with the law and penal procedure of that State.' The UK is, however, one of only six out of forty signatories not to ratify this. While professional discipline is not a criminal proceeding, many lawyers would argue that the same principles should apply. On reintegrative

justice see Braithwaite (1989, 2002) and Braithwaite and Pettit (1990). The potential for legal dissension around the actions of the CHRE should serve as a caution against treating law as any less heterogeneous than medicine.

4 Dewees *et al.* (1991) give a rate of 13.0 claims filed per 100 doctors in 1988 based on data published by the St Paul Fire and Marine Insurance Company, the largest commercial insurer of US physicians. More recent data range between 2.8 per 100 (Maryland 2002) and 30 per 100 (Louisiana 2004). These data vary considerably in the definition of a claim and tend to include all doctors, whereas the figure quoted here (from Dingwall and Fenn 1994) is restricted to hospital doctors.

5 Statutory Instrument 2002 No. 1592 The Regulatory Reform (Vaccine Damage Payments Act 1979) Order.

6 In fact the percentage of gross medical incomes spent on liability insurance was a fairly modest 5–10 per cent in the late 1980s (Dingwall *et al.* 1991: 17–18), and subsequently tended to fall relative to inflation (Quam *et al.* 1990). In 2002, Maryland doctors were reported to spend an average of only 2.4–2.9 per cent of their practice incomes on malpractice insurance costs, against a national average of 3.2 per cent (Public Citizen 2004).

7 At another level, of course, it should also remind us of the perils of treating either profession as homogeneous. Each profession faces the same problems of achieving a sufficient measure of unity for everyday activity to continue. This is an important *caveat* because a theoretical paper must necessarily deal with general tendencies and directions rather than specific events. It is always possible to produce contrary examples but the real question is whether the broad sweep is correct.

8 This is not, of course, to argue that either is an entirely satisfactory social theory. See, for example, Selznick (1992) for a helpful discussion of the problems each raises.

9 The legal profession has been a particular target in the loss of its conveyancing monopoly (Administration of Justice Act 1985; Building Societies Act 1986) and the attempts to create a more competitive environment within the profession and between lawyers and others in the Green and White Papers of 1989 (Lord Chancellors Department 1989a, 1989b) and the consequent legislation, the Courts and Legal Services Act, 1990. See also Clementi Report (2004).

References

Armstrong, D. (1983) *The Political Anatomy of the Body*, Cambridge: Cambridge University Press.

Becker, H.S. (1963) *Outsiders: Studies in the Sociology of Deviance*, New York: Free Press.

Braithwaite, J. (1989) *Crime, Shame, and Reintegration*, Cambridge: Cambridge University Press.

—— (2002) *Restorative Justice & Responsive Regulation*, Oxford: Oxford University Press.

Braithwaite, J. and Pettit, P. (1990) *Not Just Deserts: A Republican Theory of Criminal Justice*, Oxford: Clarendon Press.

Bristol Royal Infirmary Inquiry (2001) *Learning from Bristol: The Report of the Public Inquiry into Children's Heart Surgery at the Bristol Royal Infirmary 1984–1995* Cm. 5207 (I), Norwich: The Stationery Office.

Burchell, G., Gordon, C. and Miller, P. (1991) *The Foucault Effect: Studies in Governmentality*, London: Harvester Wheatsheaf.

Cain, M. (1983) 'The general practice lawyer and the client: Towards a radical conception', in Dingwall, R. and Lewis, P. (eds), *The Sociology of the Professions*, London: Macmillan.

Clementi Report (2004) *Report of the Review of the Regulatory Framework for Legal Services in England and Wales*, London: Department of Constitutional Affairs. http://www.legal-services-review.org.uk/index.htm.

Cohen, S. (1973) *Folk Devils and Moral Panics*, London: Paladin.

Cotterell, R. (1992) *The Sociology of Law*, second edn, London: Butterworths.

Critcher, C. (2004) Trust me: I'm a doctor: MMR and the politics of suspicion. Paper presented at Communication in the age of suspicion: a conference on trust, communication and culture. Bournemouth University, 20–21 February.

Department of Health (2003) Making Amends: A consultation paper setting out proposals for reforming the approach to clinical negligence in the NHS. A report by the Chief Medical Officer, London: Department of Health.

Dewees, D.N., Trebilcock, M.J. and Coyte, P.C. (1991) 'The medical malpractice crisis: A comparative empirical perspective', *Law and Contemporary Problems*, 54 (1): 217–51.

Dingwall, R. (1979) 'Inequality and the National Health Service', in Atkinson, P., Dingwall, R. and Murcott, A. (eds), *Prospects for the National Health*, London: Croom Helm.

—— (1999) 'Professions and social order in a global society', *International Review of Sociology*, 9 (1): 131–40.

Dingwall, R. and Fenn, P. (eds) (1992) *Quality and Regulation in Health Care*, London: Routledge.

—— (1994) 'Is NHS Indemnity working and is there a better way?', *British Journal of Anaesthesia*, 73: 69–77.

Dingwall, R. and Strangleman, T. (2005) 'Organizational culture', in Ferlie, E., Lynn, L.E. and Pollitt, C. (eds), *Oxford Handbook of Public Sector Management*, Oxford: Oxford University Press.

Dingwall, R., Fenn, P. and Quam, L. (1991) *Medical Negligence: A Review and Bibliography*, Oxford: Centre for Socio-Legal Studies.

Dyer, C. (2003) 'MMR legal aid funding challenge', *The Guardian*, Tuesday 7th October. www.guardian.co.uk/uk_news/story/0,,1057302.00.html.

Evetts, J. and Dingwall, R. (2002) 'Professional occupations in the UK and Europe: Legitimation and governmentality', *International Review of Sociology*, 12 (2): 159–71.

Fenn, P. and Dingwall, R. (1990) 'The problems of crown indemnity', in Gretton, J. (ed.), *Health Care UK 1989*, Birmingham: Policy Journals.

Fenn, P., Hermans, D. and Dingwall, R. (1994) 'Estimating the cost of compensating victims of medical negligence', *British Medical Journal*, 309: 389–91.

Fenn, P., Diacon, S., Gray, A., Hodges, R. and Rickman, N. (2000) 'Current cost of medical negligence in NHS hospitals: Analysis of claims database', *British Medical Journal* 2000 (320): 1567–71.

Fenn, P., Gray, A. and Rickman, N. (2004) 'The economics of clinical negligence reform in England', *Economic Journal*, 114: 272–92.

Foucault, M. (1979) *The History of Sexuality: Vol. 1. An Introduction*, London: Allen Lane.

Freidson, E. (1982) 'Review essay: Kennedy's masked future', *Sociology of Health and Illness*, 4: 95–7.

Gusfield, J. (1986) *Symbolic Crusade: American Politics and the Temperance Movement*, second edn, Urbana: University of Illinois Press (first published 1963).

Ham, C., Dingwall, R., Fenn, P. and Harris, D. (1988) *Medical Negligence: Compensation and Accountability*, London/Oxford: King's Fund/Centre for SocioLegal Studies.

Health Protection Agency (2004) Completed Primary Courses at Two Years of Age: England and Wales, 1966–1977, England only 1978 onwards. Available at www.hpa.org.uk/infections/topics_az/vaccination/cover.htm.

Hobson-West, P. (2003) 'Understanding vaccination resistance: Moving beyond risk', *Health, Risk and Society*, 5, pp. 273–83.

—— (2004) 'The construction of lay resistance to vaccination', in Shaw, I. and Kaupinen, K. (eds), *Constructions of Health and Illness: European Perspectives*, Aldershot: Ashgate Press.

House of Commons Public Accounts Committee (2002) Handling Clinical Negligence Claims in England, House of Commons Public Accounts Committee, 37th Report of Session 2001–02, HC 280.

Hughes, D. and Dingwall, R. (1990) 'Sir Henry Maine, Joseph Stalin and the Reorganisation of the National Health Service', *Journal of Social Welfare Law*: 296–309.

Illich, I. (1975) *Medical Nemesis*, London: Calder & Boyars.

—— (1977) *The Limits to Medicine*, Harmondsworth: Penguin.

Kennedy, I. (1981) *The Unmasking of Medicine*, London: Allen & Unwin.

Legal Services Commission (2003) Press release. *Decision to remove funding for MMR litigation upheld on appeal*. 1st October 2003. Available at www.mmrthefacts.nhs.uk/news/.newsitem.php?id=59.

—— (2004) Press release. 15th October 2004. *MMR appeals*. www.legalservices. gov.uk/press/press_release31.asp.

Lord Chancellors Department (1989a) *The Work and Organisation of the Legal Profession* (Cm. 571), London: HMSO.

—— (1989b) *Legal Services: A Framework for the Future* (Cm. 740), London: HMSO.

McGuire, G. (1998) *Health Update: Immunisation*, London: Health Education Authority.

National Audit Office (2001) Handling Clinical Negligence Claims in England, National Audit Office Report HC 403 2000–2001, 2 May, London.

Parsons, T. (1952) *The Social System*, London: Routledge & Kegan Paul.

Poland, G.A. and Jacobson, R.M. (2001) 'Understanding those who do not understand: A brief review of the anti-vaccine movement', *Vaccine*, 19: 2440–5.

Public Citizen (2004) *The Facts about Medical Malpractice in Maryland*, Washington, DC: Public Citizen's Congress Watch.

Pywell, S. (2002) 'The vaccine damage payment scheme: A proposal for reform', *Journal of Social Security Law*, 9: 73–93.

Quam, L., Fenn, P. and Dingwall, R. (1990) 'Malpractice liability in the US: Panic over?', *British Medical Journal*, 301: 949–50.

Selznick, P. (1992) *The Moral Commonwealth: Social Theory and the Promise of Community*, Berkeley: University of California Press.

Shipman Inquiry Fifth Report (2004) *Safeguarding Patients: Lessons from the Past – Proposals for the Future*, Independent Public Inquiry into the issues arising from the case of Harold Frederick Shipman (Chair Dame Janet Smith), Cm. 6394, http://www.the-shipman-inquiry.org.uk/fifthreport.asp.

Stacey, M. (1992) *Regulating British Medicine: The General Medical Council*, Chichester: John Wiley.

Streefland, P.H. (2001) 'Public doubts about vaccination safety and resistance against vaccination', *Health Policy*, 55: 159–72.

Strong, P.M. (1979a) 'Sociological imperialism and the profession of medicine', *Social Science and Medicine*, 13A: 199–215.

—— (1979b) *The Ceremonial Order of the Clinic*, London: Routledge & Kegan Paul.

—— (1984) 'Viewpoint: The academic encirclement of medicine', *Sociology of Health and Illness*, 6: 339–58.

Towse, A. and Danzon, P. (1999) 'Medical negligence and the NHS: An economic analysis', *Health Economics*, 8: 93–101.

Wakefield, A.J. *et al.* (1998) 'Ileal-lymphoid nodular hyperplasia, non-specific colitis, and pervasive developmental disorder in children', *The Lancet*, 351: 637–41.

Wakefield, A.J., Harvey, P. and Linnell, J. (2004) 'MMR – responding to retraction', *The Lancet*, 363: 1327–8.

Webster, C. (1990) 'Conflict and consensus: Explaining the British health service', *Twentieth Century British History*, 1: 115–51.

Wootton, B. (1959) *Social Science and Social Pathology*, London: Allen & Unwin.

4 Television and medicine
Medical dominance or trial by media?

Michael Bury and Jonathan Gabe

Introduction

In the field of health and medicine there have been, until recently, surprisingly few attempts to assess the importance of the media, outside of work in health education. In this latter, more applied, field there have been numerous studies of the impact (or lack of impact) of media on specific health campaigns, notably in HIV/AIDS (Wellings and McVey 1990), or in health promotion areas such as drugs, tobacco, alcohol, diet and exercise (Davies 1988; Flay and Burton 1990; Kotler *et al.* 2002). However, characteristic of these studies is their lack of emphasis on the sociology of the mass media and especially of television. Though the role of the media in health campaigns is regularly assessed, the representation of health and medicine in the media is not.

Following earlier attempts to tackle some of these issues with respect to one particular area of health care, namely the controversy surrounding the use of benzodiazepine tranquillisers (Gabe and Bury 1988; Bury and Gabe 1990; Gabe and Bury 1996), we attempt, in this chapter, to begin to address the broader issue of how far the media, specifically television, represent a more challenging view of medicine, both in terms of the latter's knowledge base and of its professional practice. We also address the question of how health and medicine have come to play a large part in media programming.

In approaching the issue, we begin, however, with an initial sense of paradox. On the one hand, there is a common view, sometimes expressed in academic circles, that medicine holds a dominant position in media coverage of health, specifically its view of disease and illness and its own self-image as a profession (McLaughlin 1975; Turow and Coe 1985; Turow 1989; Signorelli 1990). On the other hand, our past work on tranquilliser dependence often uncovered a strong sense of 'trial by media' amongst clinicians and medical scientists working in controversial areas. In order to explore these 'contours' of medicine and the media, the chapter examines four related themes.

First, we outline the argument that medicine has come to dominate media coverage of health and illness. The challenges that have occurred, both to medicine's knowledge base and to its power as a profession, are seen as having been largely absorbed and therefore neutralised. The exposition we examine here is of one of the few attempts to provide a broad (and historical) analysis of medicine and the media, namely that of Anne Karpf's book *Doctoring the Media* (Karpf 1988a) (see Turow (1989) for an American analysis).

Second, we go on to outline what we regard as some of the problems with this approach. In particular, we examine the difficulties in testing, empirically, the assumptions behind the analysis offered by Karpf and the questions they raise. Third, we attempt to provide the beginning of such an empirical analysis, by taking three examples of British television programmes in the 1980s and 1990s to illustrate three key formats through which television has portrayed medicine: the exposé format, the documentary and the drama. Through an examination of the form and content of these programmes we attempt to illustrate our argument that the medium, though falling short of putting medicine regularly on trial, has increasingly represented health and medicine in a more challenging light than it once did. Fourth, we briefly examine recent developments in television and the media, which have eroded some of the boundaries between these formats, and consider the greater attention now being paid to the Internet, accessed through a television or visual display unit, which can provide information for use in challenging medicine.

Medical dominance and the media

Karpf's book *Doctoring the Media* (1988a) traces the links between medicine and the media in a historical context. Although somewhat polemical in tone, it draws on sociological insights to make some of its main claims. For present purposes, we should like to draw out two main strands of Karpf's analysis of media coverage of health and medicine and the changing relationship between them. First, Karpf describes in some detail the shifting interconnections between medicine and the media in Britain between two periods, the 1930s and 1940s, and the 1950s and 1960s. The latter period, she maintains, constitutes the heyday of medical dominance of the media. Second, Karpf goes on to assess the changing relationships between medicine and the media in the 1970s and 1980s, which appear to contradict this picture, but which, Karpf argues, largely extend it. In the rest of this section we outline these two points in a little more detail.

Karpf begins by pointing to the very different cultural climate affecting perceptions of health in the early period of media development in Britain.

During the years immediately before the Second World War, according to Karpf, a tension existed between two main preoccupations, namely austerity and poverty. In health terms, this tension could be seen in the official emphasis on an individualistic approach to staying healthy, and in the public health approach to links between poor health and poverty. Nutrition and maternal and infant health were often the focus of fierce debates about these issues. Health rather than medicine therefore dominated media coverage, especially that of radio. In the main, Karpf argues, this meant an emphasis on individualistic health prevention programmes and coverage, though social issues did force themselves on to the agenda. Curative medicine was rarely touched on, partly because of its limited effectiveness and partly because the idea of broadcasting 'intimate matters' was anathema to radio and film producers.

Karpf also argues that the medical profession was reluctant to see either the media or the public meddle in what it took to be its province. Broadcasting to an 'undifferentiated audience' would only distress the frail and neurotic; hypochondria might result (Karpf 1988a: 35). The wartime 'radio doctor', Charles Hill, gave talks on such topics as how to eat and how to cook. Such advice on 'positive health' fitted in well with state control of the media's agenda and its contribution to the war effort (Karpf 1988a: 43–8).

In the 1950s and 1960s, however, a major shift in media coverage of health and medicine took place. State control of the media shifted from direct to indirect control, as institutions such as the British Broadcasting Corporation (BBC) and then Independent Television (ITV) became more influential, and as producers developed a stronger sense of the power of the media. The medical profession also altered its position, partly to meet this growing challenge, from one of reluctant involvement to one of enthusiasm and collaboration. The founding and early development of the National Health Service (NHS) had also helped in the medical profession's development of a newfound confidence, especially in the hospital sector. Technological developments and curative medicine came to occupy much greater prominence on the public policy agenda, and thence in the media. As Karpf points out, the most obvious example of this was to be found in surgery, especially transplant surgery.

Programmes such as the 'radio doctor' were soon to be seen as old-fashioned, as television opened up a whole range of possibilities to present matters medical. The expression in health terms of a language of privation and a 'collective fate' gave way to new enthusiasms for curative medicine, with an emphasis on future-oriented research. Now British television programmes, such as the BBC's *Your Life in Their Hands*, which started in 1958, provided opportunities for the scientific and technological perspective to gain ascendancy in health-related coverage. Not only that, but the medical profession's involvement also 'marked the beginning of television's infatuation with the prestigious London teaching hospitals' (Karpf 1988a: 53). The medical profession now moved centre stage to dominate the presentation of health and medicine in the media.

As leading figures within the medical profession opened up both bodies and hospitals to the public view, so television production techniques also played a part in accelerating the pace of change towards medical dominance. According to Karpf, earlier coverage had essentially been cast within the format of the illustrated lecture. Now the possibilities for drama and excitement, let alone entertainment, inherent in the hospital and medical worlds, could be explored to the full. Medical dramas, soap operas, 'hospital watch' programmes and many others proliferated.

Despite the growth of media power, the result of this interplay between a changing profession and a changing media world, Karpf maintains, brought about a period of medical dominance over the public's perceptions of both health and medicine. Earlier references to social and environmental aspects of health now almost disappeared as 'technophoria' – a strong belief in the technical role of medicine – took over. The representation of health and medicine as essentially technical issues effectively reinforced the individualistic approach to health, offering a 'dominant ideology' suggesting that health and medicine were essentially about pharmaceutical and technical progress. In drama, 'telegenic' doctors took over from the paternalistic image of the radio doctor. Under the influence of American televisions' preoccupation with medical dramas (Turow 1989), fictional Dr Kildare replaced the real-life Charles Hill in the public's affection.

However, Karpf's account does not end there. She notes that the dynamic unleashed in the immediate post-war decades has not simply led to a continuing story of the medical profession's open dominance of media coverage. Throughout the 1970s and 1980s a whole new set of possibilities developed, associated with the rise of consumerism and the patient's view. In this period, public attitudes towards science and technology became more sceptical, and the dominant position of the doctor seemed to wane.

This shift in emphasis was marked by the appearance in media coverage of voices not usually heard in public discussions of health, those of patients or client groups themselves. Women, the disabled and others all made attempts, successful at times, to gain access to the media to put forward views on health which were often critical of the dominant medical approach. Consumerist programmes counteracted the celebration of medical technology, and ethical issues cast doubt on the ever-expanding remit of hospital medicine. In a more pluralistic cultural environment, new voices were heard and new ways of portraying medicine and health care emerged. Even the heroic and glamorous 'good doctor' image gave way to a more realistic portrayal in dramas and soap operas.

For Karpf, however, these changes were more apparent than real. Consumerism, though a challenge to medicine, meant that 'medicine has simply redrawn what it can do' (1988a: 71). Indeed, 'ideologically correct' programmes on the health promotion front seemed to reinforce rather than challenge dominant ideas. The proliferation of voices did not, according to Karpf, alter fundamentally 'dominant beliefs' about medicine. Alternative medicine, for example, was much discussed in the 1980s, but was essentially incorporated without challenging orthodox approaches (Karpf 1988a: 179). The media, even in their most recent mode, 'not only shape the dominant beliefs about medicine, they help strengthen them' (Karpf 1988a: 132).

Because of limited feedback with audiences, programme makers were also seen to be incapable of fundamentally sustaining a critical view of medicine. Their preoccupation with the production of ideas, images and words seemed to overshadow the content about which they were speaking. In turn, audiences come to believe that such images 'are all' (Karpf 1988a: 235). The changes in media coverage during the decades under discussion were thus seen as having gone as far as they could in challenging the medical profession's power. Without a more fundamental shift in journalistic values and institutional change, Karpf argues, consumerist approaches to health actually reinforce the marginal status of many social groups and leave the medical profession largely untouched. Medicine and the media may no longer have colluded to tell us what to think, but they still set the health agenda.

Though a more complex picture of medicine and the media is painted by Karpf in discussing these changes, she concludes on a pessimistic note. She contends that the medical approach will 'continue to amaze and spellbind us', and that consumerism and 'look after yourself' television programmes will leave the major causes and realities of health and health disorders behind, while bringing forward ever more serried ranks of professionals, counsellors and therapists to advise us. Though medicine may feel under pressure from these changes, Karpf suggests that it need not worry: its dominance remains.

Analysing medicine and television

We hope, through this brief resumé, to have conveyed the value of Karpf's historical analysis in clearing the way for a critical approach to medicine and the media. However, Karpf's argument relies, we contend, on two kinds of widely accepted and 'received' assumptions to sustain its case. In the first place, though the media are treated sympathetically at times, Karpf relies on many of the anti-media sentiments prevalent in social commentary, inside and outside academic circles, and, indeed, within media circles themselves. Most important among these is the idea that the media necessarily trivialise serious social issues and create amusement and entertainment out of personal and social tragedy. Karpf's view of the tendency of television to 'amaze and spellbind' has echoes, for example, of Neil Postman's (1986) *Amusing Ourselves to Death*, which offers a broadside against the supposed damaging effects of television on politics and public life. A more sustained critique can also be found on the limits and constraints placed on television coverage of events such as the Falklands and Gulf Wars in Eldridge (1993). Karpf's argument, in stressing the effects of the media in depoliticising and limiting the definitions of health, echoes these approaches to the media.

Second, the linked idea of the powerful, if not dominant, role of the medical profession in public life and the media draws heavily on the polemical arguments of social critics of medicine such as Illich (1975, 1977) and Kennedy (1981), and in medical sociology on the sustained case made by Eliot Freidson (1970) in *Profession of Medicine*. Freidson's exposition of the role of medical dominance over definitions of health and illness provides the basis for a critique of the power of medicine to deflect attention from the wider social causes of ill health and the alternative ways that might be fashioned to tackle them. Thus, in drawing on this approach as well as on critical views of the media, the negative aspects of both media and medical dominance reinforce one another in the analysis.

Important though this line of argument undoubtedly is, we wish to argue that a more systematic empirical check on its validity is necessary if the social and cultural changes since the 1970s and 1980s are to be adequately evaluated. Though Karpf refers to changes in current television programmes in her analysis, these tend to be slotted into her existing framework, rather than used to test it. This leaves certain questions unanswered.

For example, though Karpf argues that 'the box continues to be doctored' (1988a: 71), the question arises as to whether television coverage actually supports a dominant medical authority or not. Following on from this, it might be asked how far the portrayal of medical treatments reflects an unchanging 'technophoria'. Furthermore, though Karpf notes the growing range and complexity of television coverage of health, the question of the impact of different programme formats remains largely unexamined. The question here is how far do these formats provide varying opportunities to challenge medical dominance? Finally, if television coverage in general is prone to trivialise serious issues of health and medicine, do programmes within different formats really demonstrate this?

In order to examine these questions, an approach needs to be developed based on an analysis of the form and content of media products and the way they are received. For, as Fiske and Hartley maintain, 'the starting point of any study of television must be with what is actually there on the screen' (1978: 21). We recognise, however, that developing a more evaluative analysis of this kind poses many difficulties, in terms of method as well as interpretation. This is especially the case with television, which, though it now plays the major role in media coverage of health and medicine, remains notoriously difficult to assess. Yet, without such a reconsideration there is a danger that putative effects are asserted on the basis of limited evidence. We are then left to either agree with the argument that the media are 'doctored', or adopt an alternative position that the media largely reflect wider social forces (see, for example, Burns (1977) for an example of this approach).

Media sociology has, however, begun to approach the multifaceted aspects of television products and their assimilation, in a more systematic fashion. Thompson (1988, 1990), for example, has identified three dimensions to analysing mass media: the historical and institutional context within which media products are made; the construction of media messages in terms of narrative and myth; and the ways in which these messages are received and appropriated by different audiences (see Seale 2004 for a recent account of how these three dimensions can be applied to media coverage of health and illness). Here we focus on the construction process and the ways in which particular programme formats have shaped the character of what is produced on television. In so doing we shall be employing a qualitative content analysis which gives priority to a formal or discursive approach to texts in an attempt to bring out the whole range of possible meanings, including those which are 'hidden' (Thompson 1988; Larsen 1991).

We shall be focusing on three kinds of programme format which we consider central to television coverage of medicine, and which allow for a closer examination of the relationship between television and medical agenda setting. Though we select just one example of each of these formats in order to provide detail of the form and content involved, we contend that they represent a growing trend in television coverage. These are: (1) the exposé format, exemplified in our analysis by the 1980s populist ITV programme *The Cook Report*; (2) the documentary format, illustrated by a programme from a 1990s Channel 4 series, *Operation Hospital*, dealing with events in a London teaching hospital; and (3) the drama format, represented here by the popular BBC1 programme *Casualty*, which began in 1986 and has run ever since (details and video clips from the various series can be seen at www.bbc.co.uk/casualty). We now provide an account of each of these programme formats.

The Cook Report

The programme from this series with which we are concerned focused on the issue of tranquilliser dependence and was transmitted in May 1988, in its weekly half-hour Tuesday evening slot, with an audience of 6 million viewers. The exposé format sets out to provide a challenge to powerful interests in an attempt to reveal alleged corruption or malpractice. Our analysis of the content of the programme on tranquilliser dependence examines how far this occurs. It provides a test case, not least because it explores a form of medical technology, which has frequently been used in hospital and primary care settings in the management of anxiety and related psychological disorders.

The programme in question began with a scene-setting comment from a lawyer to the effect that the ongoing litigation over benzodiazepine tranquillisers, including lorazapam (Ativan) – the product with which Cook was particularly concerned – looked like dwarfing previous cases concerning pharmaceutical products. Viewers were then confronted with pictures of Ativan being manufactured *en masse*, passing along conveyor belts, being poured through a funnel, wrapped in foil and packed in boxes, while being told that an estimated quarter of a million people in Britain were 'addicted' to the drug. Given the apparent size of the problem, the question was posed, 'Who is to blame?' The manufacturers, Wyeth, doctors or both?

The programme attempted to answer this question by, in the first instance, presenting the story of one long-term Ativan user's attempt to stop taking the medication. Ada, who had been using Ativan for more than a decade, having first been prescribed it following the death of her first husband, announced to the camera that she was prepared to be videoed by her second husband undergoing withdrawal because 'I'd like everyone to know what the withdrawal symptoms are' and 'I'd like something done about it'. Edited 'highlights' of her experience over the next four days were presented, with Roger Cook providing the voice-over, interspersed on no less than seven occasions with images of tablets showering down from the top of the screen in a colourful cascade. As time went by, revealed by a counter logging the hours at the bottom of the screen, Ada was shown experiencing mounting distress, complaining of numbness and shaking all over. The experience was underscored by the fear and apprehension she showed when asked by Roger Cook to step outside her house. On the fourth day, in a state of near panic, she started taking the tablets again. Finally, later in the programme, she was seen as an in-patient in a London hospital, undergoing a two-week planned withdrawal programme, and facing the prospect of a further two years' struggle to rid herself of her dependence at home.

Having established the consequences of dependence for individual users, Roger Cook undertook a relentless pursuit of those who were deemed responsible. First and foremost this meant the drug company Wyeth. The company provided an easy target for Cook given the pharmaceutical industry's long-standing role in contemporary society as a potent symbol of indefensible profit making. Here the argument against Wyeth was that it failed to warn doctors (and patients) about Ativan's 'addictive and serious side effects' when first marketed, despite research evidence of withdrawal symptoms when stopped abruptly, and preferred to 'put profits before patients' by continuing to sell the drug despite mounting evidence from 'respected sources' about the severe withdrawal symptoms experienced at high and low dose. Moreover, the chairman of Wyeth's refusal to grant an interview with Cook presented a perfect opportunity for him to confront the director in a public setting – in the event on a golf course – and ask him on behalf of 'sufferers like Ada' why the company continued to market a drug which was 'known to be addictive'. Footage was then shown of Cook being abused, threatened and kicked by the chairman before being struck with a golf club.

More importantly, Cook also turned the spotlight on the medical profession and its involvement in creating Ativan 'addicts'. Viewers witnessed Roger Cook 'doorstepping' two general practitioners (GPs) outside their surgeries on behalf of their patients. In the first case Ada's doctor was confronted by the reporter carrying a bag of the tablets, amounting to six years' supply, which Ada had hoarded, having been prescribed them on a repeat basis without apparently being seen in person. The doctor, looking shaken, at first denied that she was currently prescribing Ativan to any of her patients. Then she changed tack and argued that she was 'not the only one' and that she had warned Ada 'so many times' about the risks of dependence and had tried to wean her off them. Cook retorted that according to Ada she had been prescribed the tablets continuously until her lawyer had threatened legal action, at which point her supply had been halted abruptly. Finally, to underline his point, Cook poured Ada's stash of tablets on the driveway, next to the doctor, adding for good measure that this was hardly evidence of responsible prescribing.

This theme was developed more generally by reproducing a comment from an article in the magazine *The General Practitioner*, which suggested that the repeated prescribing of Ativan was 'unjustified and legally dangerous'. Moreover, the results of the programme's survey of 500 'Ativan addicts' suggested that the practice was widespread. Eighty-eight per cent of these 'addicts' indicated that they had received repeat prescriptions on a long-term basis without a consultation with their doctor.

Next, one of the respondents in this survey, Anne Broomfield, was interviewed briefly about her doctor's prescribing practices before he, too, was doorstepped outside his surgery. Again the doctor appeared taken aback and tried to defend himself, claiming that he had done his best to try to help the patient withdraw. Cook replied that he should have done better and actually 'got her off' the tablets, and alleged that the GP had recently advised her to accept her lot and keep taking them. As a final twist to this story, Cook announced to viewers that the doctor had subsequently telephoned Anne Broomfield and threatened to stop prescribing Ativan to her unless the filmed interview was abandoned. To underline the consequences for the patient, Anne was shown telling Cook that she was 'terrified' about being reinterviewed and that stopping the drug represented a 'real threat' to her well-being.

Like the manufacturers, Wyeth, the doctors were thus also presented as culpable. They were castigated for having failed to act responsibly or for not doing their best for their patients and for being willing to use their power to withdraw the supply of a prescribed drug on which their patients depended, in an attempt to silence criticism.

What are the implications of this analysis for the argument concerning medical dominance and 'technophoria'? It seems difficult, in examining such a programme, to continue to maintain that there has been no significant change in the media coverage of medicine. The exposé format clearly provides opportunities to challenge medical power which need to be acknowledged and analysed. As the representative of innocent and powerless patients, the reporter in the exposé format is bestowed with the moral authority to challenge, in this case, medical interests, identify malpractice and bring individual doctors to book. In so doing, patients are brought centre-stage, challenging the doctors' version of events and participating in the construction of their account of their experiences. Moreover, by presenting a critical assessment of the risks in taking Ativan, the programme explicitly cut across a 'technophoric' view of medical treatment.

At the same time, the analysis does provide some support for other aspects of the 'doctoring the media' position. By focusing almost exclusively on individual patients' problems withdrawing from Ativan, it could be argued that little attention was given to the social causes or context of use and to the gender imbalance amongst long-term users. As such, it could substantiate the claim that the media have tended to individualise the experience of health and illness. Furthermore, by focusing on individual doctors it could be said that the exposé format highlights the existence of a few 'bad apples' without questioning the general structures that make medical dominance possible.

Operation Hospital

This series, comprising six weekly programmes, was transmitted on Channel 4 in prime time on Tuesday evenings during January and February 1993, in front of an audience of approximately 1.4 million people. Here we review the first thirty-minute programme as an illustration of the documentary format. It was watched by the highest audience of the series, 1.9 million.

Documentaries treat 'particular knowledge and particular worlds – the scientific, aesthetic or political...in an attempt to broaden horizons of everyday culture' (Silverstone 1981: 83). They can comprise single films or, as in the current case, a series. One of the main differences between the documentary and the exposé concerns the role of the presenter. Instead of there being a clearly identified reporter such as Roger Cook, the documentary presenter takes on the role of a more 'heavyweight' journalist who is heard asking searching questions but is rarely seen. The drama and narrative element of the exposé are also played down in the documentary, in favour of a more factual report or record of social interest or concern which predominantly appeals to the intellect (Silverstone 1981: 82).

This particular documentary, dealing as it did with the portrayal of events over an extended period of time in a central London teaching hospital, King's College, offered a particularly useful opportunity to examine the relationship between the media and powerful medical interests. The documentary format of the programme also provided an opportunity to focus on policy concerns and highlight their consequences for everyday practice. The purported tendency of the media to trivialise such issues can therefore be examined.

The first episode of *Operation Hospital* began with pictures of night security staff on their hospital rounds on New Year's Eve 1991 with the presenter, off camera, stating that 'over the next twelve months this great hospital will be subject to a ruthless efficiency drive with everyone affected as failings are uncovered'. Examples of such failings were then catalogued briefly, ranging from dirt and decay to the unequal distribution of intensive care beds between general medicine, catering for local need, and the specialist departments with their international reputations to maintain.

As is usual in television documentaries, the opening sequence set the scene for what was to follow. It soon became clear that the focus of this programme and of the series is on managers rather than doctors (or other health care workers) and, in particular, on the recently appointed Chief Executive, Derek Smith, who was introduced as the 'new man who says he will change everything'. To underline the point, the caption 'Chief Executive' was then flashed on the screen before viewers were shown Smith driving to work in a suitably high-powered sports car. He was described as one of a new generation of 'hospital chiefs' who had been given 'more power by Government reforms than their predecessors ever dreamt of'. Interviewed in his office, Smith said he was attracted to King's because of its 'world-beating medicine', but on arrival was 'shocked by the hospital's physical condition' and by the 'attitude of the work force' and, in particular, by the absence of any clear objectives about the hospital as a whole.

This issue and the other problems identified in the opening sequence then became organised for the purpose of the programme under three headings: 'Management', 'Money' and 'Doctors', with a caption announcing each one in turn to viewers. For Derek Smith the management problem involved getting the right managers in the right place and performing to their maximum. To achieve this he had called in an outside management consultant to undertake an organisational audit and suggest ways of improving efficiency. It was intended that managers were to be given 3000 standards to meet and a deadline by which to meet them. Such a change was presented as moving from an oral to a written culture, with managers being required for the first time to think systematically about their work.

In the meantime the existing, informal way of doing things was presented as having its 'normal effect'. Patients were seen sitting in cramped conditions in the out-patients' department waiting for a doctor who had inexplicably failed to turn up, a fruitless search for a patient's notes was shown, and a Professor of Medicine described the embarrassment of having to explain to patients that their notes were missing. A coronary bypass operation was shown being successfully completed despite the failure of a vital piece of equipment, and a nurse was filmed cleaning up spilt blood in a corridor because cleaners had not been trained to do so. All these problems were used to underline the argument for decisive management in the hospital.

The next segment of the programme was devoted to money matters, listing a series of possible savings in a context of difficult choices and increasing competition between King's and other hospitals to provide services for purchasing health authorities. A balance sheet was presented listing savings if fewer beds were used, if the contract for an expensive drug was renegotiated, if private telephone calls were billed and laundry jobs frozen. According to the Chief Executive, there was 'a direct linear relationship between lowering costs and increasing quality'. However, the programme suggested that these decisions also related to spending priorities and to the outcome of King's College's bids for contracts, in the light of increasing competition from other hospitals for specialist services in the new health market. For instance, a doctor from the Accident and Emergency

Department (A and E) was shown complaining about the lack of money for beds for 'the lady round the corner' while patients needing an emergency liver transplant were flown in at great expense. Likewise, the Professor and Director of Obstetrics and Gynaecology were shown criticising the publicity surrounding the launching of an alternative, 'national' foetal health centre at the rival St Thomas's Hospital.

As well as sorting out the managers and money, Derek Smith was also presented as facing another, far more deep-rooted problem – the attitudes and inefficiency of doctors. In the final segment of the programme, the Chief Executive's efforts to check the power of the doctors at King's was addressed. It was suggested that the task would be difficult, but that the alliance he had built up with consultants who had become clinical directors would help. One of these, Dr John Costello, was said to view the particular problems in the A and E Department as 'largely the fault of doctors', many of whom were 'not interested enough in routine hospital duties' and 'too busy with other things like building their own empire'. Certainly, viewers were left in no doubt that Derek Smith meant business when he stated that 'where medical staff are not fulfilling their contractual commitment ... we shall certainly be discussing with them the fact that we discontinue their contractual arrangements with us'. The final comment of the doctor from A and E that 'I'm sure everybody wishes him well', while noting the quick turnover of previous top managers and the scepticism of senior consultants who feel 'they've seen it all before', suggested that Derek Smith would face battles with the medical staff.

What implications does this account have for the medical dominance thesis? First and foremost, it is clear that medical dominance no longer underpinned all television coverage of health and illness in the 1990s. The documentary format with its emphasis on 'heavyweight' reportage provided the means to portray the consequences of health policy developments and, in particular, the extent to which the enhanced powers of general managers provided an opportunity to challenge medical power. The fact that the programme focused on a top manager at an elite teaching hospital and treated doctors as just one group alongside other health care workers illustrates a willingness to take this issue seriously. It certainly suggests that the media had changed significantly the way they dealt with London teaching hospitals.

Second, such programmes reflect a far more critical analysis of developments in the organisation of health care. In the programme under consideration, the focus was on the experiences of a top manager rather than a leading consultant, on the display of managerial choices, the operation of vested interests and the effects of a market-oriented system. Third, where attention was being given to high-technology medicine, this was now portrayed as being constrained by the same financial crisis as the low-status A and E Department. Fourth, the medical profession was presented as deeply divided rather than as homogeneous or dominant. Thus, an A and E specialist was given the opportunity to argue the case for more money for his department, compared with that of more expensive competitors, and critical comments were expressed about colleagues in a rival hospital making grandiose claims about a new foetal health centre which would have been in competition with their own. In such a context the image of the doctor as hero, saving lives against the odds, has to compete with a new image of the doctor as a representative of sectional interests.

Casualty

Our final example takes us from the documentary to the television drama. *Casualty* was first televised in 1986 and has been shown on BBC1 in prime time on Saturday nights (and subsequently repeated later in the year on Friday nights) almost every year since. Watched by an audience, at its height, of around 15 million it is one of the most popular programmes ever shown on British television. Here we consider the fifty-minute episode, 'Point of principle', which was first screened in December 1992 and repeated in June 1993.

The medical drama has a long history although, as Raymond Williams (1990) has pointed out, it is only in the epoch of the television serial that it has received such attention. As a television format the drama offers, in narrative form, an enacted set of fictional events, usually dominated by a main plot, with sub-plots interwoven to add interest and complexity (Kozloff 1993). Within such a format a realistic narrative develops, appealing to an audience's sense of the 'psychological realism of its characters and their individuality and to the coherence of its specific chain of events' (Fiske 1987: 129).

Underlying this first-order level of meaning, as elsewhere in television, there is a second, deeper level where characters act primarily as ideological hooks for the audience (Fiske 1987: 130). This distinction is particularly useful in analysing medical dramas, as plots and characterisation make strong appeals to the emotions and values surrounding medicine and illness. Typically, in such dramas, doctors have been seen as 'benign, trusty curers' (Karpf 1988a: 183) and medical reality apparently has been frequently trivialised.

The episode with which we are concerned here opened with a man pumping up a bicycle tyre in the back garden while arguing with his wife. It seemed that he was unemployed and resented the fact that his wife was working longer hours outside the home to make ends meet. The camera then cut to Holby City Trust Hospital and a meeting between grey-suited manager Simon Eastman and the A and E consultant, Julian Chapman, in the manager's office. The very tone of the discussion indicated the existence of a major rift between them, with Julian upset about being told that his department had been unsuccessful in its bid for a trauma unit and talking about the danger of 'transferring critically ill patients around the district', while Simon was pompously dismissing his concerns as indicative of 'hurt feelings' and stressing the need to 'live in the real world'. From the word go the audience was therefore drawn into the current drama surrounding health policy and its effects. Public and private worlds were simultaneously explored.

Once the scene had been set, the main story line developed, with the consultant finding out from the charge nurse, Charlie, and the nursing sister, Duffy, that they had prior knowledge of the decision not to give Holby the trauma unit. It also became clear that management had presented the decision, in part, as a consequence of the consultant having not been supportive of the hospital's bid. The management's reluctance to appoint a replacement registrar was also reinterpreted as being linked with a prior knowledge of the outcome of the bid for the trauma unit.

These events provided the backdrop for the climax which, as Kozloff (1993) remarks, all television narratives require. In this case Julian confronted Simon in the corridor and accused him of being kept in the dark about the bid, lying about his position and acting without his support. The manager retorted: 'Your support, Julian, is convenient. It is not essential.'

Such a clear challenge to Julian's authority had dramatic consequences. Hearing from Charlie that the local press were outside, and having got wind of a staffing crisis in A and E, Julian charged out to meet them and decided to 'go public' about the way the department was being managed. He claimed that medical opinions about management decisions were being completely disregarded, patient care was deteriorating as a result of a loss of medical posts and the failure to win the bid for the trauma unit would make matters worse. In his view, this state of affairs was a direct consequence of management failing to take the needs of A and E seriously, and he went on:

> I want to be a clinician. I want my department to be a centre of excellence. That is not possible when I am fighting a reargued action against my own Manager. And now I believe I am being lied to.

Asked what he was going to do about it he replied, with a final flourish, 'I intend to resign. I have no choice.'

A little later on, after things had (temporarily) calmed down, there followed a final confrontation between Julian and Simon, with the latter telling Julian that he would not be allowed to work out his three months' notice because he had made statements to the press. The consultant, outraged, replied that the manager 'can't run a department without a consultant', that 'it's the politics of this' that excited him and that he (the manager) might as well throw out the patients too for 'cluttering up the corridors' and 'pushing up the budget'. Charlie, the charge nurse, was then seen unsuccessfully trying to persuade Julian to reconsider before the consultant delivered his parting shot by confirming to waiting journalists that his departure was a consequence of 'the management [being] against the NHS' rather than as a result of a personality clash. Even so, viewers were left with little doubt about the victor as the camera panned to the villainous Simon, in his upper-floor office, looking down triumphantly on Julian as he drove away in his open-topped car.

We should note here, however briefly, that alongside this dominant theme, sub-plots concerning patients' lives were interwoven. We have already mentioned the case of the unemployed man and his relationship with his wife. This came to a head when the man had a serious accident which took him into casualty, revealing a web of events surrounding a previous work colleague, and his wife's employment as a poorly paid 'chat line' hostess. In addition, 'cases' of a man from a poor housing estate, involved in dog fighting, and a young woman self-injuring in order to escape from a domineering father were also developed. These examples provided both dramatic and, to some extent, stereotypical images of hospital patients against a background of current social problems: unemployment, housing estate conditions and adolescence.

What, then, are the implications of this final example from the 1990s for our argument about medical dominance and health in the media? First and foremost, as in *Operation Hospital*, there was clear evidence of a major shift towards a much more challenging view of medicine and medical practice. As we have seen, the main focus was on a confrontation between the hospital manager and a consultant, with the latter winning the ethical battle but losing the war. Moreover, the fact that the nursing staff were represented as being much better informed about hospital politics than the consultant is also indicative of the shift in the portrayal of the balance of medical power. It suggests that the days of hospital drama inevitably focusing on the doctor as the dominant figure have changed significantly.

Second, the portrayal of doctors in *Casualty* only provides partial support for the argument concerning 'telegenic' doctors in medical dramas. While there was some evidence of consultant figure Julian playing the role of the glamorous, autocratic, trusty curer, he was as much preoccupied with hospital politics as with clinical care. Brief reference was made to his love life with a staff nurse and his autocratic and unfeeling manner with female nursing staff. He was also shown using his clinical skills to save the life of one patient against the odds. At the same time, he was portrayed as a member of a team of (at times divided) health care workers battling to treat an endless stream of patients under difficult circumstances. Nor was his job made any easier by a manager who seemed as concerned with balancing his budget sheet as with increasing resources to provide adequate levels of care.

Third, there was much less 'technophoria' than one might have expected. The setting of an A and E department and the use of a drama format obviously lends itself to the portrayal of life-saving, heroic medicine. 'Realistic' operations featured in most episodes. However, much of the time, events were portrayed in a much more mundane light. Many scenes were concerned with nurses cleaning and bandaging wounds and providing cups of tea, and with staff processing patients. This appeal to the audience's sense of realism offset a one-sided 'technophoric' portrayal, as did the episode's focus on the politics of health care in NHS hospitals.

Finally, though the sub-plots tended to portray patients and the public in rather stereotypical ways, there was little evidence of a systematic divorce of individuals from their social context. If anything the reverse was the case, with dramas such as *Casualty* seeming to go out of their way to give expression to current social problems. While this may seem to trivialise such problems, at the same time the drama format provides a powerful means for their expression and rehearsal. As with the dominant theme of managerial and medical conflict, it seems to us that the portrayal of patients and health was, in the 1990s, both more serious and more critical.

Developments since the 1990s

In the discussion in the previous section, we have analysed television's portrayal and engagement with medicine within three programme formats – the exposé, the documentary and the dramatic. Each has its own logic and televisual rules, though its content can be used to challenge or reinforce medical dominance. As we have seen, the 1980s and 1990s produced powerful, and in the case of *Casualty*, long-running and successful programmes within these formats. To anticipate our general conclusion, these programmes marked a shift away from the tendency to 'doctor the media' with other players – nurses and managers, for example – finding their place in media portrayal.

Since the late 1990s, television coverage has gone further than this. Two interlinked processes have been particularly noticeable: the crossing if not erosion of boundaries between programme formats, and the increasingly graphic portrayal of what Seale has referred to as the 'lives, illness and death', of patients, especially younger ones (Seale 2002: 47). Dramas, or 'soaps' such as *ER, Holby City* and *Casualty* continue to focus on hospital life and show medical dominance being attacked, undermined and challenged by 'pluralistic players' now active on the medical scene. But other television dramas have begun to go further still.

Most important is the increasingly graphic portrayal of hospital life and the way in which medical drama borrows from and mixes in elements from the documentary format. The 2004 BBC series, *Bodies*, is a noticeable case in point. Written by an erstwhile 'junior' doctor, Jed Mercurio, *Bodies* shows life in an obstetric and gynaecology department constantly bedeviled by a series of unavoidable and avoidable deaths, key examples of the latter reflecting incompetence and error on the part of a senior consultant surgeon. The hero of the drama, unsurprisingly perhaps, is a junior doctor, but he too is seen as fallible and prone to error. The medical events in the department are set within a context which conveys a sense of constant crisis, of malfeasance as well as malpractice, and a level of political chicanery, especially set in motion by the hospital managers. Few of the characters have any redeeming features.

Doctors are portrayed as being divided amongst themselves, and managers are shown as being preoccupied with achieving, and if necessary manipulating data relating to government targets. They are also shown as dealing with a series of allegations arising from a female anaesthetist 'whistle blower' who tries to get the hospital to take action against the incompetent consultant. This falls foul of the 'closed shop', through which the surgeons, including the junior doctor – the 'hero' – defend their interests. Here, the dividing lines between drama, exposé and documentary are weak. Events in the fictional hospital resonate with real events outside, especially scandals surrounding the Kent and Canterbury Hospital, and the Bristol Royal Infirmary in the UK in the mid- and late 1990s, and the subsequent enquiries into medical incompetence and poor practice by the government and the General Medical Council.

Much of the dramatic impact of *Bodies* arises from the graphic and detailed portrayal of difficult births, botched operations and procedures going wrong. Women are shown in acute physical and psychological distress, and there is much blood on the carpet with not a little on the attending staff. Additional, though less immediately gory themes of management ruthlessness, allegations of racism and sexual misconduct and adultery are spliced into the drama in ways that make *Casualty* and *ER* appear tame by comparison. The series has been so successful, that it has been repeated on prime time BBC television and a new series planned for

2005. The relevant BBC website calls the programme 'the ultimate antidote' to hospital drama. With this programme, the idea of being 'spell-bound' by the portrayal of technical medicine takes on a darker hue.

Programmes framed within an explicit exposé format have themselves become more graphic and dramatic. Technological developments such as those associated with secret filming have gone well beyond simple 'door stepping', as described above in the *Cook Report*. The ability to make high-quality video footage without the cumbersome (and visible) paraphernalia of camera and sound equipment have allowed investigators to film in ways that would have been difficult if not impossible in earlier periods. For example, in 2004 and 2005 policy and public debate in the UK focused on unhygienic hospitals and poor professional practice with reference to reducing the occurrence of MRSA – a staphylococcus infection. In January 2005 a programme in the long-running Channel 4 documentary series *Dispatches* called *Fallen Angels* was broadcast. Two nursing assistants were recruited by the programme to go 'undercover', in order to examine what was going on in two hospitals. They found plenty of apparent evidence of poor standards and practices. The programme showed 'shocking' footage, pitched in terms of 'nurses investigating nurses'. Neglectful behaviour towards patients as well as poor hygiene was captured on film. This, the programme alleged, showed that the nursing profession is in crisis and that the NHS is failing to maintain even the most basic standards. Thus, nurses as well as doctors now find themselves in the media firing line, tried and found guilty alongside their erstwhile powerful colleagues.

Finally, television programmes are not only crossing the boundaries between documentary and exposé formats; they are also becoming more graphic. We noted, at the beginning of this chapter, Karpf's discussion of the first sorties by television into the world of medical practice and especially surgery. Viewed from the vantage point of today's coverage this appears as another world. If dramas are becoming more explicit in showing medical procedures and operations, documentary programmes (even those without an exposé approach) have gone far beyond what would have been thought possible, even a few years ago. For example, whilst sociologists debate the cultural meanings surrounding such practices as body 'enhance-ments' and cosmetic surgery (Conrad and Jacobson 2003), television now shows the operations themselves in detail, and in living colour.

In 2005 ITV in the UK ran a series of programmes showing different forms of cosmetic surgery, with highlights at the end of the series in case the viewer had missed them. Further than this, the controversy surrounding Gunther von Hagen's (highly successful) exhibition of 'plastinated' body parts and whole bodies (sometimes flayed), called

Bodyworld, has been overtaken by a series of television programmes showing von Hagen carrying out autopsies and the 'plastination' process. In addition to the dissection and plastination of (volunteered) cadavers, details of each procedure in question were sketched in felt tip pen on the naked bodies of (live) assistants. Whether, under the guise of education or instruction, such programmes can be seen as simultaneously effacing a range of boundaries all at once – the commodification of the body, voyeurism, taste, respect for human life, the breaking of long-held taboos surrounding the medical handling of bodies, and even desecration – is a matter, perhaps, for wider public debate. If nothing else, these recent programmes suggest that format boundaries are permeable, and under populist conditions, liable to erosion, with challenges to medical dominance being merely one issue among many.

Finally, we should note the tendency for analysts to recognise the significance of other forms of electronic media in the home, besides television, particularly the Internet. The growing use of the Internet to access medical information has been heralded as a new resource for challenging medicine (Hardey 1999; Nettleton and Burrows 2003; Ziebland *et al.* 2004). Others have seen the framing of information on the Internet, and its use by lay people, as more ambiguous, reinforcing medical ideas and authority as much as challenging them (Seale 2002; Henwood *et al.* 2004). Either way a new chapter of medicine and the media is unfolding, though this is unlikely to mean a significant displacement of television as a major medium for dealing with matters medical.

Conclusion

This chapter has sought to examine the thesis that media coverage of health and medicine is characterised by medical dominance, that the 'box is doctored'. The evidence from British television coverage over the last twenty-five years suggests that this thesis is difficult to sustain when exposed to empirical checks. Having said this, we fully realise we have only examined a limited number of examples, and ones which best illustrate our argument. It is still quite possible to find television coverage that displays clear ideological support for the medical profession and a narrow 'technophoric' view of medical practice. However, it is also clear that the media now act as carriers and amplifiers of many challenges to medical authority. The most recent coverage crosses many boundaries and breaks many taboos, displacing previous ideas about what should and should not be seen by 'the public'.

The evidence we have presented suggests, we believe, that two broad conclusions should therefore be drawn. First, the representations of health and medicine described here reflect and reinforce the argument that major changes are under way in the 'social relations of health care' (Gabe and Bury 1991: 453). While the medical profession and the medical model of health and illness continue to hold considerable power and prestige in modern society, these are now under great pressure. A more critical view of medical knowledge and treatments, the rise of managerialism and the concomitant divisions emerging within medicine itself cut across the exercise of medical dominance.

Second, there has been a general shift in power and social influence from professional groups, including medicine, towards the media. At times this is likely to be experienced by professions as 'trial by media', a factor which Karpf (1988b) herself noted. The massive increase in the volume and scope of media products, including those on medicine and health, has inevitably brought about an increase in their influence on everyday life. 'Mediated experience' is no less important in health and medicine than in other areas of late modern culture (Giddens 1991). Thus the media not only reflect changes and conflicts in the social relations of health care (Gabe and Bury 1991), but also influence more powerfully new cultural agendas being set. The growth of explicit and graphic representation, in particular, deserves further scrutiny.

Future analysis of both the impact of medicine on the media and of arguments concerning medical dominance in sociology more generally needs to take account of these twin developments if an adequate appraisal of medical influence in contemporary social life is to be adequately understood. At the least we would argue that the medical dominance thesis is in urgent need of revision.

Acknowledgement

We should like to thank Jean Seaton for her comments on a draft of the original version of this chapter.

References

Burns, T. (1977) 'The organisation of public opinion', in Curran, J., Gurevitch, M. and Woollacott, J. (eds), *Mass Communication and Society*, London: Edward Arnold.

Bury, M. and Gabe, J. (1990) 'Hooked? Media responses to tranquillizer dependence', in Abbott, P. and Payne, G. (eds), *New Directions in the Sociology of Health*, London: Falmer Press.

Conrad, P. and Jacobson, H.T. (2003) 'Enhancing biology? Cosmetic surgery and breast augmentation', in Williams, S., Birke, L. and Bendelow, G. (eds),

Debating Biology: Sociological Reflections on Health, Medicine and Society, London: Routledge.

Davies, J.K. (1988) 'Mass media and the prevention of illicit drug use in Scotland', *Health Education Journal*, 47: 23–5.

Eldridge, J. (ed.) (1993) *Getting the Message: News, Truth and Power*, London: Routledge.

Fiske, J. (1987) *Television Culture*, London: Routledge.

Fiske, J. and Hartley, J. (1978) *Reading Television*, London: Methuen.

Flay, B. and Burton, D. (1990) 'Effective mass communication strategies for health campaigns', in Atkin, C. and Wallack, L. (eds), *Mass Communication and Public Health*, Newbury Park: Sage.

Freidson, E. (1970) *The Profession of Medicine*, New York: Dodd Mead.

Gabe, J. and Bury, M. (1988) 'Tranquillisers as a social problems', *Sociological Review*, 36: 320–52.

—— (1991) 'Tranquillisers and health care in crisis', *Social Science and Medicine*, 32: 449–54.

—— (1996) 'Halcion nights: A sociological account of a medical controversy', *Sociology*, 30, 3: 447–69.

Giddens, A. (1991) *Modernity and Self Identity*, Cambridge: Polity Press.

Hardey, M. (1999) 'Doctor in the house: The internet as a source of lay health knowledge and the challenge of expertise', *Sociology of Health and Illness*, 21, 6: 820–35.

Henwood, F., Wyatt, S., Hart, A. and Smith, J. (2004) ' "Ignorance is bliss sometimes": Constraints on the emergence of the "informed patient" in the changing landscape of health information', in Seale, C. (ed.), *Health and the Media*, Oxford: Blackwell Publishing.

Illich, I. (1975) *Medicine Nemesis*, London: Calder & Boyars.

—— (1977) *The Limits to Medicine*, Harmondsworth: Penguin.

Karpf, A. (1988a) *Doctoring the Media*, London: Routledge.

—— (1988b) 'Medicine and the media', *British Medical Journal*, 296: 1389.

Kennedy, I. (1981) *The Unmasking of Medicine*, London: Allen & Unwin.

Kotler, P., Roberto, N. and Lee, N. (2002) *Social Marketing: Improving the Quality of Life*, Thousand Oaks, CA: Sage.

Kozloff, S. (1993) 'Narrative theory and television', in Allen, R. (ed.), *Channels of Discourse Reassembled*, London: Routledge.

Larsen, P. (1991) 'Textual analysis of fictional media content', in Jensen, K.B. and Jankowski, N.W. (eds), *A Handbook of Qualitative Methodologies for Mass Communication Research*, London: Routledge.

McLaughlin, J. (1975) 'The doctor shows', *Journal of Communication*, 25: 182–4.

Nettleton, S. and Burrows, R. (2003) ' "E-scaped medicine": Information, reflexivity and health', *Critical Social Policy*, 23, 2: 165–85.

Postman, N. (1986) *Amusing Ourselves to Death: Public Discourse in the Age of Show Business*, London: Heinemann.

Seale, C. (2002) *Media and Health*, London: Sage.

—— (2004) 'Health and the media: An overview', in Seale, C. (ed.), *Health and the Media*, Oxford: Blackwell Publishing.

Signorelli, N. (1990) 'Television and health', in Atkin, C. and Wallack, L. (eds), *Mass Communication and Public Health*, Newbury Park: Sage.

Silverstone, R. (1981) *The Message of Television. Myth and Narrative in Contemporary Culture*, London: Heinemann Educational.

Thompson, J.B. (1988) 'Mass communication and modern culture: Contribution to a critical theory of ideology', *Sociology*, 22: 359–83.

—— (1990) *Ideology and Modern Culture*, Cambridge: Polity Press.

Turow, J. (1989) *Playing Doctor: Television Storytelling and Medical Power*, New York: Oxford University Press.

Turow, J. and Coe, L. (1985) 'Curing television's ills: The portrayal of health care', *Journal of Communication*, 35: 36–51.

Wellings, K. and McVey, D. (1990) 'Evaluation of HEA AIDS press campaign: December 1988 to March 1989', *Health Education Journal*, 49: 108–16.

Williams, R. (1990) *Television: Technology and Cultural Form*, second edn, London: Routledge.

Ziebland, S., Chapple, A., Dumelow, C., Evans, L., Prinjha, S. and Rozmovits, L. (2004) 'How the internet affects patients' experiences of cancer: A qualitative study', *British Medical Journal*, 328: 564–9.

5 The alternatives to medicine

Mike Saks

Consideration of the position of the alternatives to medicine is of much interest not only because of its topicality, but also because it raises the question of the extent to which popular, consumer-based demand in an increasingly market-oriented society can diminish established patterns of professional dominance. The centrality of this question is highlighted by ongoing debates in the social sciences about possible trends towards the proletarianisation and deprofessionalisation of the medical profession in the Anglo-American context – which focus, amongst other things, on how far the occupational control and cultural authority of the medical profession have been eroded in recent times (see, for instance, McKinlay and Arches 1985; Coburn 1999; Saks 2003a). In exploring the fate of professional dominance in relation to the alternatives to medicine, this chapter will also address such related issues as the occupational strategies employed by the medical profession in defending its position against external competitors and the degree to which the medical response to this challenge has been imbued with the sense of public responsibility suggested by its professional ideology. In so doing, the chapter takes a neo-Weberian perspective on the professions in general and the health professions in particular that defines such groups as monopolistic bodies seeking to regulate market conditions in their favour in face of competition from outsiders (Saks 1998). One of the more intriguing contemporary aspects of the challenge to the orthodox medical profession comes from the external competition posed by the escalating consumer support for the alternatives to medicine, to which the discussion now turns.

Growing consumer support for the alternatives to medicine: The challenge to medical orthodoxy

Alternative medicine in Britain has gained tremendously in popularity over the last thirty or forty years – a period in which a diverse range of

marginalised therapies have come more and more into the public lime-
light. At first, growing popular interest mainly lay in now better-known
therapies such as osteopathy, homoeopathy and acupuncture. Today it
focuses on an ever-wider span of areas, from crystal therapy and yoga to
aromatherapy and reflexology. While this growth of interest has a significant
self-help dimension, as indicated by the expansion of the over-the-counter
sales of health food and herbal remedies (Bakx 1991), confirmation of the
current position is provided by survey evidence that suggests that some
one in seven of the population now go to practitioners of the alternatives
to medicine for treatment (Sharma 1995) – in 1998 in England alone in
fact an estimated 22 million visits were made to practitioners of the main
alternative therapies (Thomas *et al.* 2001).

This popularity has been attributed in the literature to a number of
factors including, amongst others, growing awareness of the technical deficiencies of orthodox medicine, the development of a broader political
culture of self-determination and the search for relationships with health
practitioners in which the consumer is the engaged subject rather than
simply the object of health care (Bakx 1991). There are debates about the
relative weight that should be given to the various explanatory elements
in this equation – as, for example, the extent to which this surge of public
interest in alternative medicine is a distinctly new-age phenomenon
reflecting a fundamental revolution in consciousness, as opposed merely to
pragmatic patterns of discontent with the side effects and limited efficacy
of orthodox medicine (Coward 1989). What, however, is not in doubt is
that alternative medicine is becoming increasingly popular and that its
popularity extends not only to Britain, but also to Europe and North
America (Fisher and Ward 1994; Eisenberg *et al.* 1998).

In this wider international context, popular support for alternative
medicine has posed a potential threat to the biomedical principles underpinning the activities and professional standing of medical orthodoxy, in
which the body tends to be viewed as a machine whose parts can be
repaired on breakdown (Stacey 1988). This threat is centrally embodied
in the characteristically more holistic approach of alternative practitioners operating largely outside the orthodox profession who show a
greater degree of recognition of the importance of the relationship between
mind and body in individual diagnosis and treatment (Saks 2003a).
The ensuing conflict with the philosophy embedded in the mainstream
theory and practice of the medical profession clearly challenges the
power, status and wealth on which its empire is based in Britain and
elsewhere, and thus raises the spectre from the viewpoint of orthodox
medicine of a possible impending trend towards proletarianisation and
deprofessionalisation.

Professional dominance and the marginalisation of alternative medicine

Importantly, however, for all its force, this consumer-led challenge has not as yet fundamentally subverted the material foundations of professional dominance of British medicine, even if it has generated a greater degree of questioning of its approach. This is most clearly highlighted by the fact that the medical profession in Britain has retained the major part of its empire established following the Second World War – namely, its monopoly over National Health Service (NHS) practice on which British health care remains centrally based and from which alternative therapists without orthodox health care qualifications have been excluded as practitioners in their own right (Cant and Sharma 1999). The corollary of this is that the state-sponsored NHS has continued to be dominated by the drug treatment and surgical intervention of orthodox biomedicine, while therapies like chiropractic, healing, herbalism and osteopathy in Britain have been predominantly restricted to the private market, where the fast swelling band of non-orthodox therapists have focused their practice (Fulder 1996). Although alternative therapists in this country have the right to compete with doctors in this sector of the market within specified limits under the common law – as long as, for instance, they do not illegitimately claim to possess medical or allied health professional qualifications – access to the broad span of generally holistic therapies that they offer is obviously limited by financial barriers (Huggon and Trench 1992).

If the law in Britain places currently defined alternative practitioners in a highly disadvantageous competitive position, primarily because of their marginal status in relation to the extensive state-supported health system, this structural disadvantage is relatively new. In the eighteenth and early nineteenth centuries, before state medicine had been established and, even more importantly, before the British medical profession had gained the legislation underpinning its modern dominance, a comparatively open market existed for the wide range of therapies on offer, with many similarities to that which existed in the anti-restrictionist climate in the United States during this period (Saks 2003a). The treatments available ranged from bone-setting and healing by touch to herbal preparations and nostrums, which were offered alongside the heroic therapies of purging, sweating, vomiting and bleeding that were more strongly associated with regular practitioners in what has been termed 'the great age of quackery' (Maple 1992). At this time, all health practitioners offered their services in relatively open competition in the market place in an entrepreneurial consumerist culture, including the forerunners of the unified medical profession – the apothecaries, surgeons and physicians – who were then themselves in a minority (Porter 2001). This era, moreover, was not too alien from our own in terms of the current popular alternative health culture, in that even greater and more widespread emphasis was placed on self-help in health care and health was usually seen as the achievement of an appropriate equilibrium, involving both mind and body (Porter 1995).

However, what was to emerge from this period in Britain, following intense parliamentary debates around the mid-nineteenth century, was the 1858 Medical Registration Act, which established a unified, self-regulating and exclusionary medical profession, differentiated from its irregular competitors (Waddington 1984). This legislation had the effect of under-writing the monopoly over state medical employment by doctors, and subsequently that of such allied health professions as nurses, midwives and the professions supplementary to medicine. This was to become particularly significant with the passing of the National Health Insurance Act in 1911 and then the National Health Service Act in 1946 that underlined the ascendance of the biomedical approach associated with the heightened dominance of the medical profession in the twentieth century (Larkin 1995).

Conversely, the establishment of this state-underwritten medical ortho-doxy also had the effect of marginalising the diverse range of therapies that did not readily fit within its frame of reference and defining them for the first time as 'alternative medicine'. In this respect, it should be stressed that the term 'alternative medicine' refers not so much to the content of these therapies – which are marked by considerable heterogeneity, for all their holistic tendencies – as to their predominant outsider status within the British health care system. This is also mirrored in their relatively marginal position in areas such as official research funding and the orthodox health care curriculum, as witnessed by the low levels of spending by major state funding bodies in this field and the limited official support for programmes of training in alternative therapies (Saks 1996). The inevitable result of this marginal standing is that the contemporary scope of availability of such alternative therapies as herbalism and naturopathy in this country is restricted, even though not as greatly as in many other countries in Europe and North America where non-orthodox therapists are often outlawed (Huggon and Trench 1992; Cohen 1998).

The driving force behind this position of professional dominance as regards alternative therapies in Britain has come from the elite of the medical establishment, which – as in the United States (see, for example, Burrow 1963) – has for long mounted strong campaigns against its non-orthodox competitors in the medical journals, as well as in other public and professional forums. This was perhaps most evident in the report of the British Medical Association (BMA) (1986) on alternative medicine that extolled the scientific aspects of modern biomedicine, whilst at the same time generally depicting alternative medicine as superstitious dogma. It is precisely this kind of approach that has placed alternative medicine in a double bind situation in relation to orthodox medicine – in which its proponents are criticised for not producing enough scientific evidence to support their case, at the same time as the allocation of official research funds is heavily restricted to more conventional health care activities (Saks 1996).

The changing position of the medical profession and unorthodox practitioners: Implications for patterns of dominance and marginality

This is not to deny that there have been changes of professional position in recent times. In fact, the stance generally taken by the medical elite in Britain has until recently been at variance with developing grass-roots opinion in medicine and other orthodox health professions; while there has always been a lingering element of support in this country for alternative therapies within such professions – as represented by the small enclave of medical homoeopaths that has operated in the NHS since its foundation (Nicholls 1988) – this has grown significantly. Within the medical profession, general practitioners have become most favourably disposed towards the alternatives to medicine. Today 49 per cent of general practices now offer some access to alternative medicine on the NHS – with many general practitioners actually practising such therapies (Thomas *et al.* 2003). Most pain clinics, too, regularly employ acupuncture and other alternative therapies, which are usually administered by nurses and cognate health professional groups working under medical authority (Trevelyan and Booth 1994).

At a wider level, the report of the BMA (1993) on such therapies no longer condemned them outright, instead acknowledging their popularity and avoiding direct comment on their validity. It is therefore tempting to see this apparent revolution from within as pointing to a progressive erosion of professional dominance. Aside from apparently indicating that the profession is now subordinating itself to expanding consumer demand, it also seems to increase the challenge that alternative therapists pose to the orthodox medical profession – not least by legitimating the operation of its competitors outside the profession, whose numbers in the United Kingdom have expanded to some 60,000 practitioners (Mills and Budd 2000).

Ironically, though, these tendencies to incorporation in Britain – which were even more evident at an earlier stage in the United States (Saks 2003a) – may be more plausibly seen within the neo-Weberian approach as an interest-based occupational strategy that has served to defuse the threat to orthodox medicine as a whole and maintained the privileged standing of the profession in face of the fast-swelling ranks of the unorthodox. What is crucial in sustaining this interpretation, in which interests are defined in terms of the achievement of a positive balance between objectively determined benefits and costs, is the limited manner in which incorporation has typically occurred (Saks 1995). This can be illustrated with reference to the growing medical incorporation of acupuncture in this country, which the medical profession has primarily employed for analgesic purposes, underpinned by orthodox neurophysiological explanations. This approach has minimised the encouragement given to non-medically qualified acupuncturists, with their more challenging Yin-Yang theories and broader ranging applications, while at the same time opening up new territory for the profession (Saks 1992). Such a strategy has frequently been used in successfully combating threats from without. This is highlighted historically by the way in which the medical profession in both Britain and the United States abandoned its commitment to heroic therapies in the latter half of the nineteenth century in the light of the challenge to its developing power, status and wealth from the more popular and less arduous treatment by homoeopaths – even to the point of surreptitiously drawing on remedies with homoeopathic origins in smaller doses than would previously have been considered viable within the profession (Rothstein 1972; Nicholls 1988).

Paralleling these incorporationist trends, alternative practitioners have themselves frequently diluted the radicalism of their ideas in the contemporary era so that they are not always as challenging as those of their founders. The classic distinction between the purist 'straight' practitioners of non-orthodox therapies and the backsliding 'mixers' who have watered down their original oppositional philosophies and practice (Wardwell 1976) seems highly relevant in this context. In this vein, the Anglo-European College of Chiropractic in this country took the lead in fostering new generations of 'mixers' by making more restricted claims about the scope and efficacy of chiropractic and working in a more respectful relationship with biomedicine, in an attempt to gain greater academic and professional credibility (Christensen 1989). This ultimately culminated in the statutory regulation of chiropractic, alongside osteopathy in the 1990s in Britain (Saks 2003b). In so doing, British chiropractors have followed their Canadian counterparts, who abandoned much of their earlier radicalism and underwent partial medicalisation in order to secure licensing recognition and the inclusion of chiropractic under government health insurance (Coburn and Biggs 1986).

Vincent (1992) too has argued that radical health self-help groups are readily incorporated into professional power structures and often operate to bolster orthodox health care provision, while Bakx (1991) similarly notes that even 'straight' alternative therapists can be useful to orthodoxy in filling gaps in conventional patterns of care. This may help to explain why, despite their broader social, political and economic interests, a small proportion of doctors in Britain occasionally refer patients to alternative therapists outside of the formally recognised health professions – which they are now able to do following the lifting by the General Medical Council of ethical prohibitions on the co-operation between doctors and unorthodox practitioners in the mid-1970s (Saks 2003a).

Some alternative approaches, however, are undoubtedly less challenging to orthodox medicine than others, in part because of the differential compatibility of the epistemological, educational and therapeutic philosophies of their exponents with medical orthodoxy (Wardwell 1976). In this light, such modern trends as the selective medical incorporation of the more threatening alternative therapies and the dilution of the aims of non-orthodox health practitioners in Britain have led some commentators to suggest that the term 'alternative medicine' should now be replaced by that of 'complementary medicine' (as, for instance, Sharma 1995). This argument is intended to reflect the increased prospects of co-operation with orthodox medicine, which have already been realised to some degree in the collaboration that has now started to take place between orthodox health professionals and non-orthodox practitioners in Britain, particularly in primary health care (see, amongst others, Peters *et al.* 2002). The suggested redefinition is also supported by the fact that a major national study has shown that the preponderant contemporary use of non-orthodox therapies by the public in this country is for a restricted range of problems and as a supplement, rather than an alternative, to medical orthodoxy (Thomas *et al.* 1991). This hardly suggests a major challenge to the cultural authority of the medical profession within the terms of the deprofessionalisation thesis.

Nonetheless, although this accentuates the limits of the current challenge posed to the medical profession from unorthodox practice in Britain, it should not mask the potential for conflict. In this respect, note should be taken of the fact that the arguments for such a reconceptualisation are often politically inspired; the non-orthodox health care organisations most willing to define their activities as 'complementary medicine' tend to be those that have the strongest ideological interest in having their co-operative standing acknowledged by medical orthodoxy (Haviland 1992). It would also be foolish to ignore the many practitioners who do still actively challenge medicine by operating with starkly counterposed philosophies to biomedicine – as, for example, acupuncturists who base their practice on the existence of meridians which bear little systematic relationship to the central nervous system and homoeopaths whose view that the more dilute a substance, the more potent its effects, does not readily fit in with the biomedical model (Stanway 1994). Nor should the existence be neglected of radical, non-hierarchical forms of health self-help groups, which are unfavourably disposed towards the involvement of professional experts – not least groups with their origins in the 1960s and 1970s counter culture, such as those centred on women's issues (Saks 2000). The greatest objection to the reconceptualisation, though, is that the notion of complementary medicine plays down the institutionalised marginality of such approaches; complementarity – as previously indicated – does not currently extend to anything like comparable official funding and support of the practices concerned. This does, however, prompt the question of whether alternative medicine might make a more substantial challenge to medical orthodoxy in the years ahead.

The future challenge to medical orthodoxy from alternative therapies

If the alternatives to medicine are seriously to challenge the professional dominance of existing medical orthodoxy in Britain in the future – and therefore give a more meaningful ring to claims about the proletarianisation and deprofessionalisation of medicine in this area – this may well be more a result of wider socio-political forces than abstracted considerations about their biomedical integrity. In this regard, further pressure looks likely to continue to be exerted on the orthodox health professions by the continuing growth of public interest in non-orthodox therapies. It is interesting that, in the debate over the professional monopoly in the health sector in the Netherlands in the 1980s, the Health Ministry gave more weight to the public demand for freedom of choice in health care than to pressure for further clinical evidence on the efficacy of the therapies concerned from the medical profession (Fulder 1996). This serves as a reminder that politicians and the state can wield a crucial influence over the outcome of events in the face of a significant level of consumer demand.

From this viewpoint, alternative therapists in Britain and the United States are now better placed than they have been for some time to challenge the dominance of orthodox medicine in the division of labour. In the United States this is indicated by the decisions of some individual states to allow groups like trained acupuncturists to practise independently of the medical profession in a primarily fee-for-service system (Cohen

1998). More recently, it has been amplified by federal support for the development of the National Center for Complementary and Alternative Medicine, which has been increasingly well funded to pump-prime research in this area (Saks 2003a). In Britain the substantial political support now available to non-orthodox practitioners is underlined by the lobbying of the Parliamentary Group for Alternative and Complementary Medicine that comprises a substantial number of committed all-party MPs. This has been matched by continuing pressure for greater state recognition of alternative medicine in this country from other politically influential figures, including sponsorship by members of the royal family – such as Prince Charles, who was responsible in his role as President of the BMA in the early 1980s for instigating its inquiry into alternative therapies (Saks 2001).

Such support in Britain has come at a time when the Government itself has begun to put the professions under pressure as corporate groups, not least in the health area. Both recent Conservative and Labour Governments have done this with varying degrees of success (Baggott 2000). This stretches back to the Griffiths reforms in Britain in the early 1980s that were intended to augment the power of managers in the health service at the expense of doctors and other health professionals (Allsop 1995). More recently, the results of such pressure can be exemplified by the reform of health regulatory bodies in the wake of a series of scandals including the long undetected string of murders perpetrated by Shipman, the serial killing general practitioner (Allsop and Saks 2002). It is in this context that the Government began to show more substantial concern over the position of the alternative therapies by selectively supporting their search for greater legitimacy through regulatory and other means (Saks 2002). This support has been increased in the wake of the generally positive Report of the House of Lords Select Committee on Science and Technology (2000) on complementary and alternative medicine, which included recommendations spanning from establishing centres of research excellence to enhancing public information in this area.

However, the political process of increasing access to alternative medicine in Britain by breaching the much-prized monopoly of the medical profession within the health service is not as simple as it may at first appear. Notwithstanding claims that the American medical profession has significantly diminished in influence in recent years (see, for example, McKinlay and Stoeckle 1988), the power of the medical elite in Britain, including the Royal Colleges and the BMA, remains substantial, even though the medical-Ministry alliance no longer seems to be the impermeable block on the progress of alternative therapies that it was for a large part of this century (Larkin 1992). This is highlighted by the fact that, for all the recent interest in alternative therapies by Government, only the osteopaths and the chiropractors so far have managed to gain statutory support for regulation – and these through private members' bills (Saks 2003b).

Having said this, it should be noted that practitioners of alternative medicine in Britain have generally not helped their own case from the standpoint of pressure group politics by their manifest disunity; divisions have been particularly apparent at both the organisational level between practitioners with orthodox and non-orthodox qualifications and between alternative therapists wedded to differing principles of practice (Fulder 1996). However, although such differences have by no means been absent in other societies – as amongst indigenous healers in the United States (see, for instance, Kleinman 1985) – they were especially significant in Britain in the 1980s given the view of the Government at this time that alternative therapists should act in a more united way if their voice was to be heard (Sharma 1995). Although there were attempts to address this issue with variable success through the formation of bodies such as the Council for Complementary and Alternative Medicine (Saks 1999b), this umbrella concept of representation has fortunately now receded from the political equation. It remains to be seen, though, how far the current efforts of groups of alternative practitioners to put their own houses in order in particular areas will lead to an effective challenge to orthodox medicine. There has certainly been growing Government interest in establishing professional regulatory mechanisms in better-founded fields of alternative medicine such as herbalism and acupuncture – the latter of which has shown especially strong trends towards developing greater unity since the early 1980s (Saks 2003a).

Ultimately, though, the power of the medical profession – especially at elite level – still appears to be the largest obstacle to further diminishing the marginalisation of alternative therapists in Britain in the future, despite the current growth in consumer interest in seeking assistance from such practitioners. Marxist authors, of course, tend to dispute the neo-Weberian professional dominance thesis in medicine on the grounds that it underplays the broader influence of financial and industrial capital in capitalist societies (see, for instance, Navarro 1986). Indeed, it is on this basis that Marxist claims about the proletarianisation of the professions have been launched (Elston 1991). The marginality of alternative therapies on this perspective is typically ascribed to the power and interests of the multinational corporations dealing in pharmaceuticals and medical equipment, which are seen to be threatened by the negative impact of the growth of alternative therapies on profits from more orthodox medical products. Yet, whilst it would be unwise to ignore the power of large multinationals like Ciba-Geigy and Hoffman-La Roche, which employ massive resources to promote their wares in the health sector (Goodman 2000), their influence in the case of the alternatives to medicine should not be overstated; there are real dangers in ignoring, amongst other things, the fact that Governments in Britain to date have managed to keep their demands under reasonable control within the NHS and the diversification in product range of such corporations which gives them a stake in expanding into alternative as well as orthodox health care (Saks 1996).

The argument for the continuing dominant influence of the medical profession in this area in Britain is further reinforced by the fact that it is the elite of the profession to which the Government still formally turns for scientifically based opinions on the safety and efficacy of alternative thera-pies from the viewpoint of public policy (Sharma 1995). As such, medical orthodoxy must be seen as having played a key role in sustaining a state-supported health care system that has not fully reflected the growth of popular interest in the alternatives to medicine. This discrepancy was highlighted even as early as the late 1980s by a MORI poll that showed that three-quarters of the population wished to have the better-known forms of alternative medicine more extensively available within the NHS (Saks 2003a). Given the increasing political emphasis that has been placed on the role of the consumer in British health care – epitomised by a range of publications from *The Patient's Charter* (1991) to *The NHS Plan* (Department of Health 2000), which make firm commitments to providing a health service that is more responsive to the public – the issue of whether the medical profession as a collectivity can be seen to have acted with a due sense of public responsibility in this area clearly needs to be addressed.

The medical profession, alternative medicine and public responsibility

This issue is very significant in view of the debate in the Anglo-American social scientific literature on the professions over the extent to which such groups subordinate their own self-interests to the public interest. The traditionally more prominent trait and functionalist writers tend to take a more benevolent view of the translation of the altruistic ideologies of the professions into practice than those of contributors to the more critical current neo-Weberian and Marxist orthodoxy (Saks 1999a). It is also not an easy issue to resolve given the complex conceptual problems involved, particularly regarding the much-contested definition of the public interest. Nonetheless, judging the public responsibility of the medical profession in this country relativistically against the key social principles of the British liberal-democratic State – namely, securing justice, enhancing the general welfare and striving to maximise the amount of individual freedom consistent with these ends (Saks 1995) – doubts certainly arise about the integrity of the modern response of the medical profession to the challenge of the alternatives to medicine. As has been noted, its influence not only has curtailed the individual freedom of consumers, but may also be viewed as having disadvantaged the broader public in terms of justice. In this latter respect, despite the increasing, if limited, practice of various forms of alternative medicine by orthodox health personnel, access to alternative therapies within the NHS has been restricted, giving rise to both economic and geographic inequalities in state health care – which have been exacerbated by the uneven distribution of practitioners of alternative medicine in the private sector in this country (Sharma 1995). However, the question of whether the medical profession has or has not acted responsibly in terms of promoting the general welfare, as well as advancing individual freedom and justice, ultimately hinges on the comparative safety, efficacy and cost-effectiveness of the alternatives to medicine.

These are difficult fields in which to make judgements, not least because the concept of alternative medicine covers a wide and heterogeneous band of therapies and therapists that can be seen to have different balances of strengths and weaknesses. In terms of safety, nonetheless, there are certainly dangers associated with alternative medicine from the orthodox biomedical perspective, which are usually felt to be exacerbated in the hands of the unqualified; some herbal medicines, for example, can cause haemorrhages, while hepatitis B outbreaks have followed the administration of acupuncture using non-sterilised needles (Saks 2003a). However, problems rarely seem to be reported and the risk of their occurrence has probably been reduced by the growing number of non-orthodox practitioners who now belong to organisations that have codes of conduct and require substantial periods of training (Fulder 1996). The fact that orthodox medicine itself can also be a perilous business – as witnessed by the victims of the thalidomide and Opren disasters (Goodman 2000) – suggests that comparative safety *per se* is not a very convincing reason for the marginalisation of the alternatives to medicine.

As has been seen, though, the relative effectiveness of alternative therapies has been questioned by their detractors at the apex of the medical profession, who have claimed that they are scientifically unproven – a view also reflected by the medically inspired, 'quackbusting' Campaign Against Health Fraud, which became transformed into Healthwatch (Sharma 1995). However, promise has been shown by alternative medicine in a wide span of areas from the use of St John's wort for mild depression to the employment of yoga for the long-term treatment of hypertension (Ernst *et al.* 2001). This can be illustrated within the mainstream controlled trial methodology of the medical profession, where there are a number of studies which indicate that therapies like homoeopathy may be more effective than placebos (see, amongst others, Reilly *et al.* 1986) and that some forms of alternative medicine may offer greater therapeutic benefits than orthodox procedures – as, for instance, the use of chiropractic for back problems as compared with hospital out-patient treatment (Meade *et al.* 1990). Against this, such studies have only rarely been carried out on a significant scale and cannot as yet rival the weight of clinically based evidence underpinning some of the more significant achievements of orthodox medicine, which can dramatically transform the lives of patients through procedures ranging from the replacement of faulty heart valves to arthritic hip surgery (Le Fanu 1999).

Nevertheless, even leaving aside the vast differential in financial support given to research into orthodox as opposed to alternative medicine that has contributed to this situation, the question of the relative efficacy of such therapies still needs to be approached with caution. In the first place, there are queries as to how far the scientific medical establishment itself lives up to its own standards. This is well illustrated by the classic widely publicised medical attack on the 'gentle approach' of the Bristol Cancer Help Centre based on a study in which it was suggested that women with breast cancer attending the Centre died sooner than those given orthodox treatment (Bagenal *et al.* 1990) – despite deficiencies in the nature of the controls employed (Stacey 1991). There are also major methodological debates about whether the randomised controlled trial is the most useful method to evaluate holistically based alternative therapies in which treatments are tailored to the individual client rather than given for a standard condition; crucially, for most alternative practitioners, the placebo effect should be exploited constructively in the healing relationship, rather than eliminated from consideration in pursuit of scientific rigour (Saks 2003a). The emphasis on the mind–body relationship in alternative therapy, moreover, does seem to have produced high levels of consumer satisfaction in this country, even if this is arguably a rather blunt instrument for gauging the efficacy of such therapy (Sharma 1995). What is perhaps more significant, though, is that the greatest apparent potential of alternative medicine lies in many of the areas where orthodox health care is at its least successful – particularly in the growing range of chronic degenerative conditions associated with the extension of the human lifespan (Cant and Sharma 1999).

All of this strengthens the case for extending the accessibility of certain forms of alternative medicine to a wider public within the increasingly consumer-oriented NHS. This case is enhanced further by the fact that alternative medicine is usually less expensive than orthodox biomedical techniques, as indicated by even a cursory comparison of the costs of drugs and medical equipment with, for instance, those of the remedies used in homoeopathy or the laying on of hands in healing – which is practised by the largest number of alternative therapists in Britain (Mills and Budd 2000). This said, the average time for a consultation with an alternative therapist is up to seven times that with a general practitioner (Fulder 1996). However, in terms of cost much depends on who is delivering the alternative therapy concerned. In this respect, it should be asked whether the highly paid, biomedically educated doctor is always the most appropriately placed to practise or to have authority over diagnostic and treatment decisions associated with non-orthodox therapies, as distinct from other personnel within the broader health care division of labour (Saks 2001). This point relates as much to competencies as to financial considerations and accentuates the potential issues posed by the continuing exclusion of well-qualified non-orthodox therapists from the NHS as practitioners in their own right.

On this basis, and subject to much-needed additional research, it seems that the restrictions that the British medical profession as a collectivity has largely imposed on both the structural location and form of alternative practice, in face of escalating consumer demand, may at least be challenged in terms of the definition of public responsibility employed here – especially as regards the more established alternative therapies, such as acupuncture and homoeopathy. Similar queries can, of course, be raised about the operation of the medical profession in other industrial societies where orthodox medicine has been no less restrictive in its approach to outsiders – as, for example, in relation to the longstanding boycott by the American Medical Association of the 'unscientific cult' of chiropractic, with its large public following, which the courts subsequently forced it to reverse (Saks 2003a). Interestingly, though, doctors in an international context have often moved further towards incorporating alternative medicine into their own repertoire when the legal restrictions on their external competitors have been at their strongest. Thus in France, where tight legislative regulation exists – even of the practice of alternative medicine by the professions allied to medicine – acupuncture and homoeopathy have for long been more widely employed by qualified doctors than in Britain (Bouchayer 1991). This pattern may be related to the reduced threat that outsiders have normally thereby posed to the social, political and financial interests of members of the medical profession, as compared to Britain where more open competition exists in the private sector, through the provisions of the common law (Saks 1995).

For all this, though, the identification of a possible medically induced health crisis in the sphere of alternative medicine in Britain prompts important questions about how far the medical profession has acted altruistically and should continue to maintain the monopolistic position that underpins its current dominance in the health care market. Although the profession undoubtedly now has much more to offer from a therapeutic standpoint than when the Medical Registration Act was passed in the mid-nineteenth century – in an age before anaesthesia and antiseptic techniques were generally utilised and when hospitals were seen as 'gateways to death' (Youngson 1979) – this does not absolve it from criticism as far as the alternatives to medicine are concerned in an ever more pluralistic, consumer-based socio-political context.

Conclusion: Markets, the medical profession and alternative medicine

The main conclusion of this chapter, however, is that whilst there have been important challenges posed by alternative therapies to the medical profession in Britain, these do not seem at present to have significantly reduced the latter's dominance. The upshot of this is that the proletarianisation and deprofessionalisation theses do not currently appear to fit this area very well, although they are difficult to examine empirically because they have typically been so imprecisely formulated (Elston 1991). Having said this, the authority of the British medical profession has certainly been thrown into question by the growing public demand for the alternatives to medicine. But, for the moment – assisted by its strategic incorporation of such therapies and the lingering strategic weaknesses of its non-orthodox competitors – the legitimacy of medical authority remains broadly intact, even if the use to which it has been put might be contested in terms of the wider professional altruism ideal. This view is reinforced by the fact that the medical profession in Britain has so far generally retained its powerful position within the NHS and the right to autonomous collective self-regulation, notwithstanding the limited support that alternative medicine has won from politicians and the state. This is not, though, to deny the substantial recent changes that have occurred in this field in Britain, but simply to highlight the current need to interpret their seemingly striking effects with caution.

Nonetheless, changes in the future may cast new light on the situation – not least as the regulatory arrangements for the medical profession are reviewed in the wake of wider concerns about public protection, alongside those of other health professions, which are themselves gradually emerging from the shade of the medical umbrella (Allsop and Saks 2002). In these circumstances, consumers may be better placed to make their views on alternative medicine felt in face of the dominance of the medical profession.

Individual medical practitioners in the NHS may also in turn be more receptive to using qualified staff in this field in their highly pressurised practice environments – drawn from both orthodox health professions and the increasingly professionalised ranks of alternative therapists, as a protection against the risks of consumer litigation. Alternative therapies may therefore continue to be increasingly taken up within the NHS, but primarily in a limited manner by doctors themselves and other health professionals operating under their authority, which may not fully do justice to their broader potential. This incorporationist scenario appears the most likely outcome in view of the current power and interests of key elements of the British medical profession, and may be reinforced by the development of a Single European Market. This could constrain the widening of public access to alternative therapists by imposing more restrictive legislation on such practitioners in the public and private sectors, in line with harmonisation and mutual recognition policies in member states (Saks 2003a). In terms of the proletarianisation or deprofessionalisation of medicine, though, the traditional monopolistic power base of the medical profession still seems likely to dilute the scope of what is available, even at a time when the profession is coming under ever-greater challenge from the consumer.

References

Allsop, J. (1995) *Health Policy and the NHS*, second edn, London: Longman.

Allsop, J. and Saks, M. (eds) (2002) 'Introduction: The regulation of health professions', in *Regulating the Health Professions*, London: Sage.

Bagenal, F.S., Easton, D.F., Harris, E., Chilvers, C.E.D. and McElwain, T.J. (1990) 'Survival of patients with breast cancer attending the Bristol Cancer Help Centre', *Lancet*, 336(2): 606–10.

Baggott, R. (2000) *Public Health: Policy and Politics*, Basingstoke: Macmillan.

Bakx, K. (1991) 'The "eclipse" of folk medicine in Western society', *Sociology of Health and Illness*, 13(1): 20–38.

Bouchayer, F. (1991) 'Alternative medicines: A general approach to the French situation', in Lewith, G. and Aldridge, D. (eds), *Complementary Medicine and the European Community*, Saffron Walden: C.W. Daniel.

British Medical Association (1986) *Report of the Board of Science and Education on Alternative Therapy*, London: BMA.

—— (1993) *Complementary Medicine: New Approaches to Good Practice*, Oxford: Oxford University Press.

Burrow, J.G. (1963) *AMA: Voice of American Medicine*, Baltimore: Johns Hopkins Press.

Cant, S. and Sharma, U. (1999) *A New Medical Pluralism? Alternative Medicine, Doctors, Patients and the State*, London: UCL Press.

Christensen, A. (1989) 'Chiropractic education', *Complementary Medical Research*, 3(3): 38–40.

Coburn, D. (1999) 'Professions in transition: Globalisation, neo-liberalism and the decline of medical power', in Hellberg, I., Saks, M. and Benoit, C. (eds), *Professional Identities in Transition: Cross-Cultural Dimensions*, Södertälje: Almqvist & Wiksell International.

Coburn, D. and Biggs, C.L. (1986) 'Limits to medical dominance: The case of chiropractic', *Social Science and Medicine*, 22(10): 1035–46.

Cohen, M. (1998) *Complementary and Alternative Medicine: Legal Boundaries and Regulatory Perspectives*, Baltimore: Johns Hopkins University Press.

Coward, R. (1989) *The Whole Truth: The Myth of Alternative Health*, London: Faber & Faber.

Department of Health (1991) *The Patient's Charter*, London: HMSO.

—— (2000) *The NHS Plan*, London: The Stationery Office.

Eisenberg, D., Davis, R., Ettner, S., Appel, S., Wilkey, S., Rompay, M. and Kessler, R. (1998) 'Trends in alternative medicine use in the United States, 1990–1997', *Journal of the American Medical Association*, 280: 1569–75.

Elston, M.A. (1991) 'The politics of professional power medicine in a changing health service', in Gabe, J., Calnan, M. and Bury, M. (eds), *The Sociology of the Health Service*, London: Routledge.

Ernst, E., Pittler, M., Stevinson, C. and White, A. (eds) (2001) *The Desktop Guide to Complementary and Alternative Medicine: An Evidence-Based Approach*, London: Mosby.

Fisher, P. and Ward, A. (1994) 'Complementary medicine in Europe', *British Medical Journal*, 309: 107–11.

Fulder, S. (1996) *The Handbook of Complementary Medicine*, third edn, Oxford: Oxford University Press.

Goodman, J. (2000) 'Pharmaceutical industry', in Cooter, R. and Pickstone, J. (eds), *Medicine in the Twentieth Century*, Amsterdam: Harwood Academic Publishers.

Haviland, D. (1992) 'The differing natures of alternative and complementary medicine', *Journal of Alternative and Complementary Medicine*, 10(11): 27–8.

House of Lords Select Committee on Science and Technology (2000) *Report on Complementary and Alternative Medicine*, London: The Stationery Office.

Huggon, T. and Trench, A. (1992) 'Brussels post-1992: Protector or persecutor?', in Saks, M. (ed.), *Alternative Medicine in Britain*, Oxford: Clarendon Press.

Kleinman, A. (1985) 'Indigenous systems of healing: Questions for professional, popular, and folk care', in Salmon, J.W. (ed.), *Alternative Medicines: Popular and Policy Perspectives*, London: Tavistock.

Larkin, G. (1992) 'Orthodox and osteopathic medicine in the inter-war years', in Saks, M. (ed.), *Alternative Medicine in Britain*, Oxford: Clarendon Press.

—— (1995) 'State control and the health professions in the United Kingdom: Historical perspectives', in Johnson, T., Larkin, G. and Saks, M. (eds), *Health Professions and the State in Europe*, London: Routledge.

Le Fanu, J. (1999) *The Rise and Fall of Modern Medicine*, London: Abacus.

McKinlay, J.B. and Arches, J. (1985) 'Towards the proletarianization of physicians', *International Journal of Health Services*, 15(2): 161–95.

McKinlay, J.B. and Stoeckle, J.D. (1988) 'Corporatization and the social transformation of doctoring', *International Journal of Health Services*, 18(2): 191–205.

Maple, E. (1992) 'The great age of quackery', in Saks, M. (ed.), *Alternative Medicine in Britain*, Oxford: Clarendon Press.

Meade, T.W., Dyer, S., Browne, W., Townsend, J. and Frank, A.O. (1990) 'Low back pain of mechanical origin: Randomised comparison of chiropractic and hospital outpatient treatment', *British Medical Journal*, 300: 1431–7.

Mills, S. and Budd, S. (2000) *Professional Organisation of Complementary and Alternative Medicine in the United Kingdom. A Second Report to the Department of Health*, Exeter: University of Exeter.

Navarro, V. (1986) *Crisis, Health and Medicine*, London: Tavistock.

Nicholls, P.A. (1988) *Homoeopathy and the Medical Profession*, London: Croom Helm.

Peters, D., Chaitow, L., Harris, G. and Morrison, S. (2002) *Integrating Complementary Therapies in Primary Care*, Edinburgh: Churchill Livingstone.

Porter, R. (1995) *Disease, Medicine and Society in England 1550–1860*, second edn, London: Macmillan.

—— (2001) *Quacks: Fakers and Charlatans in English Medicine*, Stroud: Tempus Publishing.

Reilly, D.T., Taylor, M.A., McSharry, C. and Aitchison, T. (1986) 'Is homoeopathy a placebo response? Controlled trial of homoeopathic potency, with pollen in hay fever as model', *Lancet*, 333(2): 881–5.

Rothstein, W.G. (1972) *American Physicians in the Nineteenth Century*, London: Johns Hopkins University Press.

Saks, M. (1992) 'The paradox of incorporation: Acupuncture and the medical profession in modern Britain', in Saks, M. (ed.), *Alternative Medicine in Britain*, Oxford: Clarendon Press.

—— (1995) *Professions and the Public Interest: Medical Power, Altruism and Alternative Medicine*, London: Routledge.

—— (1996) 'From quackery to complementary medicine: The shifting boundaries between orthodox and unorthodox medical knowledge', in Sharma, U. and Cant, S. (eds), *Complementary Medicines: Knowledge in Practice*, London: Free Association Books.

—— (1998) 'Professionalism and health care', in Field, D. and Taylor, S. (eds), *Sociological Perspectives on Health, Illness and Health Care*, Oxford: Blackwell Science.

—— (1999a) 'Professions, markets and public responsibility', in Dent, M., O'Neill, M. and Bagley, C. (eds), *Professions, New Public Management and the European Welfare State*, Stafford: Staffordshire University Press.

—— (1999b) 'Towards integrated health care: Shifting professional interests and identities in Britain', in Hellberg, I., Saks, M. and Benoit, C. (eds), *Professional Identities in Transition: Cross-Cultural Dimensions*, Södertälje: Almqvist & Wiksell International.

—— (2000) 'Medicine and counter culture', in Cooter, R. and Pickstone, J. (eds), *Medicine in the Twentieth Century*, Amsterdam: Harwood Academic Publishers.

—— (2001) 'Alternative medicine and the health care division of labour', *Current Sociology*, 49(3): 119–34.

—— (2002) 'Professionalisation, regulation and alternative medicine', in Allsop, J. and Saks, M. (eds), *Regulating the Health Professions*, London: Sage.

—— (2003a) *Orthodox and Alternative Medicine: Politics, Professionalization and Health Care*, London: Sage.

—— (2003b) 'Professionalization, politics and complementary and alternative medicine', in Kelner, M., Pescosolido, B., Saks, M. and Wellman, B. (eds), *Complementary and Alternative Medicine: Challenge and Change*, London: Routledge.

Sharma, U. (1995) *Complementary Medicine Today: Practitioners and Patients*, revised edn, London: Routledge.

Stacey, M. (1988) *The Sociology of Health and Healing*, London: Unwin Hyman.

—— (1991) 'The potential of social science for complementary medicine', *Complementary Medical Research*, 5(3): 183–6.

Stanway, A. (1994) *Complementary Medicine: A Guide to Natural Therapies*, Harmondsworth: Penguin Books.

Thomas, K.J., Carr, J., Westlake, L. and Williams, B.T. (1991) 'Use of non-orthodox and conventional health care in Great Britain', *British Medical Journal*, 302: 207–10.

Thomas, K.J., Nicholl, J.P. and Coleman, P. (2001) 'Use and expenditure on complementary medicine in England: A population based survey', *Complementary Therapies in Medicine*, 9: 2–11.

Thomas, K.J., Coleman, P. and Nicholl, J.P. (2003) 'Trends in access to complementary or alternative medicines via primary care in England: 1995–2001', *Family Practice*, 20: 5.

Trevelyan, J. and Booth, B. (1994) *Complementary Medicine for Nurses, Midwives and Health Visitors*, London: Macmillan.

Vincent, J. (1992) 'Self-help groups and health care in contemporary Britain', in Saks, M. (ed.), *Alternative Medicine in Britain*, Oxford: Clarendon Press.

Waddington, I. (1984) *The Medical Profession in the Industrial Revolution*, London: Gill & Macmillan.

Wardwell, W.I. (1976) 'Orthodox and unorthodox practitioners: Changing relationships and the future status of chiropractors', in Wallis, R. and Morley, P. (eds), *Marginal Medicine*, London: Peter Owen.

Youngson, A. (1979) *The Scientific Revolution in Victorian Medicine*, London: Croom Helm.

6 Self-help groups and their relationship to medicine

David Kelleher

Introduction

The focus of this chapter is the relationship between self-help groups for people with a chronic medical condition and the medical profession. This will entail asking whether self-help groups are complementary to medicine and the professional health care system or part of a growing cultural challenge, questioning medical discourse and practice and playing a wider role in contributing to debate and change (Brown and Zavestoski 2004; Scambler and Kelleher 2006) in the public sphere.

The current attempt to control the cost of providing health care in both Britain and the USA is one aspect of a crisis that has led some to claim that the medical profession is experiencing proletarianisation as a result of medical work becoming subject to managerial control from above (Elston 1991). It will be argued here that there is another aspect to this crisis: a challenge to medicine from below, from patients who express their dissatisfaction with the limitations and depersonalisation of medicine by turning either to other professionals working in alternative medicine (see Chapter 5) or to each other by forming self-help groups. The proletarianising challenge from the State and the challenge from patients are not unrelated. In this chapter the theoretical perspective of Habermas (1987) will be used to suggest that the health care systems of Britain and the USA, steered in different ways by the medium of money, and as set out in a detailed argument by Brown and Zavestoski (2004), are distorted versions of the healing mission of Enlightenment science; it is in this context that self-help groups have been developed for those whom medicine cannot cure, the ten million chronically ill in the UK (Donaldson 2003).

There is no doubt that self-help groups for people with chronic illness have been growing in number in recent years. In the USA it has been reported that:

> In the late seventies it was estimated that between 15 and 20 million people were involved in 500,000 self-help groups.
>
> (Arntson and Droge 1987: 149)

Vincent (1992) identifies a similar growth of health-related self-help groups in England, but also notes the difficulty of establishing just how many do exist at any one time, as not all survive beyond the interest and enthusiasm of the founder members. On mainland Europe the increase in the number of self-help groups has been equally great and sufficient to merit the attention of the World Health Organization (WHO). In the introduction to a survey of self-help groups carried out for the WHO, Kickbusch and Hatch (1983) not only support the claim that self-help groups are indeed growing in number, but also draw attention to the idea that the growth is related to the financial crisis of health care systems.

In relation to the latter point, Nayer *et al.* (2004) discuss the usefulness of self-help groups to countries they define as low or middle income. They conclude that the growth of self-help groups in such countries, although less suitable because of different social structures, can help to achieve 'some degree of synergy between health care providers and users but cannot be prescribed to partially replace government health services... thereby reducing health care expenditure and ensuring equity in health care', thus coming down firmly against the hopes of the WHO report on self-help in Europe, quoted below, being extended to poorer countries.

> The pace at which self-help groups and organisations have come into being over the last ten years has made self-help an issue of continuing debate in both the political and professional field, leading not only to critical assessment of the quality and efficiency of the health care system in general, but also to hopes of having found a solution to its financial crisis.
>
> (Kickbusch and Hatch 1983: 2)

Clearly, though, the self-help phenomenon is something that merits further attention. A 2005 Internet search revealed that over 9000 articles have been written on self-help groups since 2000, including 442 on those for people with diabetes alone. They are clearly important in terms of what they do for individuals and what they say about the way medicine operates in contemporary society when they are seen as part of a New Social

Movement (NSM). This chapter will not attempt to provide a comprehensive account of the range of self-help groups, nor will it provide a complete list of all the activities of these groups. The intention here is to provide some description of what self-help groups do for individuals and for the wider constituency of which they are part: chronically ill people in society. This will then be used as a basis for considering what the relationship is between the groups and the medical profession, and in particular whether these groups are part of a broadly based process which is attempting to demystify and de-monopolise professional expertise in medicine. Thus, self-help groups will be considered as an aspect of high modernity where cultural values are not clearly defined and identities are at risk (Giddens 1991). A further point considered is how the Department of Health (DOH) in England has attempted to make use of one of the processes engaged in self-help groups by developing the concept of 'expert patient'.

In the final section the theoretical perspective of Jurgen Habermas (1981) will be used to explore whether self-help groups are part of a new social movement, not only offering individuals a means of reconstructing their identities, but also playing a part in reinvigorating the public sphere (Habermas 1989) where communicative action can develop mutual understandings which may challenge the authority of medicine, and in doing so play a part in developing a wider cultural challenge.

Self-help groups and their activities

A number of writers point to the diversity of self-help groups (Robinson 1980; Richardson and Goodman 1983) and some discuss whether the wide variation in the kind of activities that they engage in is a problem in terms of defining what is meant by self-help. A brief discussion of what self-help is will follow this description of the range of activities.

The medical conditions for which there are self-help groups are enormous in number, as can be seen from an Internet search or by consulting a bulletin such as that collated by the National Self-help Support Centre. Some attempts have been made to organise this wide range of groups by classifying them according to what is seen to be their main function. Katz and Bender (1976), for example, suggest that groups can be classified according to whether they are 'inner-focused' or 'outer-focused'; that is, whether they are mainly concerned with providing members with an opportunity for sharing their personal problems and feelings with fellow sufferers, or whether they concentrate on acting as a pressure group representing the needs of all those with the condition to district authorities, currently called Primary Care Trusts. While this inner/outer distinction is a helpful starting point, it can be seen from the description of the three main groups selected below that many groups engage in both kinds of activity, although they may give more emphasis to one rather than the other, and a French example adds a further, fourth, dimension. The participatory way that links patients and professionals in the French Muscular Dystrophy Organisation (Rabeharisoa 2003) will be described later in this section. In the descriptions and analysis that follow, therefore, the inner/outer distinction will be first employed as part of an analysis of the relationship that the groups have to the medical profession.

Most of the central features and activities can be seen by looking at four examples: groups which have been set up to help people with ankylosing spondylitis, those set up to help people who feel they are dependent on tranquillisers and those for people with diabetes, and lastly the French group for muscular dystrophy.

Williams (1989) describes how the National Ankylosing Spondylitis Society was set up by doctors, physiotherapists and patients at the Royal Hospital for Rheumatic Diseases in Bath during 1976. By 1986 the Society had 4000 members and a number of local branches. Williams notes that although, ostensibly, the Society's goals were shared by lay and professional members, there was a continuing tension between shared 'outer' concerns, such as acting as a pressure group to get better treatment facilities for patients and raising funds for research, and dealing with patients' concerns with personal experience. It appears from the description of the Society that, while there is some evidence to suggest that there is a demand for the personal sharing of experience which would be necessary if the group were to be classified as 'innerfocused', in practice the organisation is controlled by professionals who see such activity as either irrelevant or harmful. In this case, then, it appears that the professionals' control ensures that the National Society does not challenge medicine, although whether that control is able to continue operating effectively in local groups is another matter.

In the case of people who felt that they were dependent on tranquillisers, Gabe (1994) describes the activities of both a local group and a national organisation, TRANX. The local group was set up on a deprived housing estate by a community health worker after a survey had shown that many of the women on the estate were concerned about their drug consumption. This group met together and shared experiences in the manner of an inner-focused group, but members also developed some local initiatives as they recognised that their problems were not just personal but also part of a public issue. They made public their criticisms of the way local doctors had prescribed tranquillisers without giving them sufficient information about side effects, and this led to them being invited to other community groups to discuss what further action should be taken. This local group, then, started as an inner-focused group but became an outer-focused one which was actively concerned in interrogating the practice of medicine.

The national self-help group for people with tranquilliser problems, TRANX, had a network of local groups and offered advice and support to individuals who telephoned, until its demise in 1990. TRANX did have an outer focus as it tried to create an awareness of the problems of long-term dependence on tranquillisers (Tattersall and Hallstrom 1992), but unlike the group described previously it clearly worked with, and was guided by, the medical profession (Ettore 1986).

The third example of self-help groups, for people with diabetes, is illustrated by the work of Kelleher (1990a, 1991). He sampled the views of people with diabetes from three different populations: people with diabetes in self-help groups, those belonging to local branches of the national organisation, the British Diabetic Association (BDA) (now called Diabetes U.K.), and those who have diabetes but are not members of either a self-help group or the BDA. In addition, he interviewed a small sample of consultant diabetologists (1990b).

The BDA, which was founded in 1934 and is now a national organisation with branches in most towns, seems originally to have been conceived of as a self-help group (BDA 1980: 2). It now finances a great deal of mainly medical research, and branches organise a range of activities to raise this money; they also invite health care professionals to give talks about diabetes. Branch members do engage in discussion and support which could be classified as self-help but there is no doubt that the majority of the activities are directed to either supporting medical research, which they take little or no part in guiding the direction of, or raising issues which are of general concern to all diabetic people, such as the effects that many people reported after having had their prescription changed from animal-derived insulin to genetically engineered 'human' insulin. The BDA branches can, then, be classified as being like the national organisation TRANX, having mainly an outer focus and operating primarily in a way that is complementary to the medical profession.

The inner-focused self-help groups for people with diabetes are a more recent development and arose from a letter from a diabetic person to *Balance*, the BDA patients' magazine (Cole 1987). These are local groups affiliated to the BDA but specifically not concerned with fund raising. Rather, they are groups where individuals with diabetes and their partners meet and discuss the problems they have in managing their diabetes. In this context, members have the opportunity to talk about the problems of managing the dietary regimen given them by health care professionals and the issues involved in self-injecting. Often the dietary advice appeared complicated and restrictive to those in the groups, but in discussions with others who shared the experience of controlled eating they were able to voice their worries, confess their temptations to eat more and learn how others managed to go beyond eating salads and the special diabetic foods that they had been told to eat.

Discussions such as these led to people feeling less guilty about having to compromise their diet in order to fit their treatment regimen around other aspects of their lives and work. It could be argued that the opportunities to share in the exchange of such experiences and problems changed people from being worried individuals who confessed to doctors that they had 'been a bit naughty' to people who drew confidence from the group's identity; this psychological security is as important an aspect of managing a chronic illness as the treatment regimen is in managing the body. This kind of change in how people understand their way of managing can be described as an example of self-regulation (Conrad 1985) and taking control of one's own disorder rather than as 'naughtiness', non-compliance or deviance from the medical regimen. Such group experiences also helped people to develop a more secure identity. Diabetes U.K. does not currently (2005) maintain a separate list of self-help groups, although in their list of groups some do identify themselves as self-help groups.

In the case of groups for people with diabetes, then, the self-help groups, like the local group of women who were worried about their shared tranquilliser problem, were inner-focused. The national organisation, the BDA, like the National Ankylosing Spondylitis Society and TRANX, although principally an outer-focused group concerned with improving facilities for all diabetic people and closely linked with the medical profession, also contained within the local branches the opportunity for people to engage in mutual help. There was evidence too from the survey part of the diabetes study (Kelleher 1991) which suggested that there was a latent demand for more of this inner-focused, interpersonal activity. In the research referred to a sample of ordinary 271 BDA branch members, 60 per cent said that they found it easier to talk to another diabetic person than to a doctor or nurse, and 55 per cent also agreed with the statement that 'doctors don't encourage people to talk about their feelings'. The eight interviews with consultants supported this view (Kelleher 1990b). Arntson and Droge (1987) also report that many of the people with epilepsy in the self-help groups in their study were upset that doctors were unwilling to talk about anything other than the medical aspect of their condition, asking them only about seizures, side effects and when they had last had a blood test.

The need for people to talk about their feelings and attempt to locate the illness within the context of their lives has been well documented in the literature on chronic illness. Bury (1988) writes about the way that young people with arthritis often associate the illness with old age and find it hard to accept that they have it. Williams (1989) illustrates the importance of 'narrative reconstruction' as a way of people coming to understand the place that the illness has in their lives. Arntson and Droge (1987) relate this need to construct narratives with the work which they observed to be going on in self-help groups for people with epilepsy:

> Self-help group members provide each other with the opportunities, stories and sets of behaviours in order to increase their perceived control over their physical and social conditions.
>
> (Arntson and Droge 1987: 153)

This aspect of self-help group work does point to shortcomings in the care provided by doctors and other health care professionals (Lock 1986), but it is not necessarily evidence of self-help groups engaging in talk which challenges the authority of medicine. Most doctors would see self-help groups, where caring work is carried out or where patients 'let off steam' (Kelleher 1990b), as supportive of their own medical work but some also saw them as places where people got 'silly' ideas about the kind of lifestyle they could live with developments like the Novopen injectors. More detailed study of the activity of sharing experiences in self-help groups, however, suggests that exchanging and sharing experiences may change people's understanding of themselves and their way of managing the condition and the treatment regimen from guiltily seeing it as non-compliance to viewing it more positively. Trojan's (1989) study of sixty-five self-help groups in Germany concluded that members gained new knowledge and developed the confidence to express themselves. Gabriel (1989), in a study of long-term mental disorder in the inner city, suggests that self-help groups can help black people to discover a sense of cultural identity and self-esteem.

This confidence may lead to a person managing the condition within the parameters of the treatment regimen, in which case there is no challenge to the authority of the doctor. But when patients begin to give a higher priority to their employment, their family's needs or their social relationships than to maintaining compliance with the treatment regimen, this suggests an implicit re-evaluation of medical knowledge.

The concern of doctors is to control the disease that people have, which in the case of diabetes means controlling the level of blood glucose. This is thought to reduce the chances of a person with diabetes developing what are seen as the 'complications' of the condition; that is, damage to feet as a result of neuropathy, blindness, kidney damage and greater risk of heart disease, all of which are serious health risks. But these complications are the long-term risks of having diabetes and may not appear threatening to people in their thirties and forties. Moreover, not everyone with diabetes develops them. As Conrad (1985) shows in relation to people with epilepsy, many people have other concerns in their lives to which they may want to give priority. Diabetic people with young children, for example, may choose to put the interests of their children before considerations of their own health. Without the support of others who share such dilemmas, the practice of decision-making based on their own judgement of priorities is difficult and often guilt-ridden, as it may involve deceiving the doctor at the periodic check-ups.

Providing people with the opportunity to talk about their illness is, for many, a way of coming to terms with and working out strategies for managing it. Much of what goes on in inner-focused groups is concerned with the expression of feelings about the condition and anxieties about the long-term effects. In one of the groups observed by Kelleher (1990a) a woman felt anxious because she had been told that her diabetes could no longer be controlled by diet and tablets. Apart from her fear of having to inject herself three times a day, she was concerned that her diabetes had now become more life-threatening. In responding to her anxiety, other members gave her both practical and psychological support; some showed her how they injected, others talked about how they still felt anxious about pushing a needle into themselves, and yet others emphasised the greater freedom to self-regulate their lives that injections give, as opposed to a diet-controlled regimen.

While many doctors would not be happy with their patients putting the interests of their family or work before concerns for their own health, they would no doubt broadly approve of the support given to the woman changing from a diet regimen to one based on insulin injections. They would see this kind of support as complementary to their own work. Some, though, would have reservations about patients thinking that insulin injections were a freer way of managing their diabetes than following a diet, just as some had doubts about the use of the Novopen, which allows diabetic people to give themselves small injections of insulin during the day according to what they are doing. One consultant interviewed by Kelleher (1990b) said that the Novopen encouraged people to adopt a 'bizarre' lifestyle, by which he meant varying the time they had lunch or sometimes going without lunch. The ways in which technological developments such as the Novopen could be used to liberate life as a diabetic was an important topic for discussion in the groups, as it was seen as a way for people to gain greater control and freedom to respond spontaneously to events.

As can be seen from these examples, much of what goes on in the inner-focused self-help groups could be interpreted as complementary to medicine, as many members are clearly not overtly rejecting the medical treatment regimen prescribed for them but are simply adapting it to suit their priorities. It can also be argued though that there is, in the sharing of experiential knowledge, an acceptance that a certain level of deviation from the medical regimen is legitimate and, in the discussion of new developments such as the Novopen, an implicit challenge to medical authority which suggests a shift in power from professionals to consumers (Stewart 1990). In a survey conducted as part of research into self-help groups for people with diabetes (Kelleher 1991), 95 per cent of BDA members and 84 per cent of diabetic people who were not BDA members thought that they could gain knowledge from other diabetics about how to control their illness, whereas only 50 per cent thought that increased awareness of the complications of diabetes would increase their compliance. Even in the outer-focused groups discussed earlier – TRANX and the BDA national organisation, both of which are medically oriented – there are examples of medical prescribing practice being interrogated on the basis of lay experience. The fourth example of a French group developed by people with neuromuscular disease is in one way the most challenging example in that it controls the direction of research it funds from its large budget. In what is called a 'partnership' model the two main characters are (1) the patient organisation which is master of its research organisation and (2) the patients who are called specialists in their own right and who liase with medical specialists (Rabeharisoa 2003). Brown *et al.* (2004) give an example of a similar development in what they describe in an 'embodied' group of people with breast cancer in the USA. This group works in such a way that the 'boundary' between experts and lay people is 'obscured'. The breast cancer group is a particularly interesting example of a self-help group challenging medical knowledge pointing up the 'inadequacy of the male orientation of the medical profession to understand... an illness "that is deeply rooted in being a woman"'.

Having described the activities of self-help groups through these examples, we can now define the common elements that run through these activities. Many of the definitions of self-help groups that are offered are little more than short descriptions of what they do. The definition set out by Katz and Bender (1976: 9), for example, starts by saying: 'Self-help groups are voluntary, small group structures for mutual aid and the accomplishment of a special purpose'. Robinson and Henry (1977: 141) offer a description of self-help group activities in terms of what self-help means to the people in the groups. They conclude that self-help groups are not a political phenomenon but 'people who are coming together to share and solve their common problems, rather than put up with the frustrations and humiliations of professional services'. Some, like Wilson (1992), argue that there is clearly no evidence that self-help groups have a commitment to challenging medical practice in any fundamental way. But others like Vincent (1992: 153) argue that: 'The strength of self-help groups in health care ... lies in their empowering of their members and the challenge they may pose to medical orthodoxy.' It will be argued later in this chapter that they may also be seen as having a political role, helping to sustain a civic culture which is rapidly coming to be in a state of atrophy.

The thread running through the description of self-help groups in this chapter suggests that while many of the activities of the groups can be seen as complementary to the work of the medical profession, there is nevertheless a subversive readiness to question the knowledge of doctors and to assert that experiential knowledge has value. Although Kickbusch (1989) has reservations about the relevance and soundness of lay knowledge, it is argued here that, regardless of its soundness, self-help groups do give a legitimacy to experiential knowledge and support to the questioning of medical practice. The definition of self-help groups offered here, then, is that they are groups which place a value on experiential knowledge, thus implicitly challenging the authority of professional health care workers to define what it is to have a particular condition and how it should be managed.

Self-help groups and modern medicine coexist in contemporary culture and the needs of patients and their relationship with professionals is influenced by changes in the relationship between the health care system and the economy, as was suggested at the beginning of the chapter. It is in this context that the discussion of self-help groups and modern medicine is now located.

Self-help groups in the context of contemporary culture

Most of the contributors to the debate about the nature of contemporary society share a view of it as having become something other than the rational society of Enlightenment philosophers, where science would be used to control the natural resources for the benefit of all (Foster 1985; Giddens 1991). Just what kind of society it has become is hotly debated, but there is little disagreement that it has become a confusing place to live in for many people. According to Giddens (1990), daily life is now experienced as resembling a runaway juggernaut rather than a well-controlled car. He also suggests that in a de-traditionalised society such as contemporary Britain, identities still have to be created and sustained (Giddens 1991). Bauman (1992), in describing the post-modern features of the contemporary world, sees it as a world that has been re-enchanted, instead of one where science can explain everything. It is a world in which fear has been privatised, and although it appears that people have the freedom to do anything they want, they have no guide as to what is worth doing and what is worthless. We are, he says, vagabonds wandering in the world instead of being pilgrims guided by knowledge of the truth (Bauman 1992). In such a situation it has been suggested that there is a tendency for people to become narcissistic (Lasch 1980) and concentrate on developing themselves and their relationships with intimate others, to the exclusion of contributing to public debate (Sennett 1977). Critics of self-help groups may see them as collective confessionals, as part of the fashion for confessing and revealing one's weaknesses and for self-exploration that seems to be so attractive to people who participate in radio phone-ins, or who watch television programmes like the *Oprah Winfrey Show*, so popular in both the USA and Britain.

It is possible that some of the people who become members of self-help groups are influenced by these cultural trends, but the condition-specific nature of the groups makes it unlikely that this is the main reason for their growth. Another cultural trend that may have an influence on the development of groups is the high value that is placed on being healthy, a state of being which is so highly valued that it is sometimes described as 'healthism' (Glassner 1989; Rich 2003)

In a world in which people find it difficult to feel that they have any control over the events that shape their lives, the attraction of feeling in control of one's health may be considerable. The contemporary western world is a risk-oriented world (Giddens 1991; Beck 1992) in which people are continuously warned about the dangers of obesity, drinking polluted tap water and breathing air from a polluted environment. This pursuit of fitness puts much of the responsibility for being healthy on to lay people themselves. It is an emphasis much approved of by cost-cutting governments, who see it as a cheap way of improving the health of the population, a way that avoids confronting the social causes of ill health.

For those people who already suffer from a chronic disease such as diabetes, epilepsy or mental illness, the idea that their own faulty lifestyle may be to blame for their condition is not helpful. The chronically ill, in a period when so much emphasis is put on choosing one's own lifestyle and creating and sustaining one's identity, are subject to all the pressures to which other people are subject, but suffer an additional handicap. Some may feel stigmatised and be in need of sympathetic support (Arntson and Droge 1987) and, as discussed earlier, often fail to find it within the professional health care system. Managing the stigmatisation caused by having a medically defined identity is one of the important ways in which self-help groups help their members.

This section has briefly drawn attention to the fact that both self-help groups and medicine exist in, and are influenced by, the cultural values of the western capitalist societies in which they are located. Such societies are still mainly run by expert systems operating in corporate economies. However, Bell (1973) maintains that there has been a transformation which has brought about a disjuncture between the values of the cultural system and the workings of the economic system, thus creating many uncertainties, particularly for those not well placed to participate in the market. The role of self-help groups and modern medicine in such societies will be explored more fully using the theoretical framework of Jurgen Habermas. Before doing that, however, it is worthwhile drawing attention to the introductory comments in the interesting article referred to earlier on whether self-help groups could be of use in low- and middle-income countries (Nayar *et al.* 2004). They note that:

> We conclude that selfhelp groups can help to achieve some degree of synergy between health care providers and users but cannot be prescribed to partially replace government health services in low-income countries, thereby reducing health care expenditure and ensuring equity in health care.
>
> (Nayar *et al.* 2004; 2)

They argue that self-help groups tend to arise in countries with well-developed health care systems and with individualistic cultures such as are found in Europe and the USA.

Self-help groups as a new social movement

It is useful to apply the overall framework that Habermas (1987) develops in his *Theory of Communicative Action* to link the essential elements of self-help groups, such as the emphasis on shared understanding, the value placed on experiential knowledge and the sense of control that this may give members, with the role played by modern medicine. It will also be suggested, as indicated earlier, that they play a part in keeping alive a fading cultural sphere.

Self-help groups do this by being seen as part of a new social movement (Habermas 1981) which is resisting the domination of the life-world by expert systems, in this case the expert system of medicine. Expert systems represent one of the differentiated mechanisms of instrumental-cognitive rationality through which a society is maintained and developed. This differs from the life-world, which refers to the public sphere in which people's actions are guided mainly by traditional ideas. In the life-world, though, actions are subject to a moral-practical form of questioning, which is the basis of what Habermas calls communicative action. From this perspective, medicine is one of the expert systems and self-help groups are part of the life-world.

It was revealed earlier that one of the reasons why people become members of self-help groups is because they consider that doctors and other health care professionals do not offer them the opportunity to talk about their experience of illness, the stigma and social handicap that they may feel, or their worries about incorporating their illness into their social identity; nor do doctors willingly recognise what their patients may have learned about their illness from experience. The concerns of medicine are with controlling the symptoms of disease by using medical/scientific knowledge and checking on whether patients comply with treatment regimens, periodically testing their blood, patterns of brain activity or degree of physical movement. The argument here is not that these activities are superfluous – indeed, they may be life-saving measures – but that they define too narrowly what it is to have, for example, diabetes, epilepsy or arthritis, and ignore the social psychological issues that people say are important to them in trying to live and work with these conditions.

This state of affairs has come about, it is suggested, because medicine has lost its way; it is now driven not by the needs of patients as they are defined in the life-world, but by the demands of the system with its need for measuring success by 'activity levels' and other forms of instrumental rationality. Medicine, like other expert systems in the contemporary world, is steered by the media of power and money as it concentrates more and more on expensive drug treatments (Collier 1989), expensive screening programmes and complex surgery; it pays insufficient attention to how chronically ill people can become psychologically secure and capable of engaging fully with life.

The problem with such expert systems, Habermas (1987) suggests, is not that they involve such forms of rationality but that they have become decoupled from the life-world and its moral-practical ways of understanding human problems, thus leaving many patients with the feeling that what are to them important aspects of their condition are being neglected. This is not to say that some individual doctors, like the doctor in John Berger's (1967) story *A Fortunate Man*, do not make great efforts to understand their patients' life-world concerns, but they are working against the flow, as noted earlier by Brown and Zavestoski (2004). They suggest that medical authority has become heavily involved with state agencies and international corporations but as has been argued here these are also being challenged by self-help groups which are part of a New Social Movement which is resisting the decoupling of which Habermas writes.

Self-help groups are part of a public sphere where life-world concerns can be discussed in the language of the life-world. In providing this kind of opportunity they can be seen as part of a social movement which is resisting change, an attempt to withstand the drive to understand all human experience in ways that deny the value of knowledge constructed intersubjectively by means of communicative action. They can be seen as part of a wide-ranging resistance to system imperatives:

> In the past decade or two, conflicts have developed in advanced Western societies that deviate in various ways from the welfare state pattern of institutionalized conflict over distribution...these new conflicts arise in domains of cultural reproduction, social integration and socialization...the new conflicts are not ignited by distribution problems but by questions having to do with the grammar of life.
>
> (Habermas 1987: 392)

Habermas (1987) also suggests that not only have the system and life-world become decoupled, but that there is a tendency for the life-world to become colonised by the interests and instrumental-cognitive rationality of expert systems. This means that when medicine and the larger system of which it is a part do make an attempt to incorporate the life-world issues of patients into their gaze, as Armstrong (1984) suggests medicine does, they do so using a discourse and empiricist methods that are at odds with the real concerns of the life-world. A striking example of this is the concept of 'expert patient' developed by the DOH. This scheme, which is based on the work of Lorig and colleagues at Stanford University in the USA, is strongly promoted by the DOH. It draws on self-help ideas but aims to promote in the groups it sets up a set of generalised 'skills' such as restructuring beliefs, building confidence, learning from peers, learning skills, goal-setting and modelling behaviour (*Expert Patient Update* 2002; Donaldson 2003). The work carried on in Expert Patient groups is thus much more directed and not organic like the experience of being a member of a self-help group. It is like the difference between the salesman's talk which defines his own strategic talk in a conversation with a customer as plausible while ignoring the communicative talk of the customer. Frank uses this illustration to show how Habermas' 'notion of [communicative] talk shows a willingness to be convinced' (Frank 1989). Self-help groups therefore are important, it is argued, because they are rooted in the life-world and offer an opportunity to discuss the experience of chronic illness within a style of discourse using a moral-practical form of reasoning. They offer people the possibility of creating an alternative way of understanding what has happened to them.

The kind of exchanges which take place in self-help groups can be seen as useful in negotiating a pathway between complete compliance with the medical regimen and its instrumental rationality and the contexted life-world concerns of individuals. In the study of self-help groups for people with diabetes, referred to earlier (Kelleher 1990a, 1991), it was noticeable that, while non-compliant acts were often legitimated by being recognised as a shared way of managing illness, instances of non-members ignoring their treatment regimen or complying only haphazardly were likely to be criticised too. Stories were told of people who had required amputations or who had died as a result of wild or irregular practice of the treatment regimen. It is not that such talk always produces what an outsider would consider as the best kind of answer, but that the structure of moral-practical discourse makes it possible for life-world concerns to be subjected to the tests of truthfulness in ordinary speech (Habermas 1987) rather than dismissed by professional concerns and interests.

Conclusion

What has been argued here is that self-help groups are a challenge to modern medicine because medicine has lost much of its emancipatory drive and has come to see human suffering in a technical-instrumental way. Self-help groups are complementary to medicine in that they are a way of making good one of its shortcomings, the failure to address the expressive needs of people. But, as part of a new social movement, they are also important because they retain the possibility for seeing things differently, creating the opportunity for medicine to be challenged and interrogated. It is for this reason that the valuing of experiential knowledge is important. It is not that it is true, and biomedical scientific knowledge is false. Instead, self-help groups enable a range of concerns to be kept alive and put alongside medical controls, rather than being distorted by expert systems and QALYs (Quality Adjusted Life Years), the discourse of the market; a form of non-coercive talk becomes possible.

It has also been suggested that self-help groups play a political role in modern society in that they may provide a link between the concerns raised in families (the private sphere) to the protest or challenging aspects of culture and the public sphere or civic society. As Habermas has it,

> Civil society is composed of those more or less spontaneously emergent associations, organizations, and movements that, attuned to how societal problems resonate in the private life spheres, distil and transmit such reactions in amplified form to the public sphere.
>
> (Habermas 1987: 367)

He later wrote of the changes taking place in the 'consumerist redefinition of private spheres and personal lifestyles':

> The relations of clients to public service agencies is to be opened up and reorganized in a participatory mode, along the lines of self-help organizations. It is above all in the domains of social policy and health policy (e.g. in connection with psychiatric care) that models of reform point in this direction.
>
> (Habermas 1989: 395)

Attempts by government through such schemes as 'Expert Patient Programmes' and the co-opting of patient representatives on to doctor-dominated Primary Care Groups can be seen as no more than part of the colonisation of the life-world by the expert system of medicine however; as has been argued in this chapter they are part of a widespread and continuing process of degrading the public sphere and the denial of public debate (Scambler and Kelleher 2006). Self-help groups are part of a NSM challenge not only to the limitations of medicine, but to the power of the political world and economy and their place in society is growing.

References

Armstrong, D. (1984) 'The patient's view', *Social Science and Medicine*, 18: 737–44.

Arntson, P. and Droge, D. (1987) 'Social support in self-help groups', in Albrecht, T., Adelman, M. and associates (eds), *Communicating Social Support*, Beverly Hills: Sage.

Bauman, Z. (1992) *Intimations of Postmodernity*, London: Routledge.

Beck, U. (1992) *Risk Society*, London: Sage.

Bell, D. (1973) *The Coming of Post-Industrial Society*, New York: Basic Books.

Berger, J. (1967) *A Fortunate Man*, London: Allen Lane.

British Diabetic Association (1980) *In the Service of Diabetes*, London: British Diabetic Association.

Brown, P. and Zavestoski, S. (2004) 'Social movements in health: An introduction', *Sociology of Health and Illness*, 26, 6: 679–94.

Brown, P., Zavestoski, S., McCormick, S., Mayer, B., Morello-Frosch, R. and Altman, R.G. (2004) 'Embodied health movements: New approaches to social movements in health', *Sociology of Health and Illness*, 26, 1: 50–80.

Bury, M. (1988) 'Meanings at risk: The experience of arthritis', in Anderson, R. and Bury, M. (eds), *Living with Chronic Illness*, London: Unwin Hyman.

Cole, E. (1987) 'The Nottingham Experience: A self-help diabetes group', *Balance*, August/September: 60–1.

Collier, J. (1989) *The Health Conspiracy*, London: Century Hutchinson.

Conrad, P. (1985) 'The meaning of medications: Another look at compliance', *Social Science and Medicine*, 20: 19–37.

Donaldson, L. (2003) *British Medical Journal*, 326: 14 June.

Elston, M.A. (1991) 'The politics of professional power medicine in a changing health service', in Gabe, J., Calnan, M. and Bury, M. (eds), *The Sociology of the Health Service*, London: Routledge.

Ettore, E. (1986) 'Self-help groups as an alternative to benzodiazepine use', in Gabe, J. and Williams, P. (eds), *Tranquillisers: Social, Psychological and Clinical Perspectives*, London: Tavistock Publications.

Expert Patient Update (2000) Issue 7.

Foster, H. (1985) *Postmodern Culture*, London: Pluto Press.

Frank, A. (1989) 'Habermas' interactionism: The micro-macro link to politics', *Symbolic Interactionism*, 12, 2: 253–60.

Gabe, J. (1994) 'Promoting benzodiazepine withdrawal', *British Journal of Addiction*, 89: 1497–1504.

Gabriel, S. (1989) 'Black to black', *Community Care*, 12 October: 26.

Giddens, A. (1990) *The Consequences of Modernity*, Cambridge: Polity Press.

—— (1991) *Modernity and Self-Identity*, Cambridge: Polity Press.

Glassner, B. (1989) 'Fitness and the postmodern self', *Journal of Health and Social Behavior*, 30: 180–91.

Habermas, J. (1981) 'New social movements', *Telos*, 57: 194–205.

—— (1987) *The Theory of Communicative Action*, Cambridge: Polity Press.

—— (1989) *The Structural Transformation of the Public Sphere: An Inquiry into a Category of Bourgeois Society*, Massachusetts: MIT Press.

Katz, A. and Bender, E. (1976) *The Strength in Us*, New York: New Viewpoints.

Kelleher, D. (1990a) 'Do self-help groups help?', *International Disability Studies*, 12: 66–9.

—— (1990b) 'Consultants' views of self-help groups', unpublished.

—— (1991) 'Patients learning from each other: Self-help groups for people with diabetes', *Journal of the Royal Society of Medicine*, 84: 595–7.

Kickbusch, I. (1989) 'Self-care in health promotion', *Social Science and Medicine*, 29: 125–30.

Kickbusch, I. and Hatch, S. (eds) (1983) *Self-Help and Health in Europe*, Copenhagen: World Health Organization.

Lasch, C. (1980) *The Culture of Narcissism*, London: Sphere Books.

Lock, S. (1986) 'Self-help groups: The fourth estate in medicine', *British Medical Journal*, 292: 1596–9.

Nayar, K., Kyobutung, C. and Razum, O. (2004) 'Self-help: What future role in healthcare for low and middle income countries? *International Journal for Equity in Health*, 3: 1 doi.1186/1475-9276-3-1.

Rabeharisoa, V. (2003) 'The struggle against neuromuscular diseases in France and the emergence of the "partnership model" of patient organization', *Social Science and Medicine*, 57: 2127–36.

Rich, E. (2003) Exploring constructions of the body, (ill)health and identity in schools: The case of Anorexia Nervosa. Paper presented to 2nd Global Conference – Making sense of: Health, Illness and Disease. Oxford, U.K. 14th–17th July 2003.

Richardson, A. and Goodman, M. (1983) 'Self-help and social care: Mutual aid organisations in practice', *Policy Studies Institute*, Paper No. 612, London.

Robinson, D. (1980) 'The self-help component of primary care', *Social Science and Medicine*, 14a: 415–22.

Robinson, D. and Henry, S. (1977) *Self-Help and Health: Mutual Aid for Modern Problems*, London: Martin Robertson.

Scambler G. and Kelleher D. (2006) 'New social and health movements: Issues of representation and change. *Critical Public Health* (In press).

Sennett, R. (1977) *The Fall of Public Man*, New York: Knopf.

Stewart, M. (1990) 'Professional interface with mutual aid self-help groups: A review', *Social Science and Medicine*, 31: 1143–58.

Tattersall, M. and Hallstrom, C. (1992) 'Self-help and benzodiazepine withdrawal', *Journal of Affective Disorders*, 24: 193–8.

Trojan, A. (1989) 'Benefits of self-help groups: A survey of 232 members from 65 disease related groups', *Social Science and Medicine*, 29: 225–32.

Vincent, J. (1992) 'Self-help groups and health', in Saks, M. (ed.), *Alternative Medicine in Modern Britain*, Oxford: Clarendon Press.

Williams, G. (1989) 'Hope for the humblest? The role of self-help in chronic illness: The case of ankylosing spondylitis', *Sociology of Health and Illness*, 11: 135–59.

Wilson, J. (1992) 'Supporting self-help groups: An action research study of the work of Nottingham self-help groups project between 1982 and 1983', unpublished M.Phil. thesis, Loughborough University.

7   Lay knowledge and the privilege of experience

Gareth Williams and Jennie Popay

> One of the main intellectual activities of our century has been the questioning, not to say the undermining, of authority.[1]
>
> (Said 1993)

Introduction

The concept of lay knowledge is a recent development of the idea of lay beliefs. The study of people's beliefs about illness, health and medical care initially provided a way of understanding different forms of 'illness behaviour' and 'lay referral', particularly where 'non-compliant' behaviour suggested differences between the patient's perspectives and those of his or her physician. Research on these themes provided an empirical foundation for the argument that a patient's behaviour was influenced by his or her beliefs, and that these beliefs were a reasoned attempt to deal with the sometimes intensely contradictory demands of illness and its treatment in everyday life (Robinson 1973). However, beliefs are more than antecedents to individual behaviour, and a second line of thought was beginning to conceptualise lay beliefs about health and illness as social representations, with distinctive form and content (Herzlich 1973; Blaxter 1983; Williams 1986).

More recently, there has been an increasing move to thinking in terms of lay knowledge, rather than beliefs (Bury 1997). For the most part, however sophisticated and sociologically illuminating this lay knowledge may be, it remains disorganised and *ad hoc*, posing an implicit rather than a direct political challenge to the power of the medical profession. However much this knowledge is part of a shared culture and society, it is the expression of personal experience which remains outside the worlds of science and politics. Much of the sociological work on these issues has explored the nature of personal accounts and narratives, and the extent to which these lay perspectives embody important modes of understanding illness experiences (Pierret 2003). The substantive focus of this research has been principally upon the relationship between lay and expert knowledge in clinical and clinical-research settings, particularly in relation to the differing models, interpretations and understandings lay people and professional experts bring to the process of making sense of chronic illness (Lawton 2003), and this may in part reflect the dominant place of the hospital within modern medicine and the health services as a whole. However, there has been increasing emphasis through the last quarter of the twentieth century and into the twenty-first on avoidable ill-health (Department of Health 2004; Public Health Strategy Division 2005). This is partly because of political anxiety over the rising costs of treating people's illnesses, but it also frames a broader concern about the prevention of disease and the promotion of health, supported by a developing, impressive body of evidence on the wider personal, socio-economic and environmental determinants of health (Williams 2003). Reflecting this shift, there is a small but growing body of work exploring lay theories about the causes of health inequalities (Blaxter 1997; Popay *et al.* 2003). In so far as public health problems, by definition, transcend the problems of particular individuals, and inasmuch as public health policies can affect whole neighbourhoods, they provide an interesting and rather different case within which to consider the relationship between lay and expert knowledge.

In this chapter we argue that the intervention of lay knowledge (by invitation, insinuation or force) into the world of public and environmental health offers the possibility of a challenge to the dominance of the medical profession. However, like self-help, anti-vivisectionism (see Chapters 6 and 9) and other 'anti-modernist' developments, the relationship of this challenge to the world of expertise is an ambiguous one. The nature of the challenge discussed in this chapter is twofold. First, lay knowledge represents a challenge to the 'objectivity' of expert knowledge. It both contests the impartiality of that knowledge *vis-à-vis* other forms of knowledge, and it raises questions about the extent to which the process of objectification – upon which the truth-claims of scientific knowledge depend – permits a proper understanding of health problems in the 'new modernity' (Beck 1992a). In this sense it provides an *epistemological* challenge to expert knowledge. Second, lay knowledge represents a challenge to the authority of professionals to determine the way in which problems are defined in the policy arena. In this sense it is a *political* challenge to the institutional power of expert knowledge in general and medical knowledge in particular.

In the first part of this chapter we sketch out the broad contours of the epistemological challenge, reviewing some of the arguments about the nature of, and relationship between, lay knowledge and the knowledge of medical experts. In the subsequent section we present an example of the way in which the epistemological and political challenges are being played out. This draws on instances of what has come to be referred to as 'popular epidemiology' – situations in which lay people conceptualise and gather information on health problems and risks about which orthodox experts are perceived to be silent, excessively cautious or in some way unreliable. In these situations, we argue, lay knowledge moves beyond individual complaint to develop a public voice and provide the basis for collective action for change in policy.

In the conclusion we argue that while lay beliefs in the clinical arena provide an implicit challenge to medical knowledge by placing it in a different interpretive context, lay knowledge in the arena of public and environmental health tests medical knowledge by exposing it to debate in the public sphere (Habermas 1989; Popay and Williams 1996; Williams and Popay 2001). Both represent a struggle over meaning that is perhaps the latest manifestation of a questioning and undermining of authority. Traditional epidemiology and health services research are not well equipped to respond to this challenge. However, we maintain that a constructive response is necessary to the challenge posed by lay knowledge – defined broadly as: the ideas and perspectives employed by social actors to interpret their experiences of health and illness in everyday life (Williams 2004) – if experts, both lay and professional, are to develop effective ways of under-standing and changing those things that shape health in the modern world.

Different ways of knowing: Lay and medical knowledge

Herzlich (1973) argued that individual beliefs about health and illness are representations of the culture and society in which people live. While these representations may include medical ideas about pathology and aetiology, lay perspectives express a certain cultural autonomy and embody a wider theorisation of health and illness in relation to society. The work of Herzlich provided the intellectual foundation for two key arguments about lay beliefs. First, that lay ideas are not 'primitive' residuals stuck in the otherwise smoothly functioning bowels of modern 'scientific' societies, but complex bodies of knowledge or contextualised rationality that are central to our understanding of culture and society (Good 1994). Second, 'lay knowledge' has two key dimensions. On the one hand, it contains a robust empirical approach to the contingencies of everyday life required by people trying to make sense of health and illness in themselves, their families and the wider communities in which they live. On the other, it displays a search for meaning that goes beyond the straightforwardly empirical, situating personal experiences of health crisis in relation to broader frameworks of morality, politics and cosmology. It represents, in Max Weber's terms, understanding in terms of both cause and meaning.

An illustration of the complexity of lay knowledge can be found in Comaroff and Maguire's (1981) insightful study of 'the search for meaning' in childhood leukaemia. Modern medicine, they argued, supplies an empirical basis for explaining to parents what is happening to their children, but it provides no overarching framework through which parents can 'make sense' of what is happening. The parents in their study were asking not only what causes childhood leukaemia, but why has my child developed this disease, and why now? Perhaps it is not the business of good doctoring to answer these questions, but it does point to the tension between 'evidence-based' and 'narrative-based' approaches to health knowledge. Lay people need the evidence, but the evidence itself will not be enough to support the wider framework of interpretation needed to make sense of their child's illness.

Sociologists have focused for the most part on the experiences of individuals *qua* individuals, and on clinical interactions in institutional settings (Brown 1992). This research has uncovered the informal knowledge about health and illness held by lay people and analysed the role it plays in their dealings with experts. There have also been occasional attempts to develop a more *gemeinschaftlich* sense of a locality's own understanding of health and illness (Cornwell 1984). In contrast to the clinical focus on disease, this work has emphasised the importance of understanding the meaning of illness and health for the individual by focusing on the *consequences* of illness for ordinary, everyday life, the *significance* of symptoms and experiences for the person who has them (Bury 1991), and the linkages between biography and knowledge (Williams 1984, 2000).

This perspective on lay knowledge has certain methodological implications. Lay knowledge could not be examined in the way it has been without using certain kinds of research methods. Understanding the nature of lay knowledge requires an approach to data collection that is egalitarian and phenomenologically open. Methods like unstructured interviews have been used, therefore, which allow a story to emerge. Treating the stories or narratives that act as the vehicle for lay knowledge as forms of understanding with which social scientists and other formal experts have to engage, rather than as sub-standard forms of data, is a necessary pre-requisite for the effective analysis of lay knowledge (Popay *et al.* 1998; Williams 2004). Not only does lay knowledge pose problems for medicine because it represents a different form of knowledge, it also challenges the methods with which medical science is most comfortable, because it remains inaccessible to them.

In lying outside the conventions of positivism, lay knowledge challenges the search for abstract facts understood as things that exist independently of our interpretation of them. Lay knowledge, in being open to variation, difference and local significance, has always been post-modern. The vogue of postmodernism, with its emphasis on 'the contextuality of truth-claims' (Giddens 1990), provides a neat legitimation for lay resistance to expert systems of knowledge, and a useful theoretical justification for the empirical work by sociologists and others in this area. Lay knowledge about health and illness thus provides an epistemological challenge to medicine. It offers a view of illness that is subjective and often highly coherent. Once the narrative structure is recognised, the beliefs it carries cannot be easily dismissed as irrational, and non-compliance may be better understood as a subversion of medical dominance and a critique of objectification. However, in so far as such knowledge about illness remains private, expressed only in the clinic, the home or in casual encounters with others, it offers no direct political challenge to the power of medicine.

The defiant nature of lay knowledge becomes more explicit in relation to problems of public and environmental health. In these situations we can see the way in which the role of lay knowledge in public debate about issues relating to expert knowledge is politically unsettling for those who hold power in society, and for those who are accustomed to being able to have their truth claims vindicated by reference to a body of technical knowledge.

Popular epidemiology and public health

Although ecological critiques of the effects of industrialism and capitalism on the environment and health are not new (Williams 1989), environmental problems are increasingly prominent in contemporary debate, both globally and locally (Lancet 1991, 1992). In addition to the concerns about large-scale ecological degradation relating to ozone depletion and global warming, waste disposal (Walker 1991), the safety of drinking water (Walker 1992), air pollution (Godlee 1991) and the state of bathing beaches (Philipp *et al.* 1993) are sources of anxiety at the present time. From lay perspectives, however, 'environmental problems' are not only those high-profile spill-ages and emissions which hit the newspaper headlines. For people living in urban areas, busy roads, litter, dogs, vandalism, noise, derelict properties and poor street-lighting constitute the hazardous reality of everyday life (Percy-Smith and Sanderson 1992), and these are often prominent in people's ideas about the determinants of health (Popay *et al.* 2003).

What is the place of lay knowledge in all this? Much risk factor epidemi-ology also assumes a freedom to make healthy choices that is out of line with what many lay people experience as real possibilities in their everyday lives. For example, in a study of a deprived inner-city area in the north-west of England (Williams *et al.* 1995), we see how lay people are only too well aware of the 'political' context of explanations for ill-health in the community. In this instance, and in stark contrast with much risk factor epidemiology, the lay accounts reported illustrate the need to contextualise risks – smoking, diet, alcohol, lack of exercise – by reference to the wider material and environmental conditions in which the risks are embedded. The respondents understood the behavioural risk factors that made ill-health more likely and for which they were, in a limited sense, responsible, but they were also aware that the risks they faced were part of social conditions that they could do little to change. For these working class Salfordians, as for Herzlich's middle-class Parisians, the 'way of life' – in this case unemployment, poor housing, low income, stressful and sometimes violent lives – provided a context for 'making sense' of smoking, drinking and drug-taking and all the other 'behaviours' that risk factor epidemiologists calculate and correlate (Popay *et al.* 2003).

This more political expression of lay knowledge finds its most challenging form in the 'popular epidemiology' examined by Phil Brown (1995) and others. Studies of popular epidemiology take situations in which members of local communities have become concerned about a public health problem in their locality – the numbers of children with cancer, the high prevalence of asthma or an increase in road traffic accidents – and seek some environmental explanation for it. In these circumstances, popular epidemiology begins with lay people linking the observed increase in the health problem to some kind of social or environmental hazard – road safety, factory emissions, toxic waste, nuclear power and so on. Having made the connection, the community then tries to take action to do something about it, and finds itself in conflict with local politicians, business corporations and professional experts who disagree, for one reason or another, with the view being expressed by the community. In these situations, local people are forced to move beyond the statement of a point of view to a process in which a social movement develops, evidence is systematically collected and analysed, and scientific arguments are developed and sometimes tested in the courts. In popular epidemiology we see the blurring of the boundaries between 'lay people' and 'experts' and the nature of the complex relationships between scientific rationality, personal beliefs and political interests.

Popular epidemiology in Massachusetts

A focus on these sorts of issues has been a key feature of much of the 'citizen action for environmental health' in the USA (Freudenberg 1984), and many examples of 'popular epidemiology' (Brown 1987) arise from community responses to problems such as toxic waste (Masterson-Allen and Brown 1990). Popular epidemiology is a synthesis of political activism and lay knowledge, and a form of public participation in the pursuit of knowledge and political change. As Brown, a prominent American writer in this field, notes, it is:

> the process whereby laypersons gather scientific data and other information, and also direct and marshall the resources of experts in order to understand the epidemiology of disease.
>
> (Brown 1992: 269)

In the USA, where it has been most prominent, popular epidemiology is an extension of the community-based protest and activism which is characteristic of political culture in the USA; a culture which has often exhibited a robust disdain for the claims of experts of any kind (Walzer 1983), including politicians and experts on public health and environmental issues (Harris 1984). The empirical work from which Brown's own ideas emerged was much more than a battle between lay people and medical or scientific experts.

In the mid-1970s, the residents of Woburn, a working-class and lower-middle-class town in Massachusetts, about twelve miles north of Boston, began to worry that their children were contracting leukaemia with considerable frequency – four times higher than would normally be expected. For decades, moreover, residents had complained about the smell and taste of their drinking water. The first detection efforts were begun by one woman, Ann Anderson, whose son, Jimmy, had been diagnosed with acute lymphocytic leukaemia in 1972:

> Anderson put together information during 1973–1974 about other cases by meetings with other Woburn victims in town and at the hospital where Jimmy spent much time. Anderson hypothesised that the alarming leukaemia incidence was caused by a water-borne agent. In 1975 she asked state officials to test the water but was told that testing could not be done at an individual's initiative.
>
> (Brown 1992: 270)

The water was eventually tested but what is interesting from the point of view of our analysis here is that the community response included a refusal to accept the conclusions of the 'independent' experts sent in by the Centers for Disease Control in collaboration with the Massachusetts Department of Public Health. The official report concluded that the cases of childhood leukaemia were more than twice as high as expected. However, because the case-control method failed to find characteristics that differentiated victims from non-victims, and because there were no environmental water exposure data going back before 1979, the report argued that it was not possible to conclude that the increased incidence was related to the water supply.

The long story which was eventually told illuminated the parts played by business, government, environmental watch-dogs and governmentally employed scientists – none of whom come out of it very clean. Brown's study went on to show how the local community, in the form of a pressure group, 'For a Cleaner Environment', enlisted the help of its own experts from the Harvard School of Public Health. By jointly collecting and analysing more data, they managed to get their case heard in the courts and challenge the results of the official researchers. Brown's study, therefore, reveals the conflict between legal and medical experts over the nature of evidence and the understanding of 'cause' and 'effect' (Brown and Mikkelsen 1990), as well as the crucial role of the media in publicising people's stories and providing a place where alternative accounts of information and events can be published.

In view of the public context within which it works, popular epidemiology is very rarely a simple bilateral struggle between lay and expert scientific knowledge. There may well be a number of different lay perspectives on the situation in a given case, and also a number of different expert viewpoints. For example, there may be differences of opinion between those working in a factory and those living near it (Brown and Mikkelsen 1990; Phillimore and Moffatt 1994), and there may be disagreements between the experts called in to assess the situation. In any given case there will be a multitude of voices and a plurality of perspectives (Williams and Popay 1993). Moreover, in addition to the conflict between diverse groups with different interests, where there is a direct governmental interest in the nature of the knowledge that emerges about a situation, the State may become more directly involved.

Something that might be described as an example of popular epidemiology has appeared more recently in Britain (Phillimore and Moffatt 1994; Rice *et al.* 1994). In order to illustrate in more detail the epistemological and political challenges posed by these situations to medical and other expertise, we want to examine the events that surrounded a water contamination incident in England in 1988, and the response of the local community to it.

The case of the Camelford Poisoning

On 6 July 1988, a lorry driver accidentally tipped 20 tonnes of aluminium sulphate solution into the treated water reservoir of the Lowermoor Water

Treatment Works supplying the residents of Camelford and the surrounding area in north Cornwall. In addition to the close historical relationship between public health and the water supply (Johnson 1986), this incident was especially noticeable in view of its having taken place very soon after the Thatcher Government's privatisation of the water authorities of England and Wales. The Camelford episode was the subject of two government-backed reports by an expert group within the space of three years, the second under a Department of Health imprint, chaired by Dame Barbara Clayton, a well-respected chemical pathologist (CISDHA 1989; Department of Health 1991). This group, the Lowermoor Incident Health Advisory Group (the Clayton Committee), was set up in January 1989 at the instigation of the then Parliamentary Under Secretary of State for Health to provide 'independent expert advice' (CISDHA 1989: 1) to the Cornwall and Isles of Scilly District Health Authority.

The appointment of this expert group was the Governmental response to considerable pressure from residents and people who had been on holiday at the time, and who attributed a variety of symptoms to water contamination, remaining unconvinced by locally generated expert advice. In addition to Barbara Clayton herself, the Committee consisted of a number of different experts: a neurochemical pathologist, the Chief Scientist of the Water Research Centre and a Professor of Epidemiology and Population Sciences. The pressure from the locality came from residents who organised themselves very quickly to express their concerns. They formed both a general support group, the Lowermoor Support Group and what was called the Camelford Scientific Advisory Panel (CSAP), a local group which included individuals who themselves had considerable expertise in particular areas relevant to the incident. They monitored the incident and its effects from the outset.

In the wake of the first Clayton Report, published exactly a year after the incident, there was little disagreement between Clayton and the local residents over the immediate health effects. According to Clayton, these included: 'nausea, vomiting, diarrhoea, headaches, fatigue, itching skin, rashes, sore eyes, and mouth ulcers'. The report goes on to register that some people felt 'generally unwell', while others complained of 'aches and pains'. CSAP produced its own questionnaire which was completed by 432 respondents between mid-July and mid-August 1988. The most commonly reported complaints were similar to those which the official group had identified.

In its first report, therefore, the Clayton Committee noted that 'many of the early symptoms reported to CSAP and at our meeting in Camelford can be attributed to the incident' (CISDHA 1989: 3). However, it pointed out that 'general practitioners' consulting patterns did not show any overall increase in the number of patients seen by doctors in the month following the incident' (CISDHA 1989: 3). The Committee also argued that detailed analysis of the CSAP information was not appropriate because 'it cannot be assumed that those who responded are representative of the local population; the questionnaires were left at strategic points for collection and returned by anyone who wished to participate, so introducing an element of self selection' (CISDHA 1989: 3).

These methodological caveats appear to have provided the basis for the dispute that followed between the Clayton Committee and the local community. The disagreement centred on the validity of claims and counterclaims about the 'delayed or persistent effects' of the incident. The first report (1989) notes that the Health Authority had compiled a register of people complaining about symptoms occurring or persisting long after the incident. At the time the report was written in July 1989 there were 280 people on the register. These chronic symptoms fell into four broad categories:

1   Joint pains, exacerbation of arthritis and non-specific aches and pains
2   Memory loss, poor concentration, speech problems, depression and behavioural disorders in children
3   Rashes and mouth ulcers
4   Gastrointestinal disorder.

The Clayton Committee examined existing research evidence regarding the detrimental health effects of a variety of contaminants in the Lowermoor water using European Community standards. For lead, zinc, copper and sulphate, they concluded that the amounts likely to have been absorbed, even on worst-case assumptions ('drinking up to two litres of the most heavily contaminated water per day' (CISDHA 1989:4)), would have no long-lasting effects on the health of the population. In relation to aluminium, the major pollutant, and in view of the complaints of memory loss and the recent attention given to the possibility of a link between aluminium and Alzheimer's disease, the report presents its summary of the evidence regarding the dietary sources, metabolism and toxicology of aluminium. On the basis of this it concluded that any ill-health caused by the aluminium was temporary:

> All the known toxic effects of aluminium are associated with chronically elevated exposure and we have concluded therefore that delayed or persistent effects following such brief exposures are unlikely.
>
> (CISDHA 1989: 14)

Although the Clayton Committee claimed to refute the link between the contamination and long-term health effects, as the quote illustrates, it clearly felt obliged to offer some explanation for the health problems being reported by local residents:

> In our view it is not possible to attribute the very real current health complaints to the toxic effects of the incident, except inasmuch as they are the consequence of the sustained anxiety naturally felt by many people.
>
> (CISDHA 1989: 14)

In its criticism of the evidence produced by local residents and the local District Health Authority in support of their claims about long-term effects, the Clayton Committee commented on 'the difficulties in both carrying out and interpreting environmental epidemiological studies of acute incidents' (CISDHA 1989: 11). The Committee also targeted the local and national media for particular criticism for their role in relation to the incident:

> Some of the reporting of the incident has been inaccurate and without scientific foundation....Some statements have...in our opinion caused unnecessary anxiety and suffering.
>
> (CISDHA 1989: 12)

The press and other media played a major role in publicising the Camelford incident, and in discussing points of view opposed to the conclusions and recommendations of the Advisory Group. After the publication of the first report, local people continued to complain of symptoms of malaise, and, in particular, problems with memory and other aspects of cognitive functioning. In view of the continuing commotion, a special conference was convened by the Cornwall and Isles of Scilly Health Authority in February 1990, which gave rise to a special report (CISDHA 1990). Three papers presented at the conference fuelled the debate: a clinical biochemist found high concentrations of aluminium in blood samples one year after the incident; a neuropsychologist reported evidence 'consistent with the effects of minor brain injury'; and a clinical psychologist discovered significant memory defects. The fact that the conference report did not get published until the findings were leaked to the press, almost six months after the conference met, led some local people and journalists to feel that something was being hidden.

Throughout the period since July 1988 to now, organised opposition to the official view has been articulated by local people through the Lowermoor

Support Group and the CSAP. The latter, according to one report, is 'an *ad hoc* group of people living in the area who have academic or campaigning skills. It includes Liz Sigmund, a veteran of the campaign against chemical weapons, Dr Newman (a local GP who has himself experienced problems with memory), and Doug Cross, an environmental consultant' (Kennedy 1990).

The Department of Health reacted strongly to the accusations by local residents and the media which had given them a platform. The then Conservative Government's Health Minister, Stephen Dorrell, in a letter to the *Guardian*, criticised the newspaper for:

> grossly misrepresent[ing] the properly cautious conclusions of the [Clayton] report, based as it was on a detailed and thorough assessment of the scientific data available. No more and no less would be expected from a group of truly independent and distinguished scientists, who are acknowledged experts in the relevant fields.
>
> (Dorrell 1990)

In a parliamentary reply in July, according to a report by the *Guardian's* columnist Melanie Phillips, Stephen Dorrell characterised the local critics of the Clayton Report as 'malicious people, down there stirring things up, and worrying people for their own short-term gains' (Phillips 1990).

In addition to underlining the highly political nature of anything to do with water at the very time that the national water companies were in the process of being privatised, there is an irony in the fact that, also at the same time, the then Secretary of State for the Department of the Environment (Chris Patten, MP) was publishing a White Paper urging precisely such active citizenship in relation to our 'common inheritance' (Department of the Environment 1990).

Continuing pressure from local people, both through individual legal action and collective protest, forced the Government to decide that the Clayton Committee should be reconvened. Its terms of reference were:

> To assess reports which have become available since July 1989 of persistent symptoms and clinicopathological findings amongst people who were resident in the Camelford area at the time of the Lowermoor incident; and to advise the Department of Health and the Cornwall and Isles of Scilly District Health Authority on the implications of these findings.
>
> (Department of Health 1991: 1)

The fact that the Committee was to have the same membership, with the addition of a clinical psychologist to interpret psychometric data, was greeted with dismay by local residents and their supporters. Liz Sigmund of CSAP was quoted in the newspapers as saying: 'One whitewash will be followed by another, unless they are all prepared to admit they were wrong, which seems highly unlikely' (16 October 1990). Another leading member of the local residents wrote mockingly: 'What wonderful news for those of us labelled by the [Clayton] committee as victims of mass hysteria and what an extraordinary opportunity for the committee to examine the effects of this mass hysteria' (Burgess 1990). The fact that the second Clayton Report includes a six-page appendix listing 'people who have provided medical, scientific and technical advice' (Department of Health 1991: 40) suggests that the Committee may have anticipated the reaction. For whatever reasons, this list does not seem to include anyone, other than local general practitioners, who could have been said to have been selected to represent the views of local people. In an editorial devoted to the issue, the *Guardian* itself commented:

> There are two purposes in setting up Committees of Inquiry: to seek out the truth and to reassure the public. Clayton is perceived in Cornwall to have failed with the first; and demonstrably been unsuccessful in the second. Reconstituting the committee now to reassess the evidence will put members under intense pressure to look for facts which will justify their original conclusions, rather than objectively reviewing the new evidence to see if they were wrong.
>
> (The *Guardian* 1990)

As it turned out the second report of the Lowermoor Incident Health Advisory Group (Department of Health 1991) reiterated the conclusions of the first report: 'The research reported to us does not provide convincing evidence that harmful accumulation of aluminium has occurred, nor that there is greater prevalence of ill-health due to toxic effects of the water in the exposed population' (Department of Health 1991: 1). Although denying that the first report had intended to imply that symptoms in the population had been caused by 'hysteria', the second report nevertheless maintained that 'The physical problems associated with all the worry and concern and the psychological harm could last a long time for some people. Such a situation is well recognised following major accidents' (Department of Health 1991: 2). In response to the continuing protests, the Chief Medical Officer insisted that Clayton and her colleagues 'have again carried out a difficult task with sensitivity and integrity' (Calman 1991).

The implications of Camelford

It would be possible to regard what happened after the spillage at Camelford as idiosyncratic. Although there were a number of unusual aspects to the community response at Camelford – as there would be in any case study – they clearly fit the description of the movement against toxic waste which:

> can be seen as part of a larger social trend toward increased public demand for a role in scientific and technological decision-making which challenges scientific criteria for assessing risk and experts' claims to technical knowledge.
>
> (Masterson-Allen and Brown 1990)

The disagreements to which the Camelford incident and the various inquiries gave rise were partly to do with the nature of different kinds and sources of evidence: the carefully collated evidence of local people's own experiences, on the one hand, and the highly technical toxicological and clinical measurements of the Committee and its expert witnesses on the other. The hope of the official bodies involved was that the disagreements would be resolved once the evidence had been appraised by the experts in a sober and dispassionate manner. This did not happen and what we have described in Camelford is a profound disjuncture between the local people's and the experts' perspectives on the evidence and the way it was handled. This could be seen as a difference between 'subjectivity' and 'objectivity', or between opinion and science, and this is what the Clayton Committee seems to imply in both the first and the second report. The Committee's use of the community diagnosis of 'sustained anxiety' (CISDHA 1989: 14) to explain the local community's beliefs was a way of indicating its unreliability and, therefore, its distance from the standards of scientific discourse.

What happened at Camelford was not just a matter of the local community insisting that its own evidence was as reliable as that of the scientists, although this was primarily the level at which the debate was conducted. Local people were issuing a political challenge to biomedical knowledge in so far as they were refusing to permit the authority of scientists to be used to disempower them. And they were issuing an epistemological challenge in two ways: first by refusing to accept that the Clayton Committee's knowledge was impartial simply by virtue of having been produced by scientists, and second, by insisting that local knowledge based on shared biographical experiences cannot be invalidated by reference to some standard of objectivity derived from abstract scientific knowledge.

As was the case in Brown's study of Woburn, the role of the media was important in these challenges. From the point of view of the Clayton Committee, the role of the media was unhelpful, serving to amplify the anxieties that were already being experienced by the local community, and therefore preventing the imposition of a rational judgement (Renn *et al.* 1992). From the perspective of the local residents, however, the media could be seen as playing a role similar to that of the coffee-house in previous centuries (Sennett 1993): providing a setting within civil society in which personal troubles can be debated and taken forward into political action over public issues.

Camelford re-visited

What happened at Camelford in 1988 has continued to produce analysis, comment and disagreement in both scientific and popular media. On the tenth anniversary of 'Britain's worst mass water poisoning' (BBC Online Network 1998), those affected by what happened at Camelford made a fresh bid for a public enquiry. In 1994, 148 victims had accepted damages totalling almost £400,000 in a settlement approved by a High Court judge, but a decade on from the incident many people were still complaining of chronic symptoms such as memory loss, joint pains and general lethargy, which they attributed to the incident. To mark the anniversary of the incident, residents and supporters went to lobby the then new Prime Minister, Tony Blair, at Downing Street, reminding him of his party's demand for a public inquiry while in opposition, and tied black ribbons around the gates of the Lowermoor Water Treatment Works where the aluminium sulphate had found its way into the wrong tank. One of the original leaders of the protest, Doreen Skudder, was quoted as saying: 'We have never ever had the whole thing properly investigated, so we still need a public enquiry' (BBC Online Network 1998).

At this time the Government was said to be considering the evidence, such as it was, so long after an incident that had never been properly documented and investigated at the time it happened. The evidence included an examination by the health authority of data on deaths of former Camelford residents between 1991 and 1997. A review of hospital discharge rates in the period between the incident and its fifth anniversary had earlier found a raised standardised discharge ratio for Camelford compared with Cornwall as a whole, and had concluded that: 'The pollution of the water to the people of Camelford has raised hospital discharges' (Owen and Miles 1995: 200).

Nonetheless, in spite of this evidence of continuing effects five years after the incident, the then Environment Minister, Michael Meacher MP, visited Camelford in June 2000, a few weeks after the death from cancer of Doreen Skudder, at the age of 71, and announced that the Labour Government was rejecting calls for a public inquiry. Reports quoted him as saying that: 'The full implications of this episode for the water industry, for the environment, in respect of health policy and the legal system, have all been systematically taken on board' (BBC Online Network 2000). The local reaction to Michael Meacher's visit was critical, to say the least, suggesting that it was no more than a public relations exercise.

A little more than a year later Michael Meacher announced a new investigation into the incident, which would be 'transparent, independent and inclusive' (BBC Online Network 2001). The Minister held back from a full public enquiry on the grounds that there was no argument about what actually happened at Lowermoor in 1988, and since the incident there had been a major change in the organisation and regulation of relevant bodies, including the water industry. Members of the local action group, not surprisingly, felt less than fully reassured by this expert inquiry. Nonetheless, this partial shift in the Government's position over the course of a year appears to have been driven by a combination of continuing pressure from the local residents, many of whom were in tears when Michael Meacher made his visit (BBC Online Network 2001), and new research evidence. In a study of 55 affected people and 15 siblings nearest in age to one of the group who had not been exposed to contaminated water, it was concluded that: 'People who were exposed to the contaminated water at Camelford suffered considerable damage to cerebral function, which was not related to anxiety' (Altmann *et al.* 1999: 807). These findings seemed to confirm the warning of the second Clayton Report (Department of Health 1991) that there might be unforeseen late consequences.

In the period leading up to the report of this expert inquiry a number of other pieces of evidence were made available to the public domain. For example, following up their earlier work on hospital discharge rates, the Cornwall and Isles of Scilly Health Authority published in the *British Medical Journal* a retrospective study of mortality, comparing the death rates in the water pollution area with those in an adjacent unaffected area, as well as with county death rates and those for England and Wales as a whole, correcting for differences in age distribution and sex. This study found no statistically significant difference in deaths between the exposed and the non-exposed cohort (Owen *et al.* 2002), and gave rise to considerable criticism, including criticism from those who were involved in the Committee on Toxicity, the expert group investigating the long-term consequences of the Camelford incident on behalf of the Government (Cross 2002).

The most recent chapter in this story is the report of the expert group or, to be more precise, the Lowermoor Sub-Group (LSG) of the Committee on Toxicity (COT) of Chemicals in Food, Consumer Products and the Environment. The somewhat paradoxical overall conclusion of the report is that while no conclusive link was found between the incident in 1988 and the chronic symptoms years later, further work was recommended on the effects of the contaminants on neurological health, the effects on the development of children who were aged less than one year at the time of the incident, and the incidence of diseased joints among people living in the affected area.

The commentary on this report published in the *British Medical Journal* (Khanna 2005) produced a number of highly critical rapid responses, one with 58 signatories, many of them experts in aluminium toxicity from across the world; and another from two people who were actually Local Representatives on the sub-group of COT. The former made a number of general criticism of the COT report, arguing that '...the conclusions drawn by the subgroup concerning aluminium have been drawn from an entirely inadequate data base both with respect to the literature that has been reviewed and cited in the report and the water quality analyses provided by the SWWA (South West Water Authority)' (Exley *et al.* 2005: 275). They also allude to wider concerns regarding the production of knowledge in this process, arguing that the proposed period of consultation (approximately ten weeks), '...will be sufficient neither to remedy the deficiencies of this report nor to do justice to the concerns of the people affected by this incident' (Exley *et al.* 2005: 275). The Local Representatives went even further, referring to 'political obstruction to impartial investigation', terms of reference which prevented the sub-group looking at all available sources of data', and insisting that 'political pressure on the LSG's work must cease' (Cross and Smith 2005: 275). As we write, the consultation period on the report has not yet come to an end.

There seem to be three general conclusions about the nature of lay knowledge in public health to be drawn from this continuing saga. First, that 'bump of irreverence', which Aneurin Bevan, the founder of the NHS, argued that ordinary people need to hold and sustain when confronted by the insistent voices of professional experts, was clearly evident in Camelford, and very much part of their early resistance to pressure. However, and second, it is increasingly clear that the distinction between 'lay knowledge' and 'expert knowledge' forms too blunt a dichotomy. What started out in Camelford as shouts of concern and irreverent anger have been transformed into skilled modes of expert engagement with the worlds of science and politics. Expertise has many forms and it connects with experience at different levels (Collins and Evans 2002). Some of those involved in local action in Camelford themselves had various forms of certified expertise; but more importantly, while lay people were not in a position to transform themselves into toxicologists, they were increasingly able to bring to the discussion about Camelford a synthetic body of knowledge based on what they had experienced first hand, and what they learned in the process of engagement with scientists, bureaucrats and politicians. Finally, this leads us to conclude that the original source of lay knowledge in people's care, concern and, as we have heard, tears for themselves and their neighbours is not an impediment to rational and evidence-based discourse. It is in fact the basis for a much more complete and reasoned model of knowledge production – one that recognises the uncertain and indeterminate basis of expert evidence; the multiple perspectives on that evidence which require both more evidence and interactional forms of thought about it; and the complex interplay of evidence, experience and politics that shape the realities of something like the Camelford incident.

Conclusion

In relation to public and environmental health, challenges to experts are often dismissed by the experts themselves in a similar fashion: as capricious, unpredictable and irrational; an irritating reflection of general scientific illiteracy (Cvetkovich and Earle 1992). Popular epidemiology, both in more modern forms (Brown and Zavestoski 2004), and in the form in which the community health movement has always used it to fight against poor housing conditions and other unhealthy aspects of local environments, is also, in essence, a struggle over meaning. It is a struggle over the meaning of health, of the good life, of acceptable risk and of hazard. It is a struggle not just over the landscape but over the 'lifescape' (Eyles *et al.* 1993). However, in defining as public dangers what might otherwise be perceived as private risks (Scott *et al.* 1992), popular epidemiology poses a direct threat to those who have conventionally been invested with the authority to pronounce on the meaning and significance of public and environmental health problems. This kind of mobilisation of lay knowledge expresses a critique of the manner in which health risks are conceptualised and measured, a profound mistrust of the experts given responsibility for doing the defining (Hayes 1992), and a rejection of existing public health policies (Vaughan and Seifert 1992).

Part of what is needed to overcome these problems is greater pluralism involving more openness to lay or popular participation – a commitment to grasping lay perspectives (Kelly 1990). Such participation would need to go beyond lay discussion of the results of research to include an active role in the conceptualisation and specification of the nature of the problem, and the design and conduct of the research. This process would involve widening the portfolio of methods considered legitimate within research, and acknowledging the important input lay knowledge can make to the design of conventional research measures. The dogmatic division of knowledge into 'science' and 'non-science' will make this difficult, but as Brown argues in relation to his study of the citizens of Woburn: 'Popular epidemiology is not antiscientific. Rather, it has a different concept of what science is, whom it should serve, and who should control it' (Brown 1987: 83).

Once the struggle over meaning becomes public in this way, the question arises as to how science can be both technical and democratic at the same time (Fiorino 1989). As one enlightened epidemiologist has argued: 'Epidemiology is a human science, inevitably entangled with society...unthinking neutrality is a stance that can have even greater political implications than open commitment' (Susser 1989: 487). Once this is recognised, the epidemiologist and any other expert needs to do something other than dismiss the statements of critics as 'unscientific' or 'politically motivated'.

Epidemiology cannot resolve the public health problems of everyday life by retiring into the epistemology of medicine. The changing relationship between experts and the public means that the experts can no longer refuse to listen to people on the grounds that they are engaged in the pursuit of truth (Harris 1984). The loss of trust in expert systems (Giddens 1990) and the collapse of the 'grand narratives' within which the legitimacy of 'science' resides (Lyotard 1984) have made such deference to the authority of experts less automatic. In our own time, it is no longer possible to say that science is something separate from politics and that knowledge has nothing to do with power.

While it might be helpful to remind those with an excessively romantic attachment to popular wisdom that '...experience on its own is rarely sufficient to understand the technical complexities of disease causation' (Prior 2003: 53), one of the consequences of the 'scientisation of politics' is that issues to do with the environment and public health have tended to be reduced to the minute analysis of technical complexities. In a society in which technological risks have become endemic, discussions of public and environmental health cannot be confined to expert seminars. They need to be located within an 'ecological extension of democracy', which means:

> playing off the concert of voices and powers, the development of the independence of politics, law, the public sphere and daily life against the dangerous and false security of a 'society from the drawing board'. The public sphere, in co-operation with a kind of 'public science'

would be charged as a second centre of the 'discursive checking' of scientific laboratory results in the crossfire of opinions.

(Beck 1992b: 119)

It is important to understand that such a development would inevitably involve more than just getting the public involved in 'science'. It would mean thinking about science quite differently. Lay knowledge is a proclamation of 'the privilege of experience' (Adorno 1973: 40). Once biomedical and other scientific knowledge becomes caught in the crossfire of opinions, it inevitably involves dealing with questions like: 'How do we wish to live?' or 'Why do we feel ill all the time?' It means taking account of these questions and being prepared to discuss them in the formulation of environmental and health policies. The lay challenge to medical knowledge is not a complaint about the aesthetics of discourse, it is a political challenge to the status of scientific knowledge and the power of those whom we are encouraged to trust with such knowledge. What we have described in this chapter, therefore, in terms of a challenge to medicine is also an important characteristic of the unfolding debate on the nature of the modern world.

Notes

1 In an obituary marking Said's death on 25 September 2003, the *Guardian* writer referred to the centrality of his 'anti-authoritarian outlook'.

References

Adorno, T.W. (1973) *Negative Dialectics*, London: Routledge.
Altmann, P., Cunningham, J., Dhanesha, U., Ballard, M., Thompson, J. and Marsh, F. (1999) 'Disturbance of cerebral function in people exposed to drinking water contaminated with aluminium sulphate: Retrospective study of the Camelford water incident', *British Medical Journal*, 319: 807–11.
BBC Online Network (1998) 'Public inquiry calls mark Camelford anniversary', 6 July.
—— (2000) 'Water poisoning inquiry plea rejected', 12 June.
—— (2001) 'Health probe into Camelford poisoning', 14 August.
Beck, U. (1992a) *Risk Society: Towards a New Modernity*, London: Sage.
—— (1992b) 'From industrial society to risk society: Questions of survival, social structure and ecological enlightenment', *Theory, Culture, and Society*, 9: 97–123.
Blaxter, M. (1983) 'The causes of disease: Women talking', *Social Science and Medicine*, 17: 59–69.
Blaxter, M. (1997) 'Whose fault is it? People's own conceptions of the reasons for health inequalities', *Social Science and Medicine*, 44: 747–56.
Brown, P. (1987) 'Popular epidemiology: Community response to toxic-waste induced disease in Woburn, Massachusetts', *Science, Technology, and Human Values*, 12: 78–85.

—— (1992) 'Popular epidemiology and toxic waste contamination', *Journal of Health and Social Behaviour*, 33: 267–81.

Brown, P. (1995) Popular epidemiologist, toxic waste, and social movements', in Gabe, J. (ed.), *Medicine, Risk and Health*, Oxford: Blackwell.

Brown, P. and Mikkelsen, E.J. (1990) *No Safe Place: Toxic Waste, Leukemia, and Community Action*, Berkeley: University of California Press.

Brown, P. and Zavestoski, S. (eds) (2004) *Social Movements in Health (special issue of Sociology of Health and Illness)*, 26: 208, pp. 208.

Burgess, M. (1990) 'Cautious welcome for reconvened inquiry into water poisoning', letter, *Guardian*, 17 October.

Bury, M. (1991) 'The sociology of chronic illness: A review of research and prospects', *Sociology of Health and Illness*, 13: 451–68.

—— (1997) *Health and Illness in a Changing Society*, London: Routledge.

Calman, K. (1991) 'Camelford Report's clear lines of inquiry', letter, *Guardian*, 12 November.

Collins, H. and Evans, R. (2002) 'The third wave of science studies: Studies of expertise and experience', *Social Studies of Science*, 32: 235–96.

Comaroff, J. and Maguire, P. (1981) 'Ambiguity and the search for meaning: Childhood leukaemia in the modern clinical context', *Social Science and Medicine*, 15B: 115–23.

Cornwall and Isles of Scilly District Health Authority (CISDHA) (1989) *Water Pollution at Lowermoor North Cornwall: Report of the Lowermoor Incident Health Advisory Group* (chairperson: Professor Dame Barbara Clayton), Truro: Cornwall and Isles of Scilly District Health Authority.

—— (1990) *Lowermoor Water Incident* (conference proceedings), Truro: Cornwall and Isles of Scilly District Health Authority.

Cornwell, J. (1984) *Hard-Earned Lives: Accounts of Health and Illness from East London*, London: Tavistock.

Cross, D. (2002) 'Mortality data are not the measure of toxic effects' (Rapid Responses), *bmj.com*, 20 May.

Cross, D. and Smith, P. (2005) 'Limitations of the Camelford water inquiry' (Rapid Responses), *bmj.com*, 7 April.

Cvetkovich, G. and Earle, T.C. (1992) 'Environmental hazards and the public', *Journal of Social Issues*, 48: 1–20.

Department of the Environment (1990) *This Common Inheritance*, Government White Paper, London: HMSO.

Department of Health (1991) *Water Pollution at Lowermoor North Cornwall: Second Report of the Lowermoor Incident Health Advisory Group* (chairperson: Professor Dame Barbara Clayton), London: HMSO.

—— (2004) *Choosing Health: Making Healthier Choices Easier*, London: TSO.

Dorrell, S. (1990) 'Government concern over the suffering in Camelford', letter, *Guardian*, 27 July.

Exley, C. (and 58 other authors) (2005), 'Aluminium and Camelford' (Rapid Responses), *bmj.com*, 5 April.

Eyles, J., Taylor, M., Johnson, N. and Baxter, J. (1993) 'Worrying about waste: Living close to solid waste disposal facilities in southern Ontario', *Social Science and Medicine*, 37: 805–12.

Fiorino, D.J. (1989) 'Technical and democratic values in risk analysis', *Risk Analysis*, 9: 293–9.

Freudenberg, N. (1984) 'Citizen action for environmental health: Report on a survey of community organizations', *American Journal of Public Health*, 74: 444–8.

Giddens, A. (1990) *The Consequences of Modernity*, Oxford: Polity Press.

Godlee, F. (1991) 'Strategy for a healthy environment', *British Medical Journal*, 303: 836–8.

Good, B.J. (1994) *Medicine, Rationality and Experience: An Anthropological Perspective*, Cambridge: Cambridge University Press.

Guardian (1990) 'Muddy waters', editorial, 17 October.

Habermas, J. (1989) *The Structural Transformation of the Public Sphere: An Enquiry into a Category of Bourgeois Society*, Cambridge, MA: MIT Press.

Harris, D. (1984) 'Health department: Enemy or champion of the people?', *American Journal of Public Health*, 74: 428–30.

Hayes, M.V. (1992) 'On the epistemology of risk: Language, logic and social science', *Social Science and Medicine*, 35: 401–7.

Herzlich, C. (1973) *Health and Illness: A Socio-Psychological Approach*, London: Academic Press.

Johnson, W. (1986) 'The privatization of public health', *Radical Community Medicine*, 25: 4–11.

Kelly, M.P. (1990) 'The role of research in the new public health', *Critical Public Health*, 3: 4–9.

Kennedy, M. (1990) 'Water blunder turned the good life sour', *Guardian*, 11 June: 4.

Khanna, K. (2005) 'Inquiry questions long-term effects on health of Camelford incident', *British Medical Journal*, 330: 275.

Lancet (1991) 'What's new in public health?', editorial, 337: 1381–2.

—— (1992) 'Environmental pollution: It kills trees, but does it kill people', editorial, 340: 821–2.

Lawton, J. (2003) 'Lay experiences of health and illness: Past research and future agendas', *Sociology of Health and Illness*, 25, 23–40.

Lyotard, J.-F. (1984) *The Post-Modern Condition: A Report on Knowledge*, Manchester: Manchester University Press.

Masterson-Allen, S. and Brown, P. (1990) 'Public reaction to toxic waste contamination: Analysis of a social movement', *International Journal of Health Services*, 20: 485–500.

Owen, P.J. and Miles, D.P. (1995) 'A review of hospital discharge rates in a population around Camelford in North Cornwall up to the fifth anniversary of an episode of aluminium sulphate absorption', *Journal of Public Health Medicine*, 17, 200–204.

Owen, P.J., Miles, D.P., Draper, G. and Vincent, J. (2002) 'Retrospective study of mortality after a water pollution incident at Lowermoor in north Cornwall', *British Medical Journal*, 324: 1189.

Percy-Smith, J. and Sanderson, I. (1992) *Understanding Local Needs*, London: Institute for Public Policy Research.

Phillimore, P. and Moffatt, S. (1994) 'Discounted knowledge: Local experience, environmental pollution and health', in Popay, J. and Williams, G. (eds), *Researching the People's Health*, London: Routledge.

Philipp, R., Pond, K. and Rees, G. (1993) 'Litter and medical waste on bathing beaches in England and Wales', *British Medical Journal*, 306: 1042.

Phillips, M. (1990) 'The seeping sickness of Camelford', *Guardian*, 26 October: 19.

Pierret, J. (2003) 'The illness experience: State of knowledge and perspectives for research', *Sociology of Health and Illness*, 25: 4–22.

Popay, J. and Williams, G.H. (1996) 'Public health research and lay knowledge', *Social Science and Medicine*, 42: 759–68.

Popay, J., Williams, G.H., Thomas, C. and Gatrell, A. (1998) 'Theorising inequalities in health: The place of lay knowledge', in Bartley, M., Blane, D. and Davey Smith, G. (eds), *The Sociology of Health Inequalities*, Oxford: Blackwell.

Popay, J., Bennett, S., Thomas, C., Williams, G., Gatrell, A. and Bostock, L. (2003) 'Beyond "beer, fags, egg and chips"? Exploring lay understandings of social inequalities in health', *Sociology of Health and Illness*, 25: 1–23.

Prior, L. (2003) 'Belief, knowledge and expertise: The emergence of the lay expert in medical sociology, *Sociology of Health and Illness*, 25: 41–57.

Public Health Strategy Division (2005), *Health Challenge Wales*, Cardiff: Welsh Assembly Government.

Renn, O., Burns W.J., Kasperson, J.X., Kasperson, R.E. and Slovic, P. (1992) 'The social amplification of risk: Theoretical foundations and empirical applications', *Journal of Social Issues*, 48: 137–60.

Rice, C., Roberts, H., Smith, S.J. and Bryce, C. (1994) ' "It's like teaching your child to swim in a pool full of alligators": Lay voices and professional research on child accidents', in Popay, J. and Williams G. (eds), *Researching the People's Health*, London: Routledge.

Robinson, D. (1973) *Patients, Practitioners and Medical Care*, London: Heinemann.

Said, E. (1993) 'Speaking truth to power' (The Reith Lectures), *Independent*, 22 July: 12.

Scott, S., Williams, G., Platt, S. and Thomas, H. (eds) (1992) *Private Risks and Public Dangers*, Aldershot: Avebury.

Sennett, R. (1993) *The Fall of Public Man*, London: Faber.

Susser, M. (1989) 'Epidemiology today: "A thought-tormented world"', *International Journal of Epidemiology*, 18: 481–9.

Vaughan, E. and Seifert, M. (1992) 'Variability in framing risk issues', *Journal of Social Issues*, 48: 119–35.

Walker, A. (1991) 'Waste disposal: Fresh looks at a rotting problem', *British Medical Journal*, 303: 1391–4.

—— (1992) 'Drinking water: Doubts about quality', *British Medical Journal*, 304: 175–8.

Walzer, M. (1983) *Spheres of Justice: A Defence of Pluralism and Equality*, Oxford: Basil Blackwell.

Williams, G.H. (1984) 'The genesis of chronic illness: Narrative reconstruction', *Sociology of Health and Illness*, 6: 175–200.

—— (1986) 'Lay beliefs about the causes of rheumatoid arthritis: Their implications for rehabilitation', *International Rehabilitation Medicine*, 8: 65–8.

—— (2000) 'Knowledgeable narratives', *Anthropology and Medicine*, 7: 135–140.

—— (2003) 'The determinants of health: Structure, context and agency', *Sociology of Health and Illness*, 25: 131–54.

—— (2004) 'Lay knowledge', in Gabe, J., Bury, M. and Elston, M-A. (eds), *Key Concepts in Medical Sociology*, London: Sage.

Williams, G.H. and Popay, J. (1993) 'Researching the people's health: Dilemmas and opportunities for social scientists', in Popay, J. and Williams, G.H. (eds)

Social Research and Public Health, Salford Papers in Sociology No. 13, Department of Sociology, University of Salford.

—— (2001) 'Lay health knowledge and the concept of the lifeworld', in Scambler, G. (ed.), *Habermas, Critical Theory and Health*, London: Routledge.

Williams, G.H., Popay, J. and Bissell, P. (1995) 'Public health risks in the material world: Barriers to social movements in health', in Gabe, J. (ed.), *Medicine, Health and Risk*, Oxford: Blackwell.

Williams, R. (1989) *Resources of Hope: Culture, Democracy, and Socialism*, London: Verso.

8 Sex, gender and medicine

The case of the NHS

Lesley Doyal

Introduction

Gender issues are receiving increased attention on national and international health policy agendas. This reflects in part the health campaigns associated with 'second wave' feminism. In the 1970s activists in many of the developed countries launched campaigns to enhance the appropriateness and quality of services for women. Following the landmark UN conferences in Cairo (1994) and Beijing (1995), these goals were taken up by advocates in many different parts of the world. At the same time a new conceptual framework was developed for understanding the links between women, health and health care. In recent years both the campaigns and the analytic work have broadened with a shift from 'women' to 'gender' as the central focus of concern.

When the National Health Service (NHS) was set up in 1948 it received widespread acclaim with visitors coming from many parts of the world to see this new model for meeting the healthcare needs of an urban industrial population. Despite major financial constraints it continues to deliver good quality care at relatively low cost and compares well on most criteria with provision in other countries at similar levels of economic development. Yet there has always been disquiet about the way the service treats women.

Since the 1980s, increasing pressures to deliver more effective and efficient services have generated innovative ways of thinking about the organisation of care. These have been implemented by both Conservative and Labour governments. Traditional patterns of power and control have been partially disrupted and new mechanisms set up to express the views of the wider community. But little attention has been paid to the promotion of gender balance in these new attempts at democratisation.

As the problems of staffing the NHS have increased, the business case for gender mainstreaming in the workforce has been widely recognised.

Equal opportunities procedures have been put in place to ensure that women are able to compete on more equal terms with men, especially in medicine and senior management. Policies have also been developed to promote part-time and flexible working. However this limited progress in the workplace has not been mirrored in service delivery.

Women's health advocates in the UK have a long history of campaigning for greater gender-sensitivity in the delivery of care. In recent years, the impact of gender on male health care has also begun to receive attention and some men have followed women in campaigning for services to meet their particular needs more effectively. But despite these pressures the NHS continues to be largely blind to gender issues. Unlike many other countries, it has no policy for women's health, for men's health or for gender and health.

In recent years critics have begun to identify the constraints imposed by this gender blindness on the realisation of the 'modernisation' agenda currently being pursued so vigorously in the NHS. They have pointed out that gender inequalities not only offend the principles of distributive justice but also place constraints on both the efficiency and the effectiveness of the medical care practised within the NHS. These concerns have been highlighted by proposed changes in UK equality legislation. Plans are currently underway for the creation of a unitary Equality Body and a public sector duty to promote gender equality. It seems likely that these developments will move sex and gender issues up the NHS agenda in a way that feminist activism alone could not achieve.

Why are sex and gender important in health and health care?

Looking around the world, it is now clear that there are marked differences in the patterns of morbidity and mortality found in women and in men. In most (but not all) countries, women live longer than men and this gap in life expectancy is greatest among those who are wealthiest (UNDP 2004). On the other hand, women in many countries report greater sickness and disability than men over a lifetime. There are also significant differences in the types of diseases and other health problems faced by women and men. The reasons behind these variations are complex and they come from both the biological and the social realms.

The biological differences between women and men are obviously an important factor, shaping differences in male and female patterns of health and illness. It is widely recognised that women face a range of potential problems associated with their reproductive capacities. Unless they are able to control their fertility and go safely through pregnancy and childbirth their health may be seriously damaged. This gives women specific health care needs and these have long been recognised through the provision of specialist services including family planning and obstetric care. Women and men are also at risk of suffering from other sex-specific problems which affect particular organs: cancers of the prostate and cervix for example.

But there is a growing volume of evidence to show that biological differences between women and men go beyond the reproductive system (Wizemann and Pardue 2001). Marked sex differences exist in the incidence, symptoms and prognosis of a wide range of diseases and conditions that affect both sexes. This is very evident in the case of coronary heart disease for example, which affects more men at younger ages. It is also reflected in the epidemiology of some infectious diseases including tuberculosis to which men appear to be inherently more susceptible. Recent studies indicate that these differences are due in large part to previously unrecognised genetic, hormonal and metabolic differences between men and women.

But biology is not the only factor shaping differences in male and female patterns of heath and illness. There is also an extensive literature documenting the relationship between gender and health (Hunt and Annandale 1998; Denton and Walters 1999). Despite their superficial similarities, there are often marked differences in the lives of women and men in the same social settings and this can have significant effects on their wellbeing. Gender differences in living and working conditions and in access to a wide range of resources put males and females at differential risk of developing some health problems while protecting them from others (Annandale and Hunt 2000).

Many studies have shown how the daily lives of women may damage their wellbeing (Doyal 1995). There is evidence, for example, that the domestic responsibilities associated with their gender can have a negative impact on both physical and mental health. The higher levels of depression and anxiety reported by women have been explained in part by reference to their work in caring for others with what may be insufficient amounts of time, money and other resources. This is especially true for those women raising their families in poverty. Gender violence has also been highlighted as a major public health hazard for women (Heise *et al.* 1994).

As the links between women's lives and their health are given greater attention, the potential health risks of masculinity are also beginning to emerge. At first glance, being male might seem to be a privilege giving greater access to health promoting resources. However it may also require the taking of risks (Cameron and Bernardes 1998; Luck, Bamford and Williamson 2000; Banks 2001; Davidson and Lloyd 2001). The traditional role of breadwinner means that men are still more likely than women to die prematurely from occupational disease and injuries. Again, this is especially true of men attempting to survive in conditions of poverty. As a result of their socialisation into masculinity, men in most societies have also been more likely than women to engage in dangerous activities including smoking, excessive drinking, driving too fast and unsafe sex.

As well as being a major determinant of health itself, gender also influences the experiences of women and men as users of health care. Women are more likely than men to report practical problems in access to services. They are more likely to have caring responsibilities for example or to have transport problems. Men, on the other hand, may find it more difficult to admit weakness or to accept that they may be ill and hence may delay longer before seeking medical advice. Once in receipt of care, there also appear to be gender differences in how women and men are treated. Studies from a number of different countries have shown that health workers may make different diagnoses of men and women with the same evidence. They may also offer different treatment in what would appear to be the same clinical situations.

Sex, gender and the NHS: What do we know?

This emerging literature on sex and gender issues in health and health care has important implications for the NHS. But as we shall see, less attention has been paid to these issues in the UK than in many other countries. The available evidence is still partial and sometimes difficult to interpret but the headlines are clear. Women as a group live longer than men. In England in 1999, the average life expectancy at birth for a female child was 80.2 years compared to 75.8 for a male (Department of Health 2003). Of course longevity also varies between groups of women and groups of men. In England and Wales in 1992–93, female life expectancy at birth was 83 for children in the highest occupational group and 77 for those in the lowest. The comparable figures for male children were 78 in the highest group and only 68 in the lowest (Office for National Statistics 2002).

There are also important differences in causes of death between women and men. The major killers for both groups are circulatory disease and cancer. However women are more likely to die from the cerebrovascular disease associated with old age while male deaths are higher for ischaemic heart disease. Men die more often than women from lung cancer and also cancers of the stomach and colon. The number of deaths from less common causes also differs between women and men. Female death rates are much lower than those of males for injuries, poisonings and suicide for example and also for chronic liver disease (Department of Health 2003).

Gender differences in morbidity are much more complex and difficult to interpret. In the UK context there do not appear to be major differences in health status between women and men in the same social groups. However recent studies suggest that women and men may assess their health according to different criteria (Curtis and Lawson 2000). It is also clear that gender differences in reported morbidity vary according to the age, level of domestic commitments and paid work of those being questioned (Arber and Khlat 2002; Walters *et al.* 2002).

Figures for both primary care and hospital services show some differences in patterns of use in women and men. Women are slightly more likely than men to be admitted to hospital and they also make more use of GP services than men, but the gender gap is small. In 2000 women made an average of five visits a year to their GP compared with four for men. Not surprisingly, however, the gender gap was greater in the reproductive years with women making an average of five visits with only three for men of the same age (Dench *et al.* 2002).

Finally, it is important to note that women and men in the UK differ not only in their use of services but also in their patterns of health-related behaviour. Similar percentages of women and men smoke between the ages of 16 and 24 but there are more male smokers aged 25–64. Women then predominate over the age of 65 (Department of Health 2003). These gender differences are interlinked with social class and ethnicity (Dench *et al.* 2002). Men in all age groups are more likely than women to consume the recommended number of units of alcohol per week. Diet and lifestyle surveys now collect regular data on patterns of food consumption and again gender differences are very evident with the average diets of women being significantly better than men in the same social group. Men are more likely than women to be obese but women are less likely to participate in physical exercise on a regular basis (Department of Health 2001).

The evidence outlined above shows the potential importance of sex and gender issues for the NHS. Though much more research is needed, especially studies using more qualitative indicators, it is clear that both have an impact on patterns of health and health care in the UK. Yet they continue to be low on the agenda of policy-makers, planners and practitioners. The following sections will explore some of the reasons for this and will document the strategies deployed by women and latterly by men to try to reshape medical and wider NHS priorities.

The early years: Women document their negative experiences of health care

One of the main achievements of the NHS was to remove the financial obstacles to health care faced by the majority of British women. This was achieved through the introduction of care, free at source, and the setting up of a national network of general practitioners. Indeed, in the first years after its inception, working-class women were among the main beneficiaries of the service as their pent-up need for items such as gynaecological surgery, dental care and spectacles was at last met. However this did not mean that women were always satisfied with the services they received.

As feminist activism increased in the 1970s and 1980s, individual women talked about their negative experiences of health care encounters. These seemed to reflect both their own socialised deference towards doctors and also the stereotypical views too often held of them by health workers (Graham and Oakley 1981; Doyal 1983, 1998; Roberts 1985; Stacey 1985; O'Sullivan 1987). Many women felt unable to assert their own needs and desires while many doctors appeared to be reluctant to let women speak for themselves. Poor women in particular, as well as those from ethnic minorities, were too often treated as though they were less rational, less capable of complex decision-making and sometimes as simply less valuable than men (Douglas 1992).

The early stages of women's health activism in the UK were therefore broadly similar to those found in other developed countries such as the USA and Australia (Broom and Doyal 2004). They focussed mainly on criticisms of sexism in health care and its impact on women's experiences of oppression and social control. Some of these earlier critiques were themselves criticised for being 'over-determined' with a crude model of 'professional imperialism' (Strong 1979; Elston 1991). This was borne out to some extent as some of the most extreme manifestations of individual sexism did appear to diminish when older and more traditional doctors retired and new ideas were introduced into the medical curriculum. But more radical changes in the way services were delivered were difficult to achieve.

This reflected in part women's lack of power in the wider society. However it was also a product of the iconic status of the NHS itself which symbolised the vision of a society based on collective solidarity. This made it difficult for feminists (and others) to criticise the work of the medical profession which was embedded at the heart of this much-valued institution.

Women and the NHS in the Thatcher era: Defending the indefensible?

These constraints on women's ability to challenge gender discrimination in health care were exacerbated after 1979 by the policies of the conservative government led by Margaret Thatcher. With monetarist economic policies and a commitment to reduce public spending, it appeared that the existence of the NHS in its original form could no longer be taken for granted. The creation of an internal market and pressures towards the privatisation of service delivery put the NHS under threat. Under these circumstances the defence of the NHS itself became the major priority for many who might otherwise have been campaigning for qualitative changes in the way services were delivered.

Women are the major users of health care both for themselves and for those for whom they care. This reflects their specific needs associated with biological reproduction but also their greater longevity. They therefore have more to lose than men if the quantity and/or quality of services decline. This is especially true in the context of community services which are used most frequently by women but often receive the lowest priority in the context of fiscal restraint. Not surprisingly, therefore, women played an important part in campaigns to defend services both as workers and as patients.

As the pressures on NHS spending increased, many women reported difficulties in obtaining appropriate care. Though waiting lists and other symptoms of financial strain had an impact on both sexes, women were disproportionately affected in particular areas. Family planning services, for instance, were significantly reduced in many parts of the country (Kennir 1990). Their longer life expectancy (often in poor health) meant that older women were also more likely than their male counterparts to be affected by the withdrawal of the NHS from the provision of continuing care beds.

Thus, women from a number of different constituencies fought during the Thatcher years mainly to keep the health service they had, but also to reshape it in ways that met their needs more effectively. However this was not a hospitable climate for progressive change (Robinson and Le Grand 1993). In the United States and in Australia women were working hard to develop separate women-controlled services but in the UK this was not seen as politically appropriate at a time when the NHS itself might be under threat (Broom and Doyal 2004).

Who controls whose health: Women in the medical profession

Though the Thatcher years did not see major changes in the gender sensitivity of care offered to patients, progress was made in the promotion of greater equality of opportunity in the health care workforce. Campaigns to change modern medicine had focused for some time on gender inequalities in the distribution of power within the NHS in general and in the profession in particular. Women's lack of influence was striking in a system in which they made up about 75 per cent of workers as well as the majority of users. Most of the power remained with the medical profession and with senior managers, the majority of whom were male.

Women within the profession campaigned for changes in the organisation of medical work to make it more family-friendly for both women and men. Organisations such as the Medical Women's Federation and Women in Medicine set up support groups and developed information packs to help female colleagues to develop their careers. Spurred on by their female members, the Royal College of Surgeons set up Women in Surgery in 1991 with the aim of increasing the number of women in the specialty to 20 per cent by the year 2010. The Royal College of Physicians later followed suit with a major investigation into the obstacles women face in pursuing their careers (Royal College of Physicians 2001).

For many years women had not been allowed to enter medicine at all. After a series of hard fought battles they now make up over 50 per cent of medical students but only about a third of hospital doctors and general practitioners. About 35 per cent of consultants are female but they are concentrated in a few specialties, most of which have relatively low status (BMA 2001). In higher status areas such as surgery, women make up only about 6 per cent of consultants (McManus and Sproston 2000). As a result they continue to be under-represented on the ruling bodies of the profession such as the General Medical Council and the committees of the Royal Colleges.

Some progress has therefore been made in restructuring medical careers within the NHS and in facilitating women's competition with men on equal terms (Coyle 2003). As female entrants move through the system their representation is increasing in different sectors of the workforce. By 2001, women made up about 15 per cent of registrars in surgery and 50 per cent in gynaecology (BMA 2001). But the weight of tradition remains heavy. The initial exclusion of women from medicine and their subsequent failure to reach equal status with male colleagues were not the result of an accidental misfit between women's needs and those of the profession (Witz 1992). Rather they reflected the underlying reality that medicine has traditionally been 'male' in much of its theory and practice.

Much more remains to be done if women are to pursue a medical career on equal terms with men (Witz 1992; Pringle 1998). The 'business case' for equal opportunities in all arenas of the health care labour force has been widely accepted as staffing problems multiply. But unless further changes are made in the culture of the profession and in the terms and conditions upon which medicine is practised there will continue to be institutional bias against females. This will not only be a potential source of harm to the doctors involved but it will also play a part in sustaining the discriminatory attitudes and practices that continue to be reported by women patients.

The era of modernisation: Creating a climate for change?

In 1997 a Labour government was returned with a manifesto to maintain and improve the NHS. This meant more funds for some parts of the service and an ambitious 'modernisation' agenda (Department of Health 1997). However this did not include an increased commitment to remedying gender inequalities. During this period campaigners have therefore pursued a low-key agenda, seeking out the 'fault lines' created by modernisation and using them to push for improvements in care for women. As we shall see, the emphasis has been less on the subjective experiences of health care users and more on the objective issues of access and technical quality of care. This has required a much clearer engagement with aspects of the scientific credibility of medical theory and practice.

While the concept of equity is still a central focus, the discourse of campaigners has been extended to include greater reference to equity and efficiency. Men have joined with women in calling for much greater attention to be paid to sex and gender issues across the whole range of research and practice in health care. Both argue that men and women are too often treated in stereotypical ways. This does not respect their individual humanity and may well limit the quality of treatment they receive. Women and men are not 'minorities' requiring special treatment. All patients are either male or female and unless this is recognised, the services delivered will be less than optimal and scarce resources will be wasted.

Of course the immediate interests of women and men may well be in opposition and this has sometimes caused difficulties in the competition for scarce resources. Both male and female health groups therefore continue to campaign separately with men's activities arguably being more vigorous at this time than those of women. However there has also been a recent recognition that both groups could benefit if NHS services in general were made more gender-sensitive. Hence efforts have also been made to work collaboratively to increase the visibility of gender issues in the NHS.

The NHS Plan for Modernisation highlighted the issue of diversity and stressed the need to deliver care which is appropriate to the needs of all patients (Department of Health 1997). However critics have pointed out the relative absence of sex and gender concerns in this new paradigm for the planning and delivery of services. A recent review showed that most of the modernisation initiatives have been gender-blind. That is to say, they have failed to acknowledge the impact of gender differences on health outcomes and on the delivery of health care (Doyal *et al.* 2003).

Not surprisingly these policies do pay some attention to the different needs of women and men. However most of the strategies proposed are sex-specific. There is a recognition, for example, that improved breast screening will be required if the needs of women are to be better met. There is also a growing recognition that separate and targeted services will be needed if men are to be persuaded to take greater care of their own health. However there appears to be little recognition of the fact that sex and gender issues need to be incorporated into the planning of all health services for both women and men.

A recent consultation with the users and providers of official statistics in the UK revealed considerable dissatisfaction about the lack of separate data for males and females and also of data disaggregated by sex in relation to age, ethnicity and region (Dench *et al.* 2002). There is also a lack of evidence on health problems disproportionately affecting one group (Murgatroyd 2000). Gender violence, for example, affects women much more often than men while criminal violence is more likely to affect men but very little information is collected on the gendered health implications of these issues. Similarly, surveys on workplace health issues have tended to focus mainly on male experiences of mortality and morbidity with female experiences of occupational health problems remaining largely invisible.

There is now a strong emphasis in the NHS on what has come to be called 'evidence based medicine'. However, much of the evidence used in everyday clinical practice has been generated by studies based on the experiences of young white men both in the UK and in the US (Bandyopadhyay *et al.* 2001). This is true both of epidemiological studies and also of clinical trials. The extent of this bias has been demonstrated with particular clarity in the case of research into coronary heart disease but it is also evident in a number of other settings (Sharp 1998).

In the US this gender bias in the creation of medical knowledge has been seen as an equity issue and has received a great deal of attention (Mastroianni *et al.* 1994). In the late 1980s, some women began to claim their right to be involved in clinical trials in the same numbers as men (Fiebach *et al.* 1990; Hamilton 1996). They made the case that when studies did not include appropriate numbers of women and men the generalisability of their findings would be indeterminate and hence they would be unscientific. Drugs that were tested on men but then used on both women and men ran the risk of being less effective or more hazardous in one sex than in the other.

In response to these arguments, the US government passed a law in 1993, requiring all applications for federal funding to show that women and men (and ethnic minority groups) were represented in appropriate numbers in the proposed research design. Similar initiatives have been implemented in a number of other countries including Canada, Australia and South Africa. However these arguments have received little or no attention in the UK. Guidelines for the implementation of clinical trials show very limited awareness of either the ethical or the scientific relevance of gender issues. They are similarly absent from the current guidelines for research ethics committees. The new Research Governance Framework for the UK does talk about the need to ensure that the body of research evidence 'reflects the diversity of the population' but offers no practical guidance on how this should be achieved.

If health care is to be provided in ways that take sex and gender seriously (as they apply to both women and men) these issues need to be part of initial training as well as being incorporated into continuing professional development programmes. In a number of countries, they are now included in medical, nursing and other curricula but initiatives of this kind are scarce in the UK. A recent survey of British medical schools revealed very few examples of systematic innovation in the area of gender (Doyal 2003). A similar gap exists in the education of nurses (and other health-related professionals). While the NHS has recently developed considerable expertise in 'diversity' training for different categories of staff this has focussed mainly on race and ethnicity, and gender issues have been largely invisible.

Wider organisational learning will also be necessary if services are to meet the particular needs of women or men. Some hospitals are now offering one-stop clinics to support women in danger of miscarrying for instance, while specialist cessation clinics have been developed to support women in disadvantaged areas wishing to give up smoking (Doyal 1998). Similarly, a range of health promotion initiatives have been designed to meet what are seen to be the gender-specific needs of some men. Services are being offered through local football clubs for example, or in a barber's shop or a Harley Davidson show room. Male drop-in centres have also been set up to target gay men. However the lessons from these demonstration projects are too rarely transferred to the mainstream and important lessons remain unlearned.

Gender blindness in coronary heart disease: A case study

As part of the modernisation agenda, the Department of Health has constructed the National Service Frameworks (NSF) upon which policy and practice are to be based. The failure to take gender seriously in mainstream service delivery is well illustrated by the NSF on coronary heart disease (CHD). There is already a large body of international evidence on sex and gender differences in risk factors in heart disease, and in symptoms, use of services and diagnosis and treatment. However these are not discussed in the framework. Throughout the document, patients are referred to in gender neutral terms. Evidence concerning differences between women and men is not presented and no incentives are given for the development of gender-sensitive services.

It is known that the risk factors for CHD are broadly similar in women and in men but this does not mean that they can be treated in exactly the same way. There are marked differences in male and female patterns of smoking for instance (Bostock 2003). A number of studies have also indicated that different cessation strategies may work best for male and female smokers (Perkins 2001). Diet and exercise too are highly gendered risk factors but this is not discussed in the National Service Framework.

There is also evidence of male and female potential cardiac patients being treated differently during screening (Williams *et al.* 2003). A recent study in general practice in the Trent region showed that men were more likely than women to have their cardiovascular risk factors recorded on computer (Hippisley-Cox *et al.* 2001). Those women who had their cholesterol tested were more likely than the men to have an abnormal reading. However the men were more likely to receive lipid lowering treatment. Another study in general practices in England and Wales found that men were significantly more likely than women to be prescribed statins (Majeed *et al.* 2000).

There is also evidence of gender differences in coronary care in hospital settings. A recent study found that women with myocardial infarction were less likely to be admitted to intensive care than men in the same condition (Raine *et al.* 2002b). Another study done by the same author found no gender differences in the use of revascularisation procedures overall but men were more likely than women to be given coronary artery bypass grafting (Raine *et al.* 2002a).

A number of studies have also examined gender differentials in the use of cardiac rehabilitation services in the UK. In a recent national study, hypertensive men were found to be nearly twice as likely to undergo a rehabilitation programme as hypertensive women (Raine *et al.* 2004). There is also growing evidence that the psychological consequences of heart disease may be especially profound for men, posing threats to sexuality and masculinity, which many will find it difficult to handle (White and Johnson 2000; White and Lockyer 2001). Much more work is needed to uncover these gender differences in experiences of CHD and also to evaluate the appropriateness of existing patterns of service delivery. However this does not appear to be on the current research agenda.

Conclusion: Movement towards gender mainstreaming?

If this situation is to be changed, new policy initiatives will be needed not just in the context of coronary care but across the whole range of health care including disease prevention and health promotion as well as interventions that address the wider determinants of health. In other words sex and gender mainstreaming would be required in all the activities of the NHS and associated agencies.

This would need to start with the enhancement of existing policies and practices to promote gender equality throughout the NHS workforce. However it would need to go much further in tackling the very complex issues involved in the delivery of gender-sensitive services. Both routine data collection and medical research will need to be undertaken with a clear focus on sex and gender issues. Capacity-building would be required to ensure a workforce which is both individually and collectively capable of recognising the similarities and differences in the needs of women and men and of how to meet them in appropriate ways. Sex and gender issues would need to be integrated not just into the planning of services but also into mechanisms and criteria for quality assurance, audit and monitoring and evaluation. Finally women would need to be more actively involved in the running of the service.

But this will not be achieved without a change in political will. Despite a rhetoric of decentralisation, a wide range of strategies are used to ensure that central government political priorities come high on the agenda of doctors, managers and other health care workers. These include the setting of targets, for example, and the imposition of penalties on organisations and individuals who fail to meet these. Thus far, successive governments have defined inequalities and differences relating to class, ethnicity or (more recently) disability as more urgent than those of sex and gender. Under these circumstances there has been little incentive for those who wish to focus more closely on the differences between women and men.

However there are signs that the reshaping of the equalities agenda may change this situation. In May 2004 the government announced the creation of a new single body, the Commission for Equality and Human Rights. This will be in place by 2007 and will replace the Commission on Racial Equality, the Equal Opportunities Commission and the Disability Rights Commission. At the same time a new law will oblige public bodies (for the first time) to promote gender equality and eliminate discrimination between women and men.

The introduction of this new legislation will provide important new levers in the long-standing campaigns to make medicine more gender-sensitive. As we have seen, women's activities have played an important part in wider attempts to transform the culture and organisation of British medicine. But there have been few instances where feminist challenges alone have been powerful enough to effect major changes in medical practice. In recent years the pressures towards greater efficiency and effectiveness have challenged the power of doctors and some of their traditional power has been eroded. It remains to be seen how far the new powers relating to gender equality can be used to optimise the quality of the health care needed by both women and men.

References

Annandale, E. and Hunt, K. (2000) *Gender Inequalities in Health*. Buckingham: Open University Press.

Arber, S. and Khlat, M. (2002) 'Introduction to social and economic patterning of women's health in a changing world', *Social Science and Medicine*, 54 (5): 643–7.

Bandyopadhyay, S., Bayer, A. and O'Mahoney, M. (2001) 'Age and gender bias in clinical trials', *QJM*, 94 (3): 127–32.

Banks, I. (2001) 'No man's land: Men, illness and the NHS', *BMJ*, 323: 1058–60.

Bostock, Y. (2003) *Searching for the Solution: Women, Smoking and Inequalities in Europe*. London: Health Development Agency.

British Medical Association (2001) *Medicine: The Changing Face of Today's Doctors*. London: BMA.

Broom, D. and Doyal, L. (2004) 'Sex and gender in health care and health policy', in J. Healy and M. McKee (eds), *Accessing Health Care: Responding to Diversity*. London: Oxford University Press.

Cameron, E. and Bernardes, J. (1998) 'Gender and disadvantage in health: Men's health for a change', in M. Bartley, D. Blane and G. Davey Smith (eds), *Sociology of Health Inequalities*. Oxford: Blackwells.

Coyle, A. (2003) *Women and Flexible Working in the NHS*. Manchester: Equal Opportunities Commission.

Curtis, S. and Lawson, K. (2000) 'Gender, ethnicity and self reported health: The case of African Caribbean populations in London', *Social Science and Medicine*, 50: 365–85.

Davidson, N. and Lloyd, T. (eds) (2001) *Promoting Men's Health: A Guide for Practitioners*. London: Balliere Tindall.

Dench, S., Aston, J., Evans, C., Meager, N., Williams, M. and Willison, R. (2002) *Key Indicators of Women's Position in Britain*. London: Department of Trade and Industry/Women and Equality Unit.

Denton, M. and Walters, V. (1999) 'Gender differences in structural and behavioural determinants of health: An analysis of the structural production of health', *Social Science and Medicine*, 48: 1221–35.

Department of Health (1997) *The New NHS: Modern and Dependable*. London: Stationery Office.

—— (2001) *Health Survey for England*. London: Department of Health.

—— (2003) 'Health and Personal Social Service Statistics for England' available at *http://www.doh.gov.uk/HPSSS/INDEX.HTM*.

Douglas, J. (1992) 'Black women's health matters: Putting black women on the research agenda', in H. Roberts (ed.), *Women's Health Matters*. London: Routledge.

Doyal, L. (1983) 'Women, health and the sexual division of labour: A case study of the women's health involvement in Britain', *Critical Social Policy*, 7: 21–33.

—— (1995) *What Makes Women Sick? Gender and the Political Economy of Health.* London: Macmillan.

—— (ed.) (1998) *Women and Health Services: An Agenda for Change.* Buckingham: Open University Press.

—— (2003) Unpublished review of medical schools in Europe funded by the European Commission's 5th framework Programme on Women and Science.

Doyal, L., Payne, S. and Cameron, A. (2003) *Promoting Gender Equality in Health.* Manchester: Equal Opportunities Commission.

Elston, M. (1991) 'The politics of professional power: Medicine in a changing health service', in J. Gabe, M. Calnan and M. Bury (eds), *The Sociology of the Health Service*, London: Routledge.

Fiebach, M., Viscoli, C. and Horwitz, K. (1990) 'Differences between men and women in survival after myocardial infarction', *Journal of the American Medical Association*, 63: 1092–6.

Graham, H. and Oakley, A. (1981) 'Competing ideologies of reproduction: Medical and maternal perspectives on pregnancy', in H. Roberts (ed.), *Women, Health and Reproduction.* London: Routledge and Kegan Paul.

Hamilton, J. (1996) 'Women and health policy: On the inclusion of females in clinical trials', in C. Sargent and C. Brettell (eds), *Gender and Health: An International Perspective.* Upper Saddle River, NJ: Prentice-Hall.

Heise, L., Pitanguy, J. and Germain, A. (1994) *Violence Against Women: A Hidden Health Burden*, World Bank Discussion Paper 255. Washington DC: World Bank.

Hippisley-Cox, J., Pringle, M., Crown, N. and Wynn, A. (2001) 'Sex inequalities in ischaemic heart disease in general practice: Cross sectional survey', *BMJ*, 332: 832.

Hunt, K. and Annandale, E. (1998) 'Relocating gender and morbidity: Examining women's and men's health in contemporary western societies', *Social Science and Medicine*, 48 (1): 1–5.

Kennir, B. (1990) *Family Planning Clinic Cuts: A Survey of NHS Family Planning Clinics in Greater London.* London: Family Planning Association.

Luck, M., Bamford, M. and Williamson, P. (2000) *Men's Health: Perspectives, Diversity and Paradox.* Oxford: Blackwell Science.

McManus, I. and Sproston, K. (2000) 'Women in hospital medicine in the United Kingdom: Glass ceiling, preference prejudice or cohort effect', *Journal of Epidemiology and Community Health*, 54: 10–16.

Majeed, A., Moser, K. and Maxwell, R. (2000) 'Age, sex and practice variation in use of statins in general practice in England and Wales', *Journal of Public Health Medicine*, 22 (3): 275–9.

Mastroianni, A., Faden, R. and Federman, D. (1994) *Women and Health: Ethical and Legal Issues of Including Women in Clinical Studies*, vol. 1 and 2. Washington DC: National Academy press.

Murgatroyd, L. (2000) 'Developing gender statistics in the UK', *Radical Statistics*, 74, Spring 2000.

Office for National Statistics (2002) *Social Trends 32.* London: ONS.

O'Sullivan, S. (1987) *Women's Health: A Spare Rib Reader.* London: Pandora Press.

Perkins, K.A. (2001), 'Smoking cessation in women: Special considerations', *CNS Drugs*, 15 (5): 391–411.

Pringle, R. (1998) *Sex and Medicine: Gender, Power and Authority in the Medical Profession*. Cambridge: Cambridge University Press.

Raine, R., Black, N., Bowker, T. and Wood, D. (2002a) 'Gender differences in the management and outcome of patients with acute coronary artery disease', *Journal of Epidemiology and Community Health*, 56 (10): 791–7.

Raine, R., Goldfrad, C., Rowan, K. and Black, N. (2002b) 'Influence of patient gender on admission to intensive care', *Journal of Epidemiology and Community Health*, 56 (6): 418–23.

Raine, R., Hutchings, A. and Black, N. (2004) 'Is publicly funded health care really distributed according to need? The example of cardiac rehabilitation in the UK', *Health Policy*, 67 (2): 227–35.

Roberts, H. (1985) *The Patient Patients: Women and Their Doctors*. London: Pandora.

Robinson, R. and Le Grand, J. (1993) *Evaluating the NHS Reforms*. London: King's Fund Institute.

Royal College of Physicians (2001) *Women in Hospital Medicine: Career Challenges and Opportunities. Report of a Working Party*. London: RCP.

Sharp, I. (1998) 'Gender issues in the prevention and treatment of coronary heart disease', in L. Doyal (ed.), *Women and Health Services: An Agenda for Change*. Buckingham: Open University Press.

Stacey, M. (1985) 'Women and health: The United States and the United Kingdom compared', in E. Lewin and V. Oleson (eds), *Women, Health and Healing: Towards a New Perspective*. London: Tavistock.

Strong, P. (1979) 'Sociological imperialism and the profession of medicine: a critical examination of the thesis of medical imperialism', *Social Science and Medicine*, 13A (2): 199–215.

United Nations Development Programme (2004) *World Development Report 2003*. New York: UNDP.

Walters, V., McDonough, P. and Strohschein, L. (2002) 'The influence of work, household structure and social, personal and material resources on gender differences in health: An analysis of the 1994 Canadian National Population Health Survey', *Social Science and Medicine*, 54: 677–92.

White, A. and Johnson, M. (2000) 'Men making sense of chest pain – niggles, doubts and denials', *Journal of Clinical Nursing*, 9 (4): 534–41.

White, A. and Lockyer, L. (2001) 'Tackling coronary heart disease: A gender sensitive approach is needed', *BMJ*, 323: 1016–17.

Williams, D., Bennet, K. and Feeley, J. (2003) 'Evidence for an age and gender bias in the secondary prevention of ischaemic heart disease in primary care', *British Journal of Pharmacology*, 55 (6): 604–8.

Witz, A. (1992) *Professions and Patriarchy*. London: Routledge.

Wizemann, T. and Pardue, M. (2001) *Exploring the Biological Contributions to Human Health: Does Sex Matter?* Washington DC: National Academy Press.

9 Attacking the foundations of modern medicine?

Anti-vivisection protest and medical science

Mary Ann Elston

Introduction: Animal experimentation and modern medicine

As this chapter was being prepared, in February 2005, more than 400 different food products made by over 300 firms were being recalled by producers from shops and food outlets across the United Kingdom in the largest exercise of this kind in British retail history. The recalls followed the discovery that a batch of one manufacturer's 'Worcester' sauce contained chilli powder contaminated by an industrial dye. The dye in question, Sudan 1, is banned from human consumption because 'animal tests suggest that it is a potent carcinogen'. According to one toxicologist, 'In standard tests, in which the dye is fed to rodents for two years, at moderately high levels it caused tumours' although this scientist was also reported as declaring 'The risk [to humans] is negligible here' because high doses or prolonged exposure were so unlikely (*Daily Telegraph* 22 Feb. 2005). Thus we have an expert scientist stressing the limitations of extrapolating results from animal testing directly to humans.[1] This was presumably with a view to minimising public anxiety, given the scale of the sauce's use across the food-processing industry. And, according to some reports, there was a further twist: the reason that the particular manufacturer's version of the sauce was favoured by the food-processing industry was that, unlike the brand leader, it contained no animal products and hence could be used in products marketed as suitable for vegetarians (*Guardian* 22 Feb. 2005; *Sunday Times* 27 Feb. 2005).

The Sudan 1 episode reveals one of the underpinnings of contemporary health policy: that non-human animals are conscripted to protect humans' health by standing proxy for them in the testing of an immense range of products and processes for toxicity. Toxicological testing is only one of the ways in which living non-human animals play an integral, although often unrecognised, part in modern health care. Animal experimentation will have been involved at some stage in the development, production or testing of almost all therapeutic and clinical preventive drugs and clinical technologies currently employed in allopathic medicine. A large part of the curriculum for students of 'basic' medical sciences is derived from research with living animals. Its transmission may involve pedagogic demonstrations with live, but usually terminally anaesthetised, animals, although the extent of the latter varies between countries as well as between professions.[2] Slightly less contentious, but possibly more extensive today than the use of living animals, is the use of animals specifically bred and killed for their tissues in medical research and education, drug development and safety testing.

Not all scientific use of animals is devoted to furthering knowledge with direct human health applications. And the ascendancy of the laboratory-based approach to medicine has been neither uncontested nor total within British medicine (e.g. Lawrence 1992). But, under the statutes regulating animal experiments in Britain for over a century (Cruelty to Animals Act, 1876, and Animals (Scientific Procedures) Act, 1986), prevention, diagnosis or treatment of disease is the first stated purpose for which scientists may be licensed to perform scientific procedures on animals. The vast majority of the 2.79 million scientific procedures on animals conducted under the 1986 legislation in 2003 claimed a direct or indirect human health promoting purpose (Home Office 2004).

In short, to lead what most people would consider to be a normal life, to engage in normal health and illness behaviour in an affluent society, is to take for granted a large area of co-ordinated scientific activity involving the use of laboratory animals. Whether this situation is a morally justifiable one; whether we should eschew animal experiments and forego any putative health benefits on moral grounds; whether we might in fact be healthier if we did so; whether the same or better knowledge might be (or have been) obtained through alternative methods: these are, for some, important questions to be answered. This chapter does not, however, attempt to do so. Rather, it analyses some of the tactics and arguments deployed by those who have persistently asked such questions from an oppositional standpoint and the response of those challenged.

The chapter begins by outlining the links between the rise and the fall of the anti-vivisection movement and the medical profession's rise in status and autonomy from the 1870s to the 1960s. Against this historical background, the marked revival of anti-vivisectionist activity over the last three decades raises obvious questions, which the chapter seeks to address, about possible connections between the resurgence of public opposition to animal experiments and the themes of this book: that is, the challenge to and putative loss of medical authority in some affluent Western societies at the turn of the twenty-first century. The chapter demonstrates how current questioning of animal experimentation exemplifies and draws on the external challenges to medicine (and biomedical science) described in other contributions. The anti-vivisectionist campaign attempts to open up the 'black box' of medical knowledge and technology to public scrutiny and debate, to re-open controversy. The campaign's efforts have generated a response from the institutions of medical research that reveals some of the tensions facing those who might wish to close up the box again.[3]

A century of controversy over animal experiments

Opposition to live animal experiments is a central feature of the contemporary 'animal rights' movement. This social movement is particularly strong in Britain, the main focus of this chapter. But parallel movements have arisen in the United States (Lederer 1987; Sperling 1988; Jasper and Nelkin 1992), Australia, the Nordic countries and, to a lesser extent, in other parts of Europe (Ryder 1989). The term 'social movement' is apposite in that the animal rights campaign is a loosely structured 'collective actor constituted by individuals who understand themselves to have common interests and, for at least some significant part of their social existence, a common identity' campaigning for social change (Scott 1990: 6). Within the animal rights and anti-vivisection movements can be found many of the features of so-called 'new social movements' (NSMs). These include calls for major changes in values and lifestyle (e.g. conversion to vegetarianism if not veganism) and an emphasis on grass-roots support and direct action (liberating animals from laboratories or sabotaging fox-hunting) rather than relying on conventional political mobilisation. But, as with some other contemporary oppositional NSMs (Scott 1990), the movement for 'animal rights' represents a resurgence of long-standing concerns about human–animal relationships while also manifesting some distinctively new features. This is particularly apparent in the protest against animal experimentation.

The modern idea of animal rights is often contrasted with an allegedly more traditional concern with animal welfare. The latter implies that humans have a duty to treat animals humanely when they make use of them for (morally acceptable) human ends. An animal rights position implies that animals have a moral standing that is in some sense equivalent to that which we accord to humans.[4] Hence animals are never acceptable objects for human exploitation, not for food, sport nor entertainment, not as pets nor in science and medicine. There are, undoubtedly, important conceptual distinctions between 'animal rights' and 'animal welfare' as philosophical positions. But, in active campaigning, the distinction is not always sharp, and sustained collective action opposition to animal experiments in principle is not a new development. Nor has it ever been 'merely' about animal welfare (although it has always been about this among other things).

Concern about the morality and utility of animal experimentation dates from the practice's tentative beginnings in ancient Greece (Rupke 1987a). But it was after 1850 that vivisection expanded rapidly in parts of Europe, bringing with it major public controversy and collective opposition (French 1975). Ever since, the vivisection controversy has been a vehicle for argument about what animal experiments have come to symbolise: the claims and the power of modern science and of a form of medicine that espouses and legitimates such science.

The Victorian cause

Vivisection was an integral part of the application of the methods and values of experimental natural science to the study of living things that began in Germany and France in the mid-nineteenth century. In Britain, a movement of (largely medically trained) scientists worked to reform the medical curriculum around the new physiology from the 1850s. They shared a vision of what the education of modern medical gentlemen should be and a desire for a secure institutional base for their research activities (Butler 1981; French 1975). They acted under the protective shelter offered by the wider medical profession which thereby demonstrated its growing power and its (at least partial) espousal of the values of science. When sociologists speak of the professionalisation project of medicine employing science as a legitimation (e.g. Larson 1977) or the ascendancy of laboratory medicine as a medical cosmology (Jewson 1976), it is this process that is being referred to. Demonstrably superior healing powers of science-based medicine did not precede the conversion. Rather, science was conceived of as 'a powerful and compelling means of conferring "expert status" upon medicine, thereby consolidating its position as an "autonomous" learned profession' (Austoker 1988: 31).

This development was bitterly contested by many Victorians. From the 1870s to the early 1900s, competing reformist and abolitionist anti-vivisection societies proliferated. Some of these survive today, the major English ones being the National Anti-Vivisection Society (NAVS) and the British Union for the Abolition of Vivisection (BUAV). Within and outside these societies were hundreds of activists, mostly upper and middle-class women (Elston 1987). Their weapons were media exposure, petitions, personal lobbying and public meetings. In 1876, only the efforts of the organised medical profession turned a parliamentary bill that would have significantly curbed experimentalists' activities into the much less restrictive Cruelty to Animals Act of 1876. Anti-vivisectionists were especially embittered by what they saw as their betrayal by a medical profession corrupted by the experimental approach (French 1975).

Materialist medicine: Disputing its morality and utility

At the heart of Victorian anti-vivisectionists' passionate crusade was not only concern about cruelty to animals. To its Victorian critics, the materialist approach to knowledge that vivisection represented was itself immoral, reducing human beings to mechanical assemblages of cells. Vivisection was the weapon with which causal links between religious faith, moral conduct and physical health were being broken, for example through bacteriologists' doctrine of specific aetiology. The discoveries of those 'scientific devils' Koch and Pasteur reduced disease to a matter of chance encounter with amoral germs. In the opinion of the doyenne of the Victorian anti-vivisectionist movement, Frances Power Cobbe, this led not to the relief of suffering but to 'hygeiolatry', an obsession with health which itself increased susceptibility to disease. According to her, doctors' socialisation through vivisection was leading them down the slippery slope to experiments on humans (Cobbe 1882).

Moreover, according to its critics, the new medical profession was illegitimately claiming the right to dictate personal morality in the name of health. The anti-vivisectionist movement had strong affinities with other late nineteenth-century movements protesting against doctors' and state's arrogation of power in relation to health. These included the movements against compulsory smallpox vaccination, for women doctors and against the Contagious Diseases Acts controlling prostitutes in garrison towns (Elston 1987; French 1975; Walkowitz 1980). Anti-vivisectionists appealed particularly to women on the grounds of their greater dependency on doctors (and doctors' greater economic dependency on them). The movement's rhetoric drew heavily on a metaphor of vivisection as the 'rape of nature', linking contemporary concerns about science and medicine with those about sexual vice. Women were repeatedly invited to identify with laboratory animals, both being victims of allegedly sadistic doctors (Elston 1987).

For most Victorian anti-vivisectionists the question of the utility of animal experiments was secondary to the moral issue. For Cobbe, the idea that an evil scientific method could produce valid results was blasphemous (Elston 1987). But, from the 1880s, experimentalists' claims for the clinical utility of a materialist approach strengthened (Rupke 1987b). By 1900, George Bernard Shaw spoke for many other anti-vivisectionists when he declared that the utility of vivisection could never justify the cruelty (Shaw 1900). However, others continued to reject Shaw's implicit concession that the animal experiments might ever be useful. Attacks on animal experimentation's medical utility were proffered alongside the moral critique. Vaccinations, as against rabies and smallpox, and anti-diphtheria toxin were particular targets. Alternative approaches to health were often commended, including for example, spiritualism (Westacott 1949).

Anti-vivisectionists were a highly visible source of pressure on scientists until the First World War. But after the 1880s, their influence was reduced by the close relationships developing between biomedical scientists, the medical profession and government (French 1975). By the 1920s, the visibility of anti-vivisectionism was in sharp decline in the face of the apparently growing success of materialist medicine and the rise in state-sanctioned autonomy of scientists and the medical profession. Medical practice that explicitly shunned the products of animal experimentation became increasingly subject to professional and public censure; alternative medicine was dismissed as 'quackery' (Westacott 1949). From the 1920s to the 1960s, verbal skirmishes with 'anti-vivs' continued to be a taken-for-granted minor occupational hazard for biomedical scientists using animals (see, for example, Austoker 1988; Rose 1987). But the anti-vivisectionist message about animal research was largely being reiterated by what appeared to be a diminishing, ageing and increasingly eccentric constituency.

Thus the course of Victorian anti-vivisectionism demonstrates both the initial contestation of medical professionalisation in civil society and the profession's subsequent success in establishing itself as *the* cultural authority on matters of health. Yet, looking back from the first decade of the twenty-first century, we can ask if this was a contingent and possibly temporary achievement.

Laboratory animals' rights and wrongs: Revived concerns

The first signs of revival in the anti-vivisection movement were in the mid-1960s in Britain, simultaneous with early moves in what was to become the general animal rights movement (Ryder 1989). This was also just after the thalidomide catastrophe brought the question of drug safety testing to public notice and led to legislation mandating more extensive animal testing of all new ethical drugs in Britain (Paton 1993: 145). Against a sharp increase in the number of animal experiments, the organised anti-vivisectionist move-ment sought compromise around restrictive reforms and further development of alternatives to living animals (Hampson 1987: 316). But the newer animal rights consciousness, acting almost entirely outside the organised anti-vivisection movement, was turning its attention to laboratory animals in various ways. These included militants' attacks on research institutions and the more peaceful publications of an informal network of philosophers and others in Oxford (Henshaw 1989; Ryder 1989).

In Britain, the year 1975 marked a turning point, with a series of critical incidents including tabloid revelations that beagles were being used to test the safety of alternatives to tobacco. In the United States, a protest against the use of cats by the American Museum of Natural History in New York in 1976 marks the beginning of the contemporary protest movement (Jasper and Nelkin 1992: 26). Against this background of widespread publicity, two new 'anti-speciesist' manifestos attacking animal experiments were widely reviewed: Richard Ryder's *Victims of Science* (1975); and what became the movement's 'bible', the Australian philosopher Peter Singer's *Animal Liberation*, first published in the United States in 1975 and in the United Kingdom in 1976. An active campaign to put animals into British parliamentary politics was launched by a coalition of animal welfare and animal rights groups (Hollands 1980; Ryder 1989: 245–9). On both sides of the Atlantic, myriad local and special-cause animal rights groups began to appear from the late 1970s. New animal rights organisations were founded such as Animal Aid in Britain, in 1977, and the largest of the new American animal rights organisations, People for the Ethical Treatment of Animals (PETA), in 1980. By the 1980s, the new animal rights consciousness was affecting most of the older, often wealthy animal welfare and anti-vivisection societies. Indeed, Britain's largest animal welfare society, the Royal Society for the Prevention of Cruelty to Animals (RSPCA), has been periodically riven by internal disputes between moderates and radical animal rightists since the 1960s, with its policy on animal experiments being, at times, one of the most contested issues (Garner 1993; Ryder 1989).

So, between the mid-1970s and the 1990s, the animal rights movement as a whole grew in both public visibility and in membership on both sides of the Atlantic. Precise assessment of the growth of active support is difficult because of the very nature of social movements. The three largest organisa-tions campaigning against all animal experimentation in Britain (NAVS, BUAV and Animal Aid) had a total of 47,000 members in 1991 (but with much multiple membership) and a total annual income of £2.5 million (*Research Defence Society Newsletter*, October 1991: 8). Active campaigners now appear to be predominantly young, the rank and file still mainly female, spanning both the class and the political spectra (Henshaw 1989; Jasper and Nelkin 1992; Ryder 1989). Outside the core support, by the 1980s, there were indications of wider public uneasiness about the use of laboratory animals, especially among the young in Britain, according to surveys of public opinion (Durant *et al.* 1989; Lock and Millet 1991).

Like most social movements (Scott 1990), anti-vivisectionism and the animal protection movement generally is split into fundamentalist and pragmatic wings, although changing positions and alliances often cut across the divide. In 1983 two pragmatic reform groups, the Scottish Society for the Prevention of Vivisection (SSPV) and the Fund for the Replacement of Animals (FRAME), formed an alliance with the British Veterinary Association to influence government proposals for what became the Animals (Scientific Procedures) Act, 1986. Their support for this alleged 'Vivisectors' Charter' was opposed by a coalition of fundamentalist groups, including BUAV, NAVS and Animal Aid (Garner 1993; Hampson 1987). This coalition's title, 'Mobilisation Against the Government White Paper', epitomises the transformation of the Victorian anti-vivisectionist societies into radical animal rights organisations.

Since 1986, all sections of the British movement have continued to campaign in and, more especially, outside Parliament. Schoolchildren and students have been particular targets, with campaign buses, school visits and campus leafleting directed against animal use in education (including dissection) as well as in research and safety evaluation. Animal rights handbooks aimed at children have proliferated (e.g. James 1992; Newkirk 1991). Infiltration of scientific institutions to expose alleged malpractice has been increasingly attempted, particularly in the United States. Two American instances, the case of the 'Silver Springs monkeys' in 1981 and videotapes made in the University of Pennsylvania in 1984, were significant in generating media attention and inspiring support (Jasper and Nelkin 1992: 31). Particularly in Britain, the activities of the more militant wing have extended to planting bombs aimed at individuals and institutions (Paton 1993: 237–40).

Indeed, since the late 1990s, in the UK, the coverage of animal rights campaigning in the mass media has been dominated by stories about some animal rights groups' attempts to disrupt biomedical research by direct action. As noted at the beginning of this chapter, the scientific use of animals is, for good or ill, an integral part of a wide range of industrial and commercial activity as well as academic research. It requires staff, equipment, buildings and animals, all of which cost money. In recent years, specific organisations involved in animal research or testing have been targeted directly through picketing workplaces or staff's homes or, indirectly, through pressure on shareholders in companies connected with research and banks lending money to these companies or building contractors working on new laboratories. Several small companies breeding laboratory animals have closed as a result of this specific targeting. One contract research company, Huntingdon Life Sciences (HLS), has been a sustained focus for attack in recent years. At the time of writing, HLS survives, following government intervention to secure its continued financing. Most recently, the institutions under attack have been two of the intellectual citadels of British science, the Universities of Cambridge and Oxford, over plans to develop new animal research facilities. In the case of Cambridge, a proposed new primate research unit facility has been abandoned because of the prospective security costs that might be incurred (*Sunday Times* 8 Feb. 2004).

This kind of direct action might not be condoned by all campaigners against animal experiments. But the claims of the immorality and uselessness of the activities conducted in animal research establishments that are used to justify direct action have wider support. These claims are discussed in the next section.

Health with humanity or the cruel deception unmasked?

In retrospect, one feature of the arguments campaigners used to inspire support when the revival first began is notable. It was *not* a challenge to medical research *per se*. From the late 1960s to the 1980s, the emphasis was primarily on redefining the moral status of animals. To this was added a sustained attack on the infliction of pain and repeated calls for increased accountability of scientists. Attacks on the validity of the scientific knowledge gained were primarily claims about the difficulties of drawing inferences from data obtained with one species to another species (the problem of species error), or about the pointlessness of some animal procedures. The latter was particularly focused on behavioural research and safety testing, especially of cosmetics: such safety testing being depicted as having little relevance to preventive health but much relevance to commercial profit. According to a leading activist in the revival, by attacking the allegedly widespread use of laboratory animals 'not for strictly medical purposes, it was easier for us to erode the then widely accepted view of animal experimentation as a high-minded medical necessity involving little or no suffering for its non-human victims' (Ryder 1989: 244–5, 250–1, original emphasis). Even if distinguishing between acceptable (medical) and unacceptable (non-medical) research was only a tactical ploy (Duffy 1984: 46), the effect was to leave basic biomedical research and pharmaceutical research and development largely unchallenged. But during the 1980s, and especially after 1986, this changed. Anti-vivisectionist claims about the morality and value of animal experimentation for human health were again becoming central themes in the campaign. The BUAV launched a 'Health with Humanity' campaign in 1988 (BUAV n.d.; McIvor 1990). NAVS revised and reissued many of its old pamphlets attacking medical research.

Thus by the late 1980s and early 1990s, much anti-vivisectionist material was claiming that animal experiments were not just cruel abuses of animals, but also useless and even damaging to human health, a 'cruel deception' (Sharpe 1988). To the question 'Animals or people – which come first?' raised by defenders of animal experiments, the response became that 'the question is meaningless because vivisection benefits neither animals nor people' (McIvor 1990: 18). Most versions of this critique draw explicitly on sources that became familiar to medical sociologists during the 1970s. For example, a condemnation of the activities of the corrupt, evil and iatrogenic biomedical establishment set out in *Slaughter of the Innocent* by the controversial Swiss anti-vivisectionist Hans Ruesch (1983: 285) cited favourably 'Ivan Illich's carefully researched *Medical Nemesis*'. (Illich's (1976) book was a key influence on the more general radical critique of medicine that developed from the mid-1970s.)

The challenge to the morality of modern medicine

There have been two main strands in the renewed attack on the morality of modern medicine, both new versions of old themes. One is the idea of the corrupting, desensitising influence of the practice of vivisection, destroying the natural and healthy 'squeamishness' of the neophyte through intense pressure to conform (e.g. *Outrage*, Aug./Sept. 1990: 9). This has been alleged to lead to 'the "cut, burn, poison" approach' to patient care, and to be a step on the slippery slope towards experiments on humans (McIvor 1990: 9). The literature sometimes invites humans to empathise with animal victims, especially in the eco-feminist critiques of medical research that posit a natural affinity between women and animals (e.g. Caldecott and Leland 1983; Collard 1988). Scientists have been described as self-seeking individuals motivated by 'mere curiosity' and career advancement, blinded by their socialisation and their vested interests from adopting non-animal alternatives. From here it has been but a short step to condemning the institutions of medicine and biomedical research (e.g. Langley 1990). Such critiques reiterate much of the Marxist-influenced political economy critique of the pharmaceutical industry as profit- rather than need-driven that were prominent within medical sociology in the 1970s (e.g. Doyal 1979). Research institutions are repeatedly condemned for their 'closed doors', these being taken as indicative of there being something to hide.

Another strand in the moral argument is to draw distinctions within the medical research field, according to the degree of human culpability for diseases under investigation. A link between human conduct and health that materialist medicine was accused by Victorians of ignoring is once again being asserted in defence of animals. To make animals suffer for our own misconduct, when behavioural change would eliminate the problem, is held to be especially unacceptable. Thus the (human) 'victim-blaming' approach that has become widespread in health promotion policies since the 1970s (Crawford 1977) has been given a further twist by anti-vivisectionists. Research into the effects of tobacco or alcohol is, therefore, condemned by the whole movement (and has been very tightly regulated in the UK since 1986). But, for some critics, animal research related to any conditions where epidemiology has indicated the theoretical possibility of prevention by behavioural or social change is held to be especially egregious. Thus, on the basis of epidemiological statements that up to 90 per cent of the variance in some cancers' incidence can be statistically accounted for by known social, behavioural and environmental risks, all animal experiments in cancer research are condemned as immoral. Cancer research charities have been criticised for their alleged neglect of health education, epidemiology or clinical research (e.g. Langley 1990).

The 'facts' about modern medicine?

From the mid-1980s, alongside the critique of the morality of animal-based medical research there was also renewed emphasis on its alleged uselessness. For example, controversial doctor and journalist Vernon Coleman declared that 'Like most modern anti-vivisectionists I prefer to argue against vivisection on scientific and medical grounds' (Coleman 1991: 31). Again there have been two main themes in this critique of animal research's utility: revising the celebratory history of medicine and a strong thesis about the problem of species error. The first theme sets up a contrast between what 'people have come to believe ... that were it not for animal based medical research we would still be experiencing the appalling level of ill health which was common in Victorian times' and 'the facts [which] may come as a surprise' (BUAV n.d.: 4).

Some of these facts would have been of little surprise to medical sociologists since the 1970s, or even to most doctors and medical students, based as they are on the academic literature of the 'efficacy debate' (e.g. McKeown 1976). For example, the second edition of Singer's *Animal Liberation* included a new section on this literature (1990: 88–92). From the (undisputed) premise that the massive decline in mortality from many infectious diseases experienced by Western countries since 1800 preceded the introduction of specific chemotherapies or immunisations, questions are raised about the value of such interventions, if their research or development involved living animals, once they became available. For example, Singer's revised text concluded that 'any knowledge gained from animal experimentation has made at best a very small contribution to our increased lifespan; its contribution to improving the quality of life is more difficult to assess' (1990: 91).

With the aid of a catalogue of modern medicine's iatrogenic effects and a pessimistic picture of increasing ill-health resulting from modern life, a wide spectrum of medical interventions has been drawn into the anti-vivisectionists' critique of the effects of animal experimentation, since the 1980s. Much of the blame for the ineffectiveness of modern medicine is attributed to the allegedly false method employed in its development – the animal model. 'The fact is that animal experiments tell us about animals and not about people' (BUAV n.d.: 4). Differences between species are said to lead to the adoption of therapies that are, in fact, ineffective or even dangerous for human use, while potentially useful ones are lost.

Not surprisingly, the HIV/AIDS epidemic had attracted considerable attention in the movement's literature by the end of the 1980s. Its growing death toll was taken as evidence of the failed promise of medicine. The difficulty of reproducing AIDS symptoms in as close a relative as the chimpanzee has been taken to confirm the weakness of animal models. The use of such a sensitive species for a disease allegedly preventable by lifestyle changes has been condemned. And, for its critics, the possibility of HIV's zoonotic origins in African primate species has confirmed the dangers of meddling across species boundaries (Coleman 1991: 66; McIvor 1990; Sharpe 1988: 56). More recently, the so-called 'genomics revolution' in medical research has attracted much critical attention from anti-vivisectionists. Over the last decade, the use of genetically altered animals in biomedicine has expanded rapidly, accounting for 37 per cent of all procedures in 2003, and being largely responsible for recent annual increases in the total number of procedures (Home Office 2004). The creation of transgenic animals (where genetic material is transferred from one species to another) and the prospect of therapeutic xenotransplantation have caused particular concern, probably not just among committed critics of animal experimentation. As Brown and Webster have pointed out, 'Xenotransplantation hybrids are complex and sometimes contradictory productions which vividly trouble the boundary divisions between humans and other animals, and also between rationality and emotion, expert and lay discourse, science and culture' (2004: 111).

As Brown and Webster (2004) argue, transgenic animals and xenotransplantation bring conflicting ideas about the similarity and difference between humans and non-human animals into close proximity. But the paradoxes involved are not confined to recent arguments about the use of animals in genomic research. On the one hand, those opposed to vivisection have long accused animal experimenters of inconsistency: of invoking human–animal closeness in biological terms when arguing for the utility of animal models in research for human benefit while denying closeness in moral terms when attempting to justify using such models (Ryder 1975; Singer 1975). But the scientists' contemporary critics sometimes appear to be doing the converse. On the one hand, among the 'key ontological underpinnings of the new ethical orientations to animals are notions of [human–animal] kinship and interdependence' (Benton 1991: 8). But denial of the validity and reliability of extrapolating from animal models to humans is at the heart of the 'health with humanity' critique of vivisection.

For example, the result of such extrapolation is, according to Coleman, that, far from advancing human health, '*animal experiments kill people*' (1991: 1, original emphasis). What is required instead of animal-based research is 'REAL science: the study of human beings and human disease' (NAVS 1987: 1). Or, as 'the simple (but often overlooked) truth is that no matter how many animal tests are done the first two or three generations of people who use a new drug or technique are the real guinea pigs', so people should be the primary subjects of medical research (LIMAV/ Coleman 1991). Thus, for anti-vivisectionists, preferred methods of medical research include clinical observation studies, epidemiology, trials using human volunteers, post-marketing surveillance of therapies and more use of 'alternative' research techniques, such as those using human tissue cultures.

Arguments within medicine about the relative value, for human health and for medical students' education, of basic research based on animals, clinical research and epidemiological research have a long history (Rupke 1987b). The existence of segments or coalitions within the medical profession associated with particular positions in these debates is not in itself new. And medical reservations about the value of animal research in particular contexts is not necessarily indicative of anti-vivisectionist commitment. But there are opponents of vivisection within the medical profession. And as the anti-vivisectionist challenge revived, much has been made of any support for the cause by doctors (e.g. *Outrage*, 70 Oct./Nov. 1990: 3; Coleman 1991: 111). And new action groups explicitly including doctors and other health care professionals have emerged to add their critiques of animal experimentation. For example, in the USA there is the Americans for Medical Advancement group, and, in the UK, the Physicans' Committee for Responsible Medicine. From the 1990s, arguments within medicine about the contribution of different types of medical research and sources of knowledge to improving health outcomes have been given new force by the rise of the evidence-based medicine movement committed to ensuring 'that a particular (explicit) form of evidence, epitomized by the randomized controlled trial, is incorporated into medicine' (Pope 2003: 269). Accordingly, there have been recent calls, in the UK, to apply the precepts of evidence-based medicine to animal research and to claims about its contribution to clinical knowledge from the Society for Accountability of Animal Studies in Biomedical Research and Education (SABRE), formed in 2002 by 'researchers, health policy makers and patients', and the RATS (Reviewing Animal Trials Systematically) group (Pound *et al.* 2004; SABRE 2004).

Challenging medical science: Why the shift in focus?

Most modern anti-vivisectionists, like their predecessors, probably still see their campaign as primarily a moral one. Many might still argue, as did Shaw in 1900, that attacking the utility of an immoral method is not the central point (e.g. Singer 1990: 92). This chapter does not claim that critiques of the utility for human health of medical research and safety testing using animals have become the sole platform of modern anti-vivisectionist argument. But the view that 'humans are arguably suffering as a result of animal research' (Pound 2001: 1252) is much more widely promulgated than it was thirty years ago. So it is worth considering why the animal rights-influenced contemporary movement has returned to some of their Victorian predecessors concerns with the implications for health of animal-based research.

One factor may be simply the rediscovery of the movement's history as younger animal rightists have taken over the anti-vivisection organisations. In Britain, the critique of medical research clearly gained momentum when the campaigning groups needed a fresh focus after new legislation in 1986. But, faced with the institutionalised pervasiveness of science and medicine, it may be hard to achieve radical change in the use of animals by appeal to moral principles alone (cf. Benton 1993). Legitimations that appeal to scientific authority may carry some force, even for a movement opposed to one institutionalised form of scientific activity. If animal experiments can be shown to be useless or even damaging for human health, the main defence of the practice is removed, and self-interested grounds for public opposition provided. The renewed attack on medical research from anti-vivisectionists has clearly gathered momentum and ammunition from the other contemporary challenges to medicine discussed in this book. Medicine's record of achievement, its practitioners, its knowledge base and its scientists are attackable in the early twenty-first century in a way that was not conceivable when the revival of anti-vivisectionism began. But, even if more challengeable, the strength of the institutions of biomedical research are, of course, quite different now than a hundred years ago when the first-wave of anti-vivisection protest was at its height.

Responding to 'anti-vivisectionists' critique of the value of animal research[5]

For much of the last century, responses by either individual biomedical researchers or scientific institutions to public campaigning against animal experimentation were relatively low-key. There are many reasons for this, not least that those engaged in scientific and medical research may have had other priorities. Between the 1920s and the 1970s, to have responded vigorously might have seemed to give the challenge undue credence and invited further unwanted attention. Ever since violent direct action protests began, in the late 1960s, with the activities of the Animal Liberation Front, reluctance to 'stick one's head above the parapet' has been an understandable response from the scientists. Even after animals had been placed on the parliamentary political agenda in the late 1970s, the biomedical research community in Britain initially concentrated on securing 'bureaucratic accommodation' with realistic reformers rather than on public campaigning. This reflected the characteristic British style of public policy making through seeking negotiated consensus between 'insider groups' and probably still plays a large part, in shaping, for example, the regulations under which animal experimentation is conducted. In the 1970s and 1980s, in the more openly adversarial political culture of the United States, the scientists' response was much more publicly aggressive from the start (cf. Gluck and Kubacki 1991). This is in part because American scientists were still contesting the principle of government regulation of animal experimentation itself, a principle British scientists have worked under since 1876 (Elston 1992).

But, of course, even in Britain there have been moves to engage public opinion in support of animal research, especially during the peaks of anti-vivisectionist challenge, the 1880s (Rupke 1987b), the 1900s, and the last two decades. In 1908, the Research Defence Society (RDS) was founded specifically for this purpose and has published many pamphlets extolling the contribution of animal experiments to human health (e.g. RDS 1908). However, from the 1950s to the late 1980s, the RDS worked primarily as an 'insider group', mainly representing graduate biomedical researchers, especially in academia. But during the long negotiations leading up to the Animals (Scientific Procedures) Act in 1986, the RDS ran a national advertising campaign. Pharmacologist Sir William Paton published a book-length defence of animal experiments emphasising the practical benefits for humans (Paton 1984). At the same time the Association of the British Pharmaceutical Industry established the Animals in Medicines Research Information Centre (AMRIC) to inform the public about the use of animals in the pharmaceutical industry.

But a much more active public campaign on the part of British medical researchers and their organisations developed from the late 1980s. Besides producing new educational material, researchers have been encouraged to 'go public' in the mass media and before lay audiences, above all in schools. The RDS took on a much more public profile, seeking to enrol prominent scientists and leading members of the medical profession as public supporters of their cause. For example, in 1990 the British Association for the Advancement of Science (BA) launched a Declaration on Animals in Medical Research, which supports the case for animal experiments in biomedical research while urging scientists to respect animal life. A year later, the BA's Declaration had been signed by 'nearly 1000 eminent doctors, scientists and organisations' (*RDS News*, Summer 1991).

In 1991, the major medical research funding charities launched the Research for Health Charities Group. Its objectives include increasing public understanding of the role played by animals in medical research funded by research charities as well as encouraging good research practice among its members (*RDS Newsletter*, Jan. 1992). The British Medical Association (BMA) agreed to mount a campaign 'informing the public of the importance of animal experiments in the fight against disease' after a 'lively debate' at its 1992 Annual Representative Meeting (*RDS Newsletter*, July 1992). The voice of the patient has also been raised through such groups as Seriously Ill for Medical Research (SIMR), founded in 1991 (*Hope*, SIMR Quarterly Newsletter 1, July 1991), and its much larger American counterpart Incurably Ill for Animal Research (iiFAR) (Jasper and Nelkin 1992: 134).

By the late 1980s, the biomedical research community seems to have come to the view that the animal rights movement had been winning the public debate 'by default', aided by the mass media's interest in controversy and hence in the protest movement. Their response was, therefore, in part, a reaction to the success of the pro-animal movement in integrating some of its concerns into public (including scientists') consciousness and political life in Britain. Biomedical scientists and their institutions had to learn new strategies for responding to direct action and mass media attacks. But the upturn in overt response from the research side followed after the animal rights movement's shift to attacking the utility of animal research for human health. This might have been a sign of confidence about the new territory being contested as much as an indication of concern. It is not just that scientists may feel more confident debating claims about science than the finer points of moral philosophy. Rather, in the late twentieth century, medicine and science could not claim any exclusive or special authority in moral debates. But if a dispute centred on claims about 'scientific facts', specialist expertise could be invoked to try to close off controversy (cf. Michael and Birke 1994).

So, for nearly two decades, what biomedical scientists widely refer to as a 'battle for (the) hearts and minds' of the public has been waged, particularly in the classroom and the mass media. On the one hand, scientists defending animal experiments have sought to emphasise their moral probity, the tightness of regulation (stressing this as particularly strict in Britain) and their commitment to animal welfare. For example the legal obligation to use non-animal techniques where possible and to refine methods and reduce numbers of animals used have been given institutional support in the form of the National Centre for the 3Rs [reduction, replacement, and refinement] launched in 2004. But countering anti-vivisectionists' claims about the contribution (or lack of it) of animal experimentation to medical progress is the dominant theme in the scientists' campaign for the public's attention. For example, corrective accounts are given of oft-repeated anti-vivisectionist allegations about the role of animal tests in the thalidomide disaster or the isolation of insulin, or about species error in safety testing. The celebratory history of animal research is perhaps somewhat more qualified after having been placed in a highly critical spotlight (e.g. LaFollette and Shanks 1996). The importance of social factors for increases in life expectancy in the past and the role of behavioural factors and prevention are all more explicitly recognised now than twenty years ago. But many of the specific inferences made by anti-vivisectionists are rejected as invalid and claims of the general weaknesses of animal model are vigorously contested.

As the volume of 'pro-research' information and educational material increased since the mid-1980s, there have been changes in style and tone. The presentation of 'both sides' has been increasingly incorporated into the structure of pamphlets and videos with less reliance on 'authoritative' voices alone. For example, AMRIC's 1993 video for schools, *Life on the Line*, took the form of a class project investigating the topic, not, as in previous ones, a voiced-over documentary or a famous scientist or distinguished clinician giving their (and it was usually his) view. The Biomedical Research Education Trust, an educational charity associated with the RDS, produced a video, *A Question of Care*, in 2003, that is structured by the questions asked by three sixth-formers on visits to laboratory animal facilities. This shift in format partly reflected the importance placed on material that could be used by teachers. But it also suggests a recognition that it might not be possible to settle the debate by appeals to the authority of science and medicine alone, or even desirable to try. When individuals are shown presenting the arguments in defence of using animals, as in the leaflets and newsletters issued by the Coalition for Medical Progress launched in 2003 (www.medicalprogress.org.), they are now more likely to be young and female than twenty years ago. The research community appears to have learnt that, to use Wynne's phrase, scientists' 'body language' – how they put their message across – may be as important as its content in influencing public response, especially among young people (Wynne 1991: 119).

In some respects, since the 1990s, the immediate battleground over animal research in the UK has shifted from disputes about the merits of using animal models to promote human health, to questions of law and order, and safeguarding the rights of protest versus protecting legally permitted industrial and scientific activity. But the direct action is itself a direct challenge to the foundations of modern medical practice. The campaign against HLS has been described by the RDS as, 'In many ways...an attack on the whole of pharmaceutical and life science research in the UK' because of the integration of companies like HLS 'into the whole [pharmaceutical] development process' (*RDS News* Jan. 2000: 1). The scientific community (both academic and commercial) have increasingly sought both public expressions and tangible measures of support from government. And government's expressions of support are, of course, couched in terms that modern anti-vivisectionists dispute, the putative contribution of scientific procedures on animals to the public's health (and of biomedical science and technology to the economy's health). Thus the foreword to a 2003 government paper on policies for dealing with so-called 'extremists' by Prime Minister Tony Blair and the then Home Secretary, David Blunkett, declared that,

> Research using animals has helped save hundreds of millions of lives...British scientists, institutions and firms are at the forefront of this remarkable research...they continue to make a huge contribution to human health and well-being.
>
> (Home Office *et al.* 2004)

Conclusion

This chapter has demonstrated how, in disputing the value of a key route to knowledge, the anti-vivisection movement explicitly challenges the claims of medical research to scientific rationality, technical prowess and moral probity. Anti-vivisectionism has undoubtedly had an impact, albeit intermittently, on medical research in Britain over the past century. The contemporary movement has undoubtedly achieved public recognition of some of its concerns. Its pressure was a major factor bringing about new legislation regulating animal experimentation in Britain in 1986 (although the fundamentalist wing had little direct influence on the law's contents). Biomedical researchers have increasingly had to set out public defences of their contentious activities on both moral and scientific grounds.

Returning to the more general themes of this book, it is clear that the level of support for anti-vivisectionism in general and the focus of its claims have varied with the strength of other challenges to the social and cultural authority of medicine and medical research. Lay perceptions of doctors and their work have probably never taken the form of blind faith nor, indeed, of total scepticism. Rather, medical sociology has documented a complex mixture of the two, the balance shifting pragmatically according to particular contexts (e.g. Calnan and Williams 1992). But there is good reason to think that the scales may have tipped, at least a bit, towards scepticism since the 1970s (Elston 1991). In the last twenty-five years, public knowledge and concern about the risks and limitations of modern medicine and safety testing has been increasing, alongside more general questioning of and reduced deference to expertise and professionalism (Scott *et al.* 1992). On the one hand, concerns about risks posed by, for example, industrial chemicals can generate calls for more precautionary testing, which still generally means more animal testing. On the other hand, awareness that extrapolating to human health from animal tests is an uncertain process has probably increased, partly through anti-vivisectionist campaigning. This is one product of what Giddens calls the 'reflexivity of modernity' (1990: 36). The arguments about health and medicine deployed by the contemporary anti-vivisection movement demonstrate the reflexivity of modern knowledge about medicine very vividly. The debates about medicine's effectiveness within academic social science and medicine became the basis of an external critique of the utility of medicine which has sought to penetrate to the heart of the expert system itself. Evidence of the fallibility of scientific knowledge, of disagreement between medical scientists, of false trails, all these are taken by critics as evidence of the need for distrust of medical science. Yet the anti-vivisection movement, in giving its supporters a social identity, is itself, in part, an 'adaptive reaction' to any growing distrust of medicine and science (cf. Giddens 1990: 134, 137).

So implicit trust in both the individuals who practise medicine and in the underlying system of knowledge that sustains it may have been weakening. Whether this points to a post-modernist eclipse of scientific medical authority (cf. Bakx 1991) is less clear. Certainly, there is much that is new about the animal rights movement but there is also sufficient continuity with the past, at least in relation to anti-vivisectionism, to suggest that building a grand theory of social change on its 'newness' might be foolhardy. There is also much that fits with the changes identified by deprofessionalisation theorists (e.g. Haug 1988). Medical research's claims may have become more challengeable. But the continued appeal to scientific authority, the importance placed on 'real' medical research by the anti-vivisectionist movement, and the calls for systematic reviews of animal research's contribution to clinical research, suggest that the post-modernist cultural world is still some way off. More generally, what many deprofessionalisation and post-modernist cultural theories neglect is the institutionalised permeation of everyday life by biomedical science and technology which rely on, among many other methods, the use of animals. The revival of anti-vivisection protest has made the public more aware of this reliance, and of some of the uncertainties that surround extrapolation from non-human animals to humans. But, to judge from the Sudan 1 episode, neither politicians and regulators nor the general public appear to be ready to discount the possibility that eating dyes that cause cancer when fed to rodents might be harmful to human health.

Notes

1 The terminology in the controversy I am outlining here is contentious. I shall use 'animal' to refer to non-human creatures only, except where special emphasis is called for. Those working with laboratory animals reject the term 'vivisection', with its literal connotation of cutting open living creatures, as too emotive to apply to the vast majority of scientific procedures carried out on animals today. When discussing the scientific use of animals, terms such as 'animal research' and 'animal experiments' should be taken to cover the use of animals for safety testing as well as the pursuit of new knowledge, unless explicitly indicated.

2 Students of human and veterinary medicine generally have much more direct exposure to animal experimentation than those in so-called 'paramedical fields' such as physiotherapy. British medical students do not normally perform experiments (Smith and Boyd 1991: 233).

3 The term 'black box' has been adopted within the sociology of science from its use in engineering to refer to technologies that can be treated as uncontroversial, predictable input/output systems without consideration of their internal mechanisms (e.g. Latour 1987).

4 The term 'animal rights' is being used here to refer to the contemporary movement in general. Not all the philosophers associated with the movement employ the philosophical concept of 'rights' and, for some purposes, it is important to distinguish between 'animal rights' and 'animal liberation' segments of the movement.

5 The focus of this necessarily brief discussion is on the public response of the biomedical research community to the high-profile radical animal rights challenge. It does not attempt to consider any ongoing debates about the use of animals

within the research community or the less public dialogues about laboratory animal welfare between animal researchers and more pragmatic reformers.

References

Austoker, J. (1988) A *History of the Imperial Cancer Research Fund 1902–1986*, Oxford: Oxford University Press.

Bakx, K. (1991) 'The "eclipse" of folk medicine in western society?', *Sociology of Health and Illness*, 13: 20–38.

Benton, T. (1991) 'Biology and social science: Why the return of the repressed should be given a (cautious) welcome', *Sociology*, 25: 1–29.

—— (1993) *Natural Relations: Ecology, Animal Rights and Social Justice*, London: Verso.

British Union for the Abolition of Vivisection (BUAV) (n.d.) *Health with Humanity*, London: BUAV.

Brown, N. and Webster, A. (2004) *New Medical Technologies and Society: Reordering Life*, Cambridge: Polity.

Butler, S.V. (1981) 'Science and the education of doctors in the nineteenth century: A study of British medical schools with special reference to the development and uses of physiology', unpublished Ph.D. thesis, University of Manchester.

Caldecott, L. and Leland, S. (eds) (1983) *Women Reclaim the Earth*, London: Women's Press.

Calnan, M. and Williams, S. (1992) 'Images of scientific medicine', *Sociology of Health and Illness*, 14(2): 233–54.

Cobbe, F.P. (1882) ' "Hygeiolatry" and "Sacrificial Medicine" ', in Cobbe, F.F. (ed.), *Peak of Darien*, London: Williams & Norgate.

Coleman, V. (1991) *Why Animal Experiments Must Stop: And How You Can Help Stop Them*, London: Green Print.

Collard, A. with Contrucci, J. (1988) *Rape of the Wild*, London: Women's Press.

Crawford, R. (1977) 'You are dangerous to your health: Ideology and politics of victim blaming', *International Journal of Health Services*, 7: 663–80.

Doyal, L. with Pennell, I. (1979) *The Political Economy of Health*, London: Pluto.

Duffy, M. (1984) *Men and Beasts: An Animal Rights Handbook*, London: Paladin.

Durant, J., Evans, G.A. and Thomas, G.P. (1989) 'The public understanding of science', *Nature*, 340: 11–14.

Elston, M.A. (1987) 'Women and anti-vivisection in Victorian England, 1870–1900', in Rupke, N. (ed.), *Vivisection in Historical Perspective*, London: Croom Helm.

—— (1991) 'The politics of professional power: Medicine in a changing society', in Gabe, J., Calnan, M. and Bury, M. (eds), *The Sociology of the Health Service*, London: Routledge.

—— (1992) 'The "animal question" in the British science press: The case of *New Scientist*, 1970–1991', in Hicks, E.K. (ed.), *Science and the Human-Animal Relationship*, Amsterdam: SISWO.

French, R.D. (1975) *Antivivisection and Medical Science in Victorian Society*, Princeton: Princeton University Press.

Garner, R. (1993) *Animals, Politics and Morality*, Manchester: Manchester University Press.

Giddens, A. (1990) *The Consequences of Modernity*, Cambridge: Polity Press.

Gluck, J.P. and Kubacki, S.R. (1991) 'Animals in biomedical research: The undermining effect of the rhetoric of the besieged', *Ethics and Behaviour*, 1(3): 157–73.

Hampson, J. (1987) 'Legislation: A practical solution to the vivisection dilemma?', in Rupke, N. (ed.), *Vivisection in Historical Perspective*, London: Croom Helm.

Haug, M. (1988) 'A re-examination of the hypothesis of deprofessionalization', *Milbank Quarterly*, 66(Suppl. 2): 48–56.

Henshaw, D. (1989) *Animal Warfare: The Story of the Animal Liberation Front*, London: Fontana.

Hollands, C. (1980) *Compassion is the Bugler: The Struggle for Animal Rights*, Edinburgh: MacDonald Publishers.

Home Office (2004) *Statistics of Scientific Procedures on Living Animals Great Britain, 2003*. London: Home Office. www.officialdocuments.co.uk/document/cm58/5886/5886.pdf.

Home Office, Department of Trade & Industry, the Office of the Attorney General (2004) *Animal Welfare – Human Right: Protecting People from Animal Rights Extremists*. http://www.homeoffice.gov.uk/docs3/humanrights.pdf. (Accessed Nov. 2004).

Illich, I. (1976) *Medical Nemesis*, New York: Pantheon Books.

James, B. (1992) *The Young Person's Action Guide to Animal Rights*, London: Virago.

Jasper, J.M. and Nelkin, D. (1992) *The Animal Rights Crusade: The Growth of a Moral Protest*, Chicago: Free Press.

Jewson, N. (1976) 'The disappearance of the sick-man from medical cosmology, 1770–1870', *Sociology*, 10: 225–44.

LaFollette, H. and Shanks, N. (1996) *Dilemmas of Animal Experimentation*, London: Routledge.

Langley, G. (1990) *Faith, Hope and Charity?*, London: BUAV.

Larson, M.S. (1977) *The Rise of Professionalism: A Sociological Analysis*, Berkeley: University of California Press.

Latour, B. (1987) *Science in Action*, Milton Keynes: Open University Press.

Lawrence, C. (1992) 'Experiment and experience in anaesthesia: Alfred Goodman Levy and chloroform death, 1910–1960', in Lawrence, C. (ed.), *Medical Theory, Surgical Practice: Studies in the History of Surgery*, London: Routledge.

Lederer, S. (1987) 'The controversy over animal experiments in America, 1880–1914', in Rupke, N. (ed.), *Vivisection in Historical Perspective*, London: Croom Helm.

LIMAV (League Internationale Médecins pour l'Abolition de la Vivisection)/Coleman, V. (1991) *Why Animal Experiments Must Be Stopped*, Arbedo: LIMAV.

Lock, R. and Millet, K. (1991) *The Animals and Science Education Project, 1990–91*, Birmingham: University of Birmingham School of Education.

McIvor, S. (ed.) (1990) *Health with Humanity: The Case against Using Animals for Medical Research*, London: BUAV.

McKeown, T. (1976) *The Role of Medicine: Dream, Mirage or Nemesis*, London: Nuffield Provincial Hospitals Trust.

Michael, M. and Birke, L. (1994) 'Animal experimentation: Enrolling the core set', *Social Studies of Science*, 24: 81–95.

National Anti-Vivisection Society (NAVS) (1987) *Biohazard: The Silent Threat from Biomedical Research and the Creation of AIDS*, London: NAVS.

Newkirk, I. (1991) *Save the Animals: 101 Easy Things You Can Do*, London: Angus.

Paton, W. (1984) *Man and Mouse: Animals in Medical Research*, Oxford: Oxford University Press.

—— (1993) *Man and Mouse: Animals in Medical Research*, new edn, Oxford: Oxford University Press.

Pope, C. (2003) 'Resisting evidence: The study of evidence-based medicine as a contemporary social movement', *Health*, 7(3), 267–82.

Pound, P. (2001) 'Scientific debate on animal models in research is needed', Letter, *British Medical Journal*, 323: 1252.

Pound, P., Ebrahim, S., Sandercock, P., Bracken, M.B. and Roberts, I. (2004) 'Where is the evidence that animal research benefits humans?', *British Medical Journal*, 328: 514–17.

Research Defence Society (RDS) (1908) *Experiments on Animals: Pamphlets Issued by the Research Defence Society, February–August, 1908*, London: Research Defence Society.

Rose, S. (1987) *Molecules and Minds*, Milton Keynes: Open University Press.

Ruesch, H. (1983) *Slaughter of the Innocent*, Klosters: Civitas (first published New York: Bantam Books, 1978).

Rupke, N. (ed.) (1987a) 'Introduction', *Vivisection in Historical Perspective*, London: Croom Helm.

—— (ed.) (1987b) 'Pro-vivisection in England in the early 1880s: Arguments and motives', *Vivisection in Historical Perspective*, London: Croom Helm.

Ryder, R.D. (1975) *Victims of Science: The Use of Animals in Research*, London: Davis-Poynter (second edn 1983, London: National Anti-Vivisection Society).

—— (1989) *Animal Revolution: Changing Attitudes Towards Speciesism*, Oxford: Blackwell.

SABRE (Society for Accountability of Animal Studies in Biomedical Research and Education (2004) 'Animal research – the need to evaluate'. http://www.s-a-b-r-e.org (Accessed Feb 2005).

Scott, A. (1990) *Ideology and the New Social Movements*, London: Unwin Hyman.

Scott, S., Williams, G. and Thomas, H. (eds) (1992) *Private Risks and Public Dangers*, Aldershot: Avebury.

Sharpe, R. (1988) *The Cruel Deception: The Use of Animals in Medical Research*, London: Thorsons.

Shaw, G.B. (1900) *The Dynamitards of Science*, London: London Anti-Vivisection Society.

Singer, P. (1975) *Animal Liberation: A New Ethic for Our Treatment of Animals*, New York: New York Review of Books (British edn 1976, London: Thorsons).

—— (1990) *Animal Liberation*, second edn, New York: New York Review of Books.

Smith, J. and Boyd, K. (eds) (1991) *Lives in the Balance: The Ethics of Using Animals in Biomedical Research*, Oxford: Oxford University Press.

Sperling, S. (1988) *Animal Liberators: Research and Morality*, Berkeley, CA: University of California Press.

Walkowitz, J. (1980) *Prostitution and Victorian Society: Women, Class, and the State*, Cambridge: Cambridge University Press.

Westacott, E. (1949) *A Century of Vivisection and Anti-Vivisection*, Rochford, Essex: C.W. Daniel.

Wynne, B. (1991) 'Knowledges in context', *Science, Technology and Human Values*, 16(1): 111–21.

Index